DRYWALL CONSTRUCTION HANDBOOK

Robert Scharff and the Editors of Walls & Ceilings Magazine

McGraw-Hill, Inc.

New York San Francisco Washington, D.C. Auckland Bogotá
Caracas Lisbon London Madrid Mexico City Milan
Montreal New Delhi San Juan Singapore
Sydney Tokyo Toronto

Library of Congress Cataloging-in-Publication Data

Scharff, Robert.
    Drywall construction handbook / by Robert Scharff and the editors
of Walls & Ceilings magazine
        p.   cm.
    Includes index.
    ISBN 0-07-057124-4
    1. Drywall.   I. Walls & ceilings.   II. Title.
TH2239.S33   1995
693'.6—dc20   95-17262
                                                                        CIP

hc   2 3 4 5 6 7 8 9 0   DOC/DOC   9 9 8 7 6

ISBN 0-07-057124-4

*The sponsoring editor of this book was April D. Nolan, the copy-editor
was Sally Anne Glover, and the production supervisor was Katherine G.
Brown. This book was set in ITC Century Light. It was composed in Blue
Ridge Summit, Pa.*

Printed and bound by R.R. Donnelley & Sons Company.

CONTENTS

ACKNOWLEDGMENTS

The author would like to thank the following people, corporations, and associations for helping to furnish materials used in the text of this book:

- William D. Leavitt, Dennis Ford, Matt Gonring, and United States Gypsum Company for the use of materials and illustrations from U.S.G.'s *Gypsum Construction Handbook*.
- J.R. Walker and Robert Ek of National Gypsum Company.
- Terry Westerman and Kevin Gramley of Unimast Inc.
- Kimberly Drew of Georgia-Pacific Corporation.
- Lee Rector, Barbara Castelli, and Greg V. Campbell of *Walls & Ceilings*.
- Jerry Walker and Robert Wessel of The Gypsum Association.
- James Gerhart, Leon Korejwo, and Pamela Korejwo of Scharff Corporation for editing and coordinating the text and art for this book.

INTRODUCTION

This book was written for the drywall contractor and the various drywall tradespeople such as drywall hangers, mechanics, and finishers. It will serve equally well as a valuable reference guide for those with broad experience and those who wish to learn more about drywall construction: architects, engineers, general contractors, builders, dealers, building inspectors, and building-code officials.

With more than 375 illustrations, this book, written in clear, easy-to-understand language, contains step-by-step construction procedures as well as the most up-to-date product information and techniques. To accomplish this task, the necessary subject matter was broken down into 11 chapters plus a glossary.

Chapter 1 covers the growth of the gypsum-drywall industry, how the panels are made, and the many advantages gypsum panels offer the construction field.

Chapter 2 describes the many types of gypsum board and accessories available, including sizes, uses, and basic installation procedures.

Chapter 3 explains the various tools (both common and specialized) used in hanging drywall and the purpose each serves.

Chapter 4 goes into the importance of planning a drywall job, how to estimate both material and labor costs, and how to safely handle and store gypsum board on and off the job site.

Chapter 5 details the techniques of working with drywall panels. It covers the most current, proven methods for cutting and fastening the material to wood and steel framing using screws, nails, clips, and adhesives.

Chapter 6 contains in-depth procedures necessary to install gypsum-drywall partitions over wood framing, the most popular method for residential structures.

Chapter 7 details the use of steel framing. A construction material that has generally been used in commercial structures, steel framing is now being widely used in residential construction as support for drywall panels. This is explained, along with the techniques necessary for applying drywall panels over steel framing.

Chapter 8 covers the various special installation techniques required for curved surfaces, interior and exterior soffits, prefinished materials, installing tile, covering interior masonry walls, hanging fixtures and cabinets, and doing remodeling work.

Chapter 9 provides valuable and important information concerning the installation of fire-resistant and sound-control assemblies.

Chapter 10 describes the various levels of gypsum-drywall panel finishing, including mixing and using joint compound, the tools used, installing trim and tape, joint treatments, sanding walls, mechanical taping devices, and the final finishes that are available.

Chapter 11 analyzes the major problems that can arise in any drywall installation, how to avoid them, and the methods for correcting them.

A glossary defines drywall terms; appendix A lists the manufacturers that contributed the various illustrations in this book, and appendix B provides metric conversion tables.

CHAPTER 1
DRYWALL CONSTRUCTION

Robert Scharff
Walls & Ceilings Magazine

Prior to the drywall revolution after World War II, plaster was the number one material for the interiors of homes, office buildings, stores, and various other structures. At that time, the definition of the word drywall was any wall-covering base material that did not require a finishing coat of plaster. This is not to imply that plaster was not an excellent wall material; it still is. But its application takes considerably more labor, and the material is messy and leaves the structure saturated with moisture that must evaporate before painting or any other finishing operation can be started. Drywall construction overcame these problems. As a result, since 1945 to the present, the use of drywall construction has jumped from about 15 percent to well over 90 percent in residential and small commercial buildings.

Today, drywall means gypsum-board construction. *Gypsum board* is the generic term for a family of panel products composed of a noncombustible gypsum core encased in a heavy natural-finish paper on the face side and a strong liner paper on the back side. The face paper is folded around the long edges to reinforce and protect the core. The ends are square-cut and finished smooth. Long edges of panels are usually tapered, allowing joints to be reinforced, and concealed with a joint treatment system.

Gypsum board is often called wallboard, plasterboard, gypboard, Sheetrock, or just drywall. It differs from the other so-called "drywall" materials such as wood paneling, plywood, hardboard, and fiberboard, because of its fire-resistant core. It is designed to provide a monolithic surface when joints and fastener heads are covered with a joint compound system. This book is devoted to the use, application, and finishing procedures of gypsum-board construction in both residential and commercial buildings (Figure 1.1).

FIGURE 1.1A   Drywall construction in a residential structure.

FIGURE 1.1B   Drywall construction in a commercial structure.

THE MANUFACTURE OF GYPSUM BOARD

Gypsum is a basic mineral found in sedimentary rock formations in a crystalline form known as calcium sulfate dihydrate, $CaSO_4 \cdot 2H_2O$. One hundred pounds of gypsum rock contains approximately 21 pounds (or 10 quarts) of chemically combined water. This is the feature that gives gypsum its fire-resistive qualities and makes it so adaptable for construction purposes.

After the gypsum rock is mined or quarried, it is crushed, dried, and ground to flour fineness (Figure 1.2). It is then heated to about 350°F, driving off three-fourths of the chemically combined water in a process called *calcining*. The calcined gypsum (or hemihydrate) $CaSO_4 \cdot \frac{1}{2}H_2O$, is then used as the base for gypsum plaster, gypsum board, and other gypsum products.

FIGURE 1.2 After the gypsum rock is quarried, it is crushed and ground to a flour fineness.

The calcined gypsum, commonly called *plaster of paris*, is mixed with water and additives, forming a slurry that is fed between continuous layers of paper on a board machine. As the board moves down a conveyer line (Figure 1.3), the calcium sulfate recrystallizes or rehydrates, reverting to its original rock state. The paper becomes chemically and mechanically bonded to the core. After the gypsum core has set, the boards are cut to length, dried, prefinished, if required, and packaged for shipment. All processing is in strict accordance with specifications to meet quality standards.

FIGURE 1.3   Cutting and processing of gypsum-drywall panels.

As described in chapter 2, there are several different types of gypsum boards: regular (standard) board, high fire resistance type-X board, predecorated board, moisture-resistant (MR) board, foil-backed board, high-strength ceiling board, shaft liner board, sound deadening board, soffit board, sheathing, deck roof board, and special gypsum board for veneer plaster. The application of these various types of gypsum-board construction is covered in subsequent chapters of this book.

ADVANTAGES OF GYPSUM BOARD CONSTRUCTION

Gypsum board walls and ceilings have several outstanding advantages over other interior materials. They are:

- Fire resistance
- Sound control
- Durability
- Dry construction
- Light weight
- Low installation costs
- Fast installation
- Easily decorated
- Versatility

Let's look at these advantages in more detail.

Fire resistance

Gypsum board is an excellent fire-resistant material. Its core will not support combustion or transmit temperatures greatly in excess of 212°F. Actually, its noncombustible core contains chemically combined water, which under high heat is slowly released as steam, effectively retarding heat transfer. Even after complete calcination, when all the water has been released, it continues to act as a heat-insulating barrier (Figure 1.4). In addition, tests conducted by the American Society of Testing and Material (ASTM) standard show that gypsum board has a low flame-spread index and smoke-density index. These tests and ratings, based on full-scale tests, are generally recognized by building-code authorities and fire-insurance rating bureaus. Fire-resistance ratings of up to 4 hours for partitions, 3 hours for floor-ceilings, and 4 hours for column and shaft fireproofing assemblies are available with specific assemblies. Fire-resistant ratings represent the results of tests on assemblies made up of specific materials in a specific configuration. When selecting construction assemblies to meet certain fire-resistance requirements, caution must be used to ensure that each component of the assembly is the one specified in the test. Further, precaution should be taken that assembly procedure is in accordance with that of the tested assembly. (See chapter 9 for specific ratings and related assemblies.)

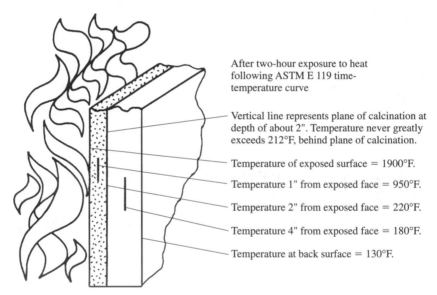

After two-hour exposure to heat following ASTM E 119 time-temperature curve

Vertical line represents plane of calcination at depth of about 2". Temperature never greatly exceeds 212°F, behind plane of calcination.

Temperature of exposed surface = 1900°F.

Temperature 1" from exposed face = 950°F.

Temperature 2" from exposed face = 220°F.

Temperature 4" from exposed face = 180°F.

Temperature at back surface = 130°F.

FIGURE 1.4   How gypsum board retards heat transmission. (Data from the Underwriters Laboratories, Inc.)

Sound control

Control of unwanted sound that might be transmitted to adjoining rooms is a key consideration in the design stage of a building, taking into account the environment described for the particular activity of the occupants. Gypsum construction offers excellent resistance to airborne and impact sound transmission without excessive bulk or weight. Resilient attachment of gypsum panels or bases and/or the addition of sound-insulating blankets further improves sound ratings and makes partitions ideally suited for party walls. Drywall construction systems are laboratory tested to establish their sound-insulation characteristics. Airborne sound insulation is reported as the sound transmission class (STC), whereas impact noise, tested on floor-ceiling systems only, is reported as the impact insulation class (IIC). Suggested construction techniques for sound isolation are described and illustrated in chapter 9, along with recommended procedures and materials necessary to obtain adequate sound control.

Durability

Gypsum board can be used to construct strong, high-quality walls and ceilings with excellent dimensional stability and durability. Bonded together as described in chapters 6 to 10, gypsum panels will form walls and ceilings that resist cracking caused by minor structural movement as well as variations in humidity and temperature.

Dry construction

Factory-produced panels do not contribute moisture in construction; plaster construction does.

Light weight

Gypsum partition systems weigh appreciably less than masonry assemblies of the same thickness. They reduce material-handling expense and permit the use of lighter structural members, floors, and footings. Gypsum drywall is considerably lighter than conventional plaster.

Low installation cost

Gypsum systems provide lower installation costs than more massive constructions (Figure 1.5). The lighter-weight systems reduce materials-handling costs. The hollow-type constructions provide an ample cavity for thermal and sound insulation, simplifying fixture attachment and mechanical installation. It is easy to cut and install (Figure 1.6). Low material cost and large, quickly erected panels combine to provide a lower cost for gypsum drywall systems than conventional plaster. Gypsum can be attached with nails (Figure 1.7A), screws (Figure 1.7B), or adhesives.

Fast installation

Gypsum construction eliminates costly winter construction delays and permits earlier completion and occupancy of buildings. Gypsum panels are job-stocked, ready for use, easily cut, and quickly applied. They can be applied over either wood or metal framing.

Easily decorated

Gypsum construction offers smooth surfaces that readily accept paint, wallpaper, vinyl coverings, or wall tile. Gypsum also permits repeated decoration throughout the life of the building (Figure 1.8). Plain or aggregated textures are easily applied to gypsum board. This is available with vinyl-faced prefinished or predecorated panels. With these, joint finishing and decorating are eliminated, and maintenance is minimized.

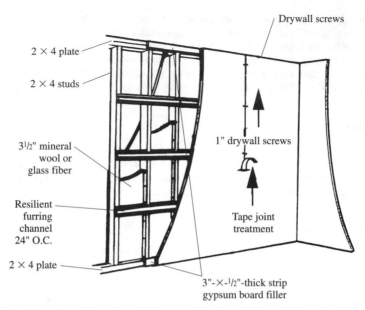

Drywall screws

2 × 4 plate

2 × 4 studs

3¹/₂" mineral
wool or
glass fiber

1" drywall screws

Resilient
furring
channel
24" O.C.

Tape joint
treatment

2 × 4 plate

3"-×-¹/₂"-thick strip
gypsum board filler

FIGURE 1.5   Drywall panels are suitable for and will cover either wood (as shown above) or metal framing.

FIGURE 1.6   To cut large panels, score the surface paper with a utility knife, then snap and cut the back paper with the same knife.

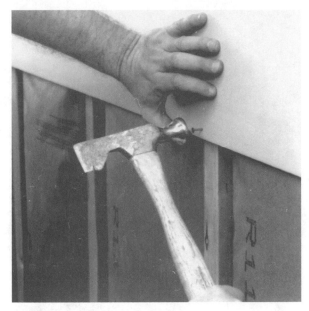

FIGURE 1.7A Panels secured with nails.

FIGURE 1.7B Panels secured with screws.

FIGURE 1.8   The decorating surface of drywall construction offers a number of easy-to-decorate finishes.

Versatility

Gypsum is suitable as party dividers, corridor walls, pipe-chase and shaft enclosures, radiant-heat ceilings, exterior walls and wall furring, and membrane fire-resistant constructions. Gypsum is adaptable for use in every type of new construction—commercial, institutional, industrial and residential—and in remodeling. It produces attractive, joint-free walls and ceilings (Figure 1.9), and it is easily adaptable to most contours, modules, and dimensions (Figure 1.10).

The advantages of drywall construction just described have made it the choice material for residential, commercial, and industrial wall treatment. These drywall applications have become so successful that there is a growing demand for the drywall product and for personnel to install it. Today a trained drywall mechanic or installer has tremendous opportunities available in this expanding field of construction.

FIGURE 1.9   Drywall construction offers joint-free walls and ceilings.

FIGURE 1.10   Drywall construction is easily adaptable to most contours and dimensions.

CHAPTER 2
GYPSUM-BOARD PRODUCTS AND ACCESSORIES

Robert Scharff
Walls & Ceilings Magazine

The drywall contractor or installer has a variety of gypsum-board sizes and types to work with. The regular (standard) gypsum board is used primarily as an interior wall and ceiling surface for finishes such as paint, wallpaper, and other wall coverings. It is also available prefinished in colorful textures, vinyl, or fabric-surfaced panels. In addition, there are gypsum boards on the market that can be used for ceramic, metal, and plastic tile; as area separation walls between occupancies; for exterior soffits; as an underlayer on exterior walls; as a component in shaft-wall construction; and to provide fire protection to structural elements. Many of these gypsum boards can be purchased with aluminum-foil backing, which provides an effective vapor retarder for exterior walls when applied with the foil surface against the framing.

Regular (standard) gypsum boards

Regular or standard-core gypsum boards are usually manufactured in 8-, 10-, 12- and 14-foot-long panels. The length of panels used will depend on the application and the panel thickness (see Table 2.1). Longer sheets are heavier and are more difficult to handle. If not handled carefully, they have a tendency to snap. Weigh the advantages of longer boards with fewer joints against the inconvenience of handling longer sheets.

The standard width of a gypsum board is 4 feet, which is compatible with the framing of studs or joists spaced 16 inches and 24 inches on center (O.C.) and room heights of 8 feet. But because of the popularity of 9-foot ceilings in some residential and commercial buildings, some manufacturers are making a 54-inch-wide board. With these additional 6 inches of width, two horizontally placed pieces fit perfectly on 9-foot walls with no extra cutting, taping, or finishing (Figure 2.1). Other lengths and widths of gypsum boards are available from manufacturers on special order.

TABLE 2.1 Gypsum Board Sizes

TYPICAL USES

1/4"	—remodeling, double layer walls, covering old walls/ceilings
5/16"	—manufactured housing walls and ceilings
3/8"	—remodeling, base for rigid panels, double layer walls/ceilings
1/2 & 5/8"	—any interior and some protected exterior uses
3/4 & 1"	—coreboards and liner board for shafts, area separation walls, party walls, fire walls, stairways, duct enclosures

SIZES(1)(3) WIDTH-FT.	2	2	2	2	4	4	4	4	4	4
LENGTH-FT.	8	9	10	12	8	9	10	12	14	16
1/4"					•	•	•			
5/16"					•	•	•	•		
3/8"					•	•	•			
1/2"*(2)(7)	•(4)				•	•	•	•	•	•
5/8"*(2)(7)	•(4)				•	•	•	•	•	•
3/4"*(5)(6)(7)	•	•	•	•						

NOTE:
(1) All boards available with regular core.
(2) 1/2", 5/8" also available with Type X core.
(3) Boards of other dimensions are available on special order.
(4) Gypsum Sheathing Only.
(5) Gypsum Liner Board – custom cut, lengths to 14' may be available.
(6) May be available with fire resistive core (See manufacturer).
(7) Available in 24" and 30" width for movable partitions (See manufacturer).

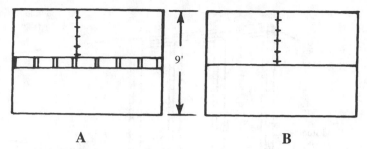

FIGURE 2.1   How a special 54-inch-wide panel saves cutting and joint treatment in a 9-foot-high wall area.

Regular boards are generally available in six thicknesses:

- ¼ inch. A lightweight, low-cost utility gypsum panel used as a base layer for improving sound control in multilayer partitions and in covering old wall and ceiling surfaces. Also, it is used for forming curved surfaces with short radii.
- ⁵⁄₁₆ inch. A gypsum board usually employed in mobile homes to keep weight to a minimum.
- ⅜ inch. A lightweight panel applied principally in repair and remodel working over existing surfaces. Also, it is used frequently in the double-layer wall system.
- ½ inch. This is the most common thickness used in single-layer application in both new construction and remodeling. It can also be in double-layer systems for greater sound and fire ratings.
- ⅝ inch. It is recommended for the finest single-layer drywall construction. The greater thickness provides higher rigidity and increased resistance to fire exposure and transmission of sound.
- ¾ and 1 inch. Sometimes known as coreboards, these are used in solid drywall partitions, shaft walls, stairwells, chaseways, area separation walls, and corridor ceilings.

Regular gypsum boards have a paper covering on each side and on the edges. The backs of the boards are surfaced with a gray liner paper. The facing is generally a light gray manilla paper that extends over the long edges. The surface is smooth and will take a wide variety of finishes. They can be applied in one or more layers directly to wood framing members, to steel studs or channels, or to interior masonry surfaces.

Single-layer or single-ply gypsum-board construction is the most commonly used system in residential and light commercial construction (Figure 2.2). The single-ply uses just one layer of gypsum drywall and is usually adequate to meet many fire-resistance and sound-control requirements.

Multi-ply or multilayer construction consists of a face layer of gypsum applied over a base layer of gypsum board that is directly attached to the framing members (Figure 2.3). This construction can offer greater strength and higher resistance to fire and sound transmission, compared to single-ply applications. When adhesively laminated, double-ply construction is especially resistant to cracking and provides the finest, strongest wall available. These adhesively laminated constructions are highly resistant to sag and joint deformation. In double-ply construction, always apply all base-layer board in each room before beginning face-ply application. This is because the face plies are laminated over base layers, thereby reducing the number of fasteners. As a result, surface joints of the face

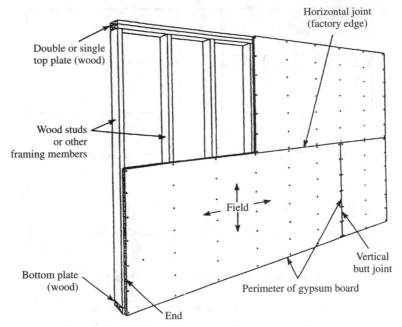

FIGURE 2.2   A single-layer or single-ply gypsum wall.

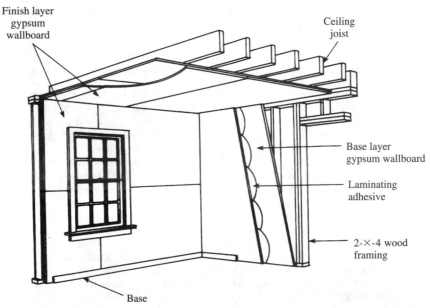

FIGURE 2.3   A double-layer or double-ply wall using an adhesive laminate between the base ply and finished layer.

layer are reinforced by the continuous base layers of gypsum board. Nail popping and ridging problems are less frequent, and imperfectly aligned supports have less effect on the finished surface.

As shown in Figure 2.4, regular board edges can be tapered (or recessed) (T), rounded (or featured edges) (RE or SWJ), double beveled (B), square edge (S), and tongue-and-groove (T&G). A taper with round edges (often called a *featured eased edge*) has a tapered and slightly rounded or beveled factory edge MB. This design helps minimize ridging or beading and other joint imperfections. When joint compound is applied, it firmly bonds the tape to the board and the panel "V" edges to each other making a strong, rigid joint (Figure 2.5).

The following are some limitations on the use of regular gypsum board:

• Exposure to excessive or continuous moisture and extreme temperatures should be avoided. To prevent weakening due to calcining, gypsum board should not be exposed to temperatures more than 125°F for extended periods of time. Not recommended for use in solar or other heating systems when board will be in continuous direct contact with surfaces exceeding 125°F.

• Must be adequately protected against wetting when used as a base for ceramic or other wall tile. Water-resistant panels are the recommended products for partitions in moisture-prone areas.

• Maximum stud spacing for single-layer application of ½-inch and ⅝-inch gypsum wallboard is 24 inches O.C. If ⅜-inch gypsum wallboard is used, it must be applied in two layers, with the second layer adhesively applied; 24-inches O.C. stud spacing might be used. Regular gypsum panels ⅜ and ¼ inch are not for use on steel framing or as base for water-based texturing materials.

• Application of gypsum panels over ¾-inch wood furring applied across framing is not recommended since the relative flexibility of the furring under impact of the hammer tends to loosen nails already driven. Furring should be 2-×-2 inch minimum (might be 1-×-3 if panels are to be screw-attached).

• Where long, continuous runs of this wall system are employed, control joints must be provided every 30 feet or less.

• Where structural movement might impose direct loads on these systems, isolation details are required.

• Partitions should not be used where frequently exposed to excessive moisture unless all surfaces are waterproofed.

• The application of gypsum panels over an insulating blanket that has first been installed continuously across the face of the framing members is not recommended. Blankets should be recessed and blanket flanges attached to sides of studs or joists. Insulation that fits tightly between metal studs requires no fastener (Figure 2.6).

• To produce final intended results, certain recommendations regarding surface preparation, painting products and systems must be adhered to for satisfactory results.

Type-X gypsum board

This board combines all the advantages of standard panels with additional resistance to fire exposure—the result of a specially formulated core containing special additives that enhance the integrity of the core under fire exposure. That is, the gypsum core of a type-X board works as a natural "sprinkler system." As noted in chapter 1, gypsum naturally contains about 21 percent water. When the board is heated, the water in the core begins to

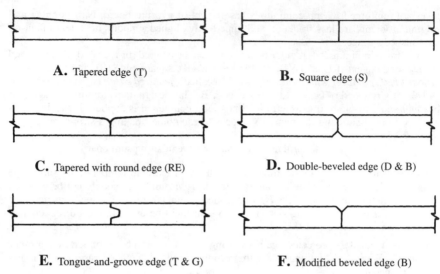

A. Tapered edge (T)   **B.** Square edge (S)

C. Tapered with round edge (RE)   **D.** Double-beveled edge (D & B)

E. Tongue-and-groove edge (T & G)   **F.** Modified beveled edge (B)

FIGURE 2.4   Regular board edges. (A) Tapered edge. (B) Square edge. (C) Tapered with round edge. (D) Double-beveled edge. (E) Tongue and groove. (F) Modified beveled edge.

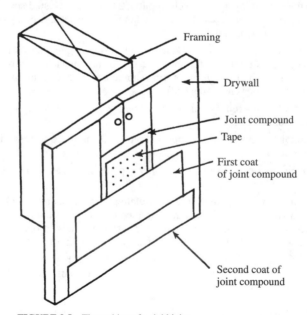

FIGURE 2.5   The making of a rigid joint.

evaporate and is released as steam, retarding heat transfer. Type-X wallboard remains in-combustible, however, as shrinkage occurs. Because of the loss of water volume, cracks de-velop that might permit passage of fire and heat. To lessen this process, type-X wallboard is formulated by adding incombustible fibers to the gypsum to help maintain the integrity of the core as water volume is lost, while providing greater resistance to heat transfer.

FIGURE 2.6 Blanket insulation can be installed between metal studs with no fasteners.

Fire ratings of from 45 minutes to 3 hours or more are available in both wood or steel framing systems in various wall, floor, and ceiling assemblies as well as for steel column and beam protection. When used on both sides of a load-bearing wood stud partition, a ⅝-inch type-X board has a 1 hour fire rating while ½-inch type-X board provides a 45 minute assembly rating. Fire-resistant gypsum panels are generally available in 4-foot widths and in lengths from 8 to 12 feet.

Proprietary type-X gypsum board is available in ½-inch and ⅝-inch thicknesses, and is required in some fire rated assemblies; additional additives give this product improved fire resistive properties. For more details on the important subject of fire ratings, see chapter 9.

Predecorated gypsum board

This gypsum board has a decorative surface which does not require any further treatment (Figure 2.7). The surfaces might be coated, printed, or have a vinyl film. Other predecorated finishes include factory painted and various textured patterns. It can be installed with color matched nails or adhesive. Predecorated panels are also available with type-X core.

The panels edges are either square or tapered and are butted together. Matching or contrasting moldings are available to conceal the joints and protect the panels from damage.

FIGURE 2.7 An example of a room finished with predecorated wallboard.

Moisture-resistant (MR) or water-resistant (WR) gypsum board

MR or WR board is a specially processed gypsum wallboard for use as a base for ceramic tile and other nonabsorbent finish materials in wet areas (Figure 2.8). The core, face paper and back paper of MR board are treated to withstand the effects of moisture and high humidity. MR board is available in the standard 4-foot width and 8-foot and 12-foot lengths. Its facing paper is colored green (hence it is often called "green board" by drywall mechanics) so as to make it readily distinguishable from regular gypsum wallboard. It is also available in ½-inch regular, and ½-inch or ⅝-inch type-X core. MR or WR board might be extended beyond the area to be tiled. A tapered edge is provided so that joints can be treated in the normal manner where MR board extends beyond the tiled area. No special tapes or edge sealants are required. Tile adhesive eliminates the need for further corner treatment, nail spotting and edge sealing, or filling the edge taper in the area to be tiled.

There are, however, a few limitations that should be kept in mind when considering the use and handling of MR or WR board. They are:

- MR board is not recommended for use where there will be direct exposure to water or continuous high humidity, such as in saunas, steam baths, gang shower rooms, or swimming pool enclosures. Cementitious tile backer board should be considered for these areas.
- No vapor retarder should be placed behind the MR board where tile is to be applied to the face. A vapor retarder can be created on the face of the MR board by applying a skim coat of tile adhesive or by using a silicone grout for tile.
- The MR board should not be used on exterior ceilings. Soffit board is recommended for protected exterior ceiling applications.

- The MR board should not be used on interior ceilings unless extra framing is provided; spacing of framing members should not exceed 12 inches O.C. Consult the local building code for compliance.

- Do not apply joint compound to joints or fasteners to be tiled. This requirement might be waived if the applied tile in combination with the bonding adhesive employed fully protects the gypsum board and water sensitive materials, if present (such as when joint compound is used), from penetration of water. Responsibility for performance of completed installations should rest with the surfacing material manufacturer and/or the surfacing material applicator.

- Adherence to the recommendations concerning sealing exposed edges, painting, tile adhesives, framing and installation is necessary for satisfactory performance. For high-humidity or "wet" areas, cement board should be considered as an alternative. Cement board exhibits most of the features of drywall but is unaffected by water.

Foil-backed gypsum board

These boards are made by laminating special kraft-back aluminum foil to the back surface of regular or X-type panels. Where required in cold climates, these boards form an effective vapor retarder for walls and ceilings, when applied with foil surfaces next to the framing on the interior side of an exterior wall in single-layer applications, ceiling, when applications, or as the base layer in a multilayer system. Foil-backed gypsum panels provide a water vapor retarder to help prevent interior moisture from entering wall and ceiling spaces. In tests per ASTM C355 (desiccant method), ½-inch foil-backed panels showed a vapor permeability of 0.06 permeance. The permeance of the total exterior wall is dependent on the closure of leaks with sealants at the periphery and penetrations such as outlet boxes.

Foil-backed gypsum panels are designed for use with furred masonry, wood, or steel framing (Figure 2.9). They are generally available in ⅜, ½ and ⅝-inch thicknesses and sizes, edges and finishes the same as for regular panels. Foil-backed gypsum board is also

FIGURE 2.8   Moisture-resistant (MR) or water-resistant (WR) board can be used as a base for ceramic tile.

FIGURE 2.9   Typical installation of foil-backed gypsum board.

available with an X-type core. The in-place cost of a foil-backed drywall installation is lower per thousand square feet than a similar installation for regular gypsum wallboard and polyethylene-film retarder installed separately.

This gypsum panel board has the following limitations:

- Not recommended for use where exposure to moisture and high outside temperature is extreme and continuous. Under these conditions, a qualified mechanical engineer should determine location of the vapor retarder.

- Foil-backed gypsum board should not be used as a base for ceramic or other tile or as a base layer for prefinished vinyl wall panels in double-layer assemblies. Also, not to be used as a base for adhesively applied vinyl or other highly water-vapor-resistant wall coverings.

- To prevent objectionable sag in ceilings, weight of overlaid unsupported insulation should not exceed: 1.3 pounds/square foot for ½-inch-thick panels with frame spacing 24 inches; 2.2 pounds/square foot for panels with frame spacing 16 inches. Panels ⅜ inch thick must not be overlaid with unsupported insulation. Unheated attic spaces should be properly ventilated.

- Foil-backed gypsum wallboard is not recommended for use in hot, humid climates such as the Southern Atlantic and Gulf Coast areas.

High-strength ceiling board

Some gypsum board manufacturers provide a ½-inch, high-strength ceiling board as a cost-saving alternative to ⅝-inch wallboard for ceilings. High-strength ceiling board has a specially formulated core that resists the natural tendency to sag when attached to ceiling joists and trusses spaced 24 inches and where heavy water-based textures are applied.

Gypsum ceiling panels

Gypsum ceiling panels have a noncombustible gypsum core with high light reflection and attractive predecorated surfaces. The panels install easily in standard exposed-grid systems. Because ceiling panels have a rigid gypsum core, they resist sagging and warping, and they do not require clips to offset bowing. In addition, they can be easily cut by simply scoring and snapping. As little as 1 inch of material can be cut from the panels with virtually no crumbling of the edges. Most gypsum ceiling panels are accepted by the United States Department of Agriculture (USDA) for use in food service and food-processing areas. Most gypsum ceiling panels are ½ inch thick with a 2-mil, white, stipple-textured vinyl laminate for high light reflection and easy cleaning. They are available in 2-×-2-foot and 2-×-4-foot panels for interior and unexposed exterior applications. In accordance with industry practice, these dimensions are nominal. Actual sizes, correspondingly are:

$$2 \times 2 \text{ feet} = 23\frac{3}{4} \times 23\frac{3}{4} \text{ inches}$$
$$2 \times 4 \text{ feet} = 23\frac{3}{4} \times 47\frac{3}{4} \text{ inches}$$

Custom sizes are available from most manufacturers by special order.

Gypsum shaft liner

Gypsum shaft liner is used for the construction of elevator, air, and mechanical shafts (Figure 2.10), stair walls, and general partitions. It is designed for use on building construction that requires a 2-hour fire-resistance rating. An arrangement constructed with nonload-bearing metal framing, a 1-inch type-X shaft liner panel, and 2 layers of regular ½-inch or ⅝-inch gypsum boards will help to protect the framing members and prevent or delay the spread of fire from one area to another. With the addition of insulation or resilient channels, the construction will effectively reduce sound transmission, too.

Liner board is available in ¾- or ½-inch thicknesses in widths of 24 or 48 inches, and with square edges (sometimes eased square edges). Shaft liners are designed to be non-load-bearing.

Gypsum sound-deadening board

When used in conjunction with either ½- or ⅝-inch type-X board, a ¼-inch sound-deadening board will provide an excellent sound- and fire-resistant installation. The ¼-inch sound-deadening board is noncombustible and easy to apply, and it adds structural integrity. In UL designs, one layer of ½-inch type-X panel with one layer of ¼-inch sound-deadening board on each side of wood or metal studs will provide 1 hour of fire protection and 45- to 50-STC sound isolation (see chapter 9).

Other gypsum-board products

There are other gypsum-board products that are used by the construction industry, but they are generally installed by other professional craftspeople. However, some drywall firms do install them. These gypsum products include the following:

Exterior soffit board. Gypsum exterior soffit board is a special paper-and-core-formulated noncombustible gypsum board developed for exterior use in outdoor-building soffits, carports, ceilings of outdoor shopping malls, and other applications where there is no

FIGURE 2.10 Gypsum shaft-liner board being installed in an elevator shaft.

direct exposure to weather. Soffit board has a special water-resistant, green-colored face paper bonded to a reinforced core, and it is available in ½- or ⅝-inch thicknesses that are 4 feet wide with lengths of 8 to 12 feet. It is also available with a type-X core.

Gypsum sheathing. Gypsum sheathing is used as a protective fire-resistant membrane under exterior wall-surfacing materials such as wood siding, masonry veneer, stucco, and shingles (Figure 2.11). It also provides protection against the passage of water and wind and adds structural rigidity to either wood or metal framing systems. The noncombustible core is surfaced with water-repellent paper; it might also have a water-resistant core. Some boards are available that are covered with fiberglass mat that provides an alkali-resistant surface. This facing also resists wicking, moisture penetration, and delamination caused by surface water exposure. The alkali-resistant surface coating means that it is not necessary to apply a primer/sealer with an exterior installation finish system. Gypsum sheathing is available in 2- and 4-foot widths, ½- and ⅝-inch thicknesses, and it is available with a type-X core.

There is also a paperless exterior sheathing available that is especially suitable for exterior insulation finish systems (EIFS). The panel will not blister, delaminate, or lose bonding qualities for up to six months of outdoor weathering prior to the installation of finishing materials. It consists of a specially treated gypsum core reinforced at both surfaces with a nonwoven glass-fiber mat. The glass-reinforcing mat on the exterior face of the sheathing has been embedded under a polymer-coated gypsum layer. The panels are usually 4 × 8 feet and in ½- and ⅝-inch thicknesses.

Deck gypsum roof board. This is a nonstructural product that has a silicone-treated, water-resistant gypsum core (Figure 2.12). It might have either a fiberglass or galvanized steel mesh embedded into it. It comes in a 4-foot width that is 8 feet in length, with standard thicknesses of ½ inch. The type-X core is ⅝ inch. It is used for commercial roof assemblies.

FIGURE 2.11 Gypsum sheathing can be used for exterior surfacing materials such as wood siding, masonry veneer, stucco, and various shingles.

FIGURE 2.12 Examples of typical gypsum roof board.

Another nonstructural gypsum roof product is the so-called "form board." These boards serve as a form for poured gypsum concrete roof decks. They are fastened to the joists or beams, and then the gypsum concrete is poured into the form. The form boards are left after the concrete sets up. These panels are generally 1 inch thick, 8, 10, or 12 feet long, and they come in widths of 24, 32, or 48 inches. They are faced with either manila paper suitable for decorating or vinyl that requires no further finishing. Since form board is considered nonstructural, it is not necessary to consider it in calculating the load-carrying capacity of the completed roof.

Gypsum base for veneer plaster.   Gypsum base for veneer plaster is used as a base for thin coats of durable, high-strength, surface-abrasion-resistant gypsum veneer plaster. The gypsum boards come in 4-foot widths with square-cut edges. Standard veneer-base drywall is ⅜, ½, or ⅝ inch thick. Type-X drywall is only available in widths of ½ or ⅝ inch. Both types come in 8-, 10-, and 12-foot lengths. The gypsum core is faced with specially treated, multilayered paper designed to provide a maximum bond to veneer plaster finishes. The paper's absorbent outer layers quickly and uniformly draw moisture from the veneer plaster finish for proper application and finishing; the moisture-resistant inner layers keep the core dry and rigid to resist sagging. The face paper is folded around the long edges.

FIGURE 2.13   Applying veneer plaster to a gypsum base board.

Gypsum bases finished with veneer plasters are recommended for interior walls and ceilings in all types of construction (Figure 2.13). For these interiors, a veneer of specially formulated gypsum plaster is applied in one coat (1/16 to 3/32 inch thick) or two coats (⅛ to 3/16 inch thick) over the base. The resulting smooth or textured monolithic surfaces are preferred for hard-wear locations where durability and resistance to abrasion are required.

Gypsum base board for veneer plaster is hung in the same manner as regular or type-X board. For this reason, this board is sometimes hung by the drywall mechanic. But veneer plastering is a specialized trade and is seldom done by drywall contractors. The General Service Administration has canceled many of the federal procurement documents and replaced them with the federal specifications as given in Table 2.2.

GYPSUM LATH

Gypsum lath has a core of gypsum plaster between two layers of absorbent paper. It might be plain, perforated with ¾-inch holes on 4-inch centers, or insulating lath backed with aluminum foil to provide a vapor barrier and reflective insulation. It is available in ⅜- and ½-inch thicknesses, in sheets 16 or 24 inches wide, and in 4- or 8-foot lengths. Gypsum lath requires about 45 percent less base-coat plaster than with metal lath. Gypsum lath is designed for fast attachment to framing, either wood studs (with nails or staples) or steel studs, furring channels, or suspended metal grille.

TABLE 2.2 Federal Specification Designations

Type	Grade	Class	Form	Style
TYPE I Lath	R-Regular core X-Fire-retardant core	1-Plain face	a-Plain back b-Perforated c-Foil back	1-Square edge 5-Round edge
TYPE II Sheathing	R-Regular core W-Water-resistant core X-Fire-retardant core	2-Water-resistant surface	a-Plain back	1-Square edge 2-V-tongue-and- groove edge
TYPE III Wallboard	R-Regular X-Fire-retardant core	1-Plain face 3-Predecorated surface	a-Plain back c-Foil back	1-Square edge 3-Taper or recess edge 4-Featured joint edge 6-Taper, featured edge
TYPE IV Backer board	R-Regular core X-Fire-retardant core	1-Plain face	a-Plain back c-Foil back	1-Square edge 2-V-tongue-and- groove edge 3-Taper or recess edge
TYPE V Formboard	R-Regular core	4-Fungus-resistant surface	a-Plain back	1-Square edge
TYPE VI Veneer plaster base	R-Regular core X-Fire-retardant core	1-Plain face	a-Plain back c-Foil back	1-Square edge 3-Taper or recess edge 6-Taper, featured edge
TYPE VII Water-resistant backing board	R-Regular core W-Water-resistant treated core X-Fire-retardant core	2-Water-resistant surfaces	a-Plain back	1-Square edge 3-Taper or recess edge

* As an aid in the identification of gypsum wallboard products, classifications are set forth as in Federal Specifications SS-L30D.

DRYWALL ACCESSORIES

The drywall mechanic or contractor has many items to consider in the application of gypsum drywall panels. These include such accessories as trim, framing components, sound control and insulation products, fasteners, joint compounds, and reinforcing tapes. Trim accessories are shown in Figure 2.14, and their applications are described in chapter 10. Other metal accessories that are used are illustrated in Figure 2.15.

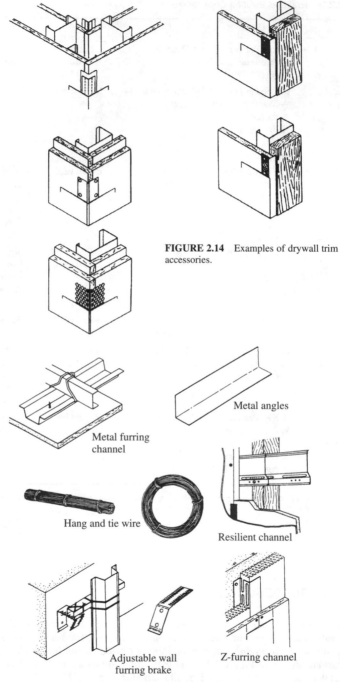

FIGURE 2.14   Examples of drywall trim accessories.

Metal angles

Metal furring channel

Hang and tie wire

Resilient channel

Adjustable wall furring brake

Z-furring channel

FIGURE 2.15   Other metal products used by drywall installers.

Trim accessories

Trim accessories include corner reinforcements, beads, trims, control joints, and decorative moldings.

FRAMING COMPONENTS

As stated in chapter 1, gypsum board can be applied over wood framing, metal framing, or furring. It can be applied to masonry and concrete surfaces, either directly or to wood or metal furring strips. If the board is to be applied directly, any irregularities in the masonry or concrete surfaces must be smoothed or filled. Furring is a means to provide a flat surface for standard fastener application as well as provide separation to overcome dampness in exterior walls. Gypsum board must not come in direct contact with surfaces such as concrete or soil, which can have high moisture content.

Wood framing

The interior walls in a wood-framed structure with conventional joist-and-rafter roof construction are normally placed so that they serve as bearing walls for the ceiling joists as well as room dividers. Walls located parallel to the direction of the joists are commonly nonbearing. Studs are a nominal 2-×-4 inches and can be spaced either 16 or 24 inches apart. Actually, spacing of the studs is usually controlled by the thickness of the covering material. For example, 24-inch stud spacing will require ½-inch gypsum board for drywall interior covering.

While the drywall contractor does not erect the wall framing or have anything to do with the selection of the framing material, he/she must make sure that all wood framing and furring must be accurately aligned in the same plane so that the gypsum boards fit flat against it at all points. If warped or crooked studs and joists have been used, they should be replaced with straight lumber. Gypsum board cannot compensate for improper or misaligned framing. Full details on installing gypsum board over wood framing can be found in chapter 6.

Metal framing

The advantages of metal framing are noncombustibility, uniformity of dimension, lightness of weight, freedom from rot problems, and relative ease of erection. The components of metal frame systems are manufactured to fit together easily, and they generally are friction fit. Except at doors, windows, etc., no other fasteners are really necessary to erect a framing wall (Figure 2.16). It is important, however, that light-gauge steel components such as steel studs and runners, furring channels, and resilient channels be adequately protected against rusting in the warehouse and on the job site. In marine areas such as the Caribbean, Florida, and the Gulf Coast, where salt-air conditions exist with high humidity, components that offer increased protection against corrosion should be used.

A multi-ply drywall sound-insulating partition can be easily erected by placing steel studs in metal runners. The runners are usually installed on the floor and ceiling first, and the studs are located 16 or 24 inches apart in the runners. While this fit is a friction fit, many contractors fasten the runners and studs with metal screws.

Studs and runners are generally of the channel type, roll-formed from corrosion-resistant steel, and designed for quick screw attachment of facing materials. They are good for

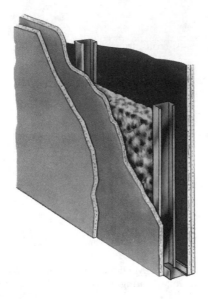

FIGURE 2.16 Double-layer installation onto metal studs with insulation installed in between.

strong, nonload-bearing construction. Limited chaseways for electrical and plumbing services are provided by punchouts in the stud web. Full details on installing gypsum drywall panels using metal framing can be found in chapter 7.

GYPSUM-BOARD FASTENERS

Nails and screws are commonly used to attach gypsum board in both single and multi-ply installations. Clips and staples are used only to attach the base layer in multi-ply construction. Special drywall adhesives can be used to secure single-ply gypsum board to framing and furring or masonry and concrete. These adhesives can also be used to laminate a face ply to a base layer of gypsum board or other base material. Adhesives must be supplemented with mechanical fasteners. These fasteners might be temporary or permanent, depending on the application.

Where fasteners are used at the board perimeter, they should be placed at least ⅜ inch from board edges and ends. Fastening should start in the middle of the board and proceed outward toward the perimeter. Fasteners should be driven as near to perpendicular as possible while the board is held firmly against the supporting construction.

Nails

When gypsum board was first used, a common problem was *nail pops*, which are raised circles in the gypsum panel where nails are pushed out of framing members as they move with settling or changes in temperature and moisture conditions. To prevent this problem, the best nail to use is an annular ring nail (Figure 2.17). It is made in two lengths: 1¼ inches for wallboards up to ½ inch thick, and 1⅜ inches for ⅝-inch gypsum board.

FIGURE 2.17 The annular ring is the best nail for drywall.

Examples of other acceptable nails for gypsum board application are shown in Figure 2.18. Preferably, the nails should have heads that are flat or concave and thin at the rim. The heads should be at least ¼ inch in diameter and not more than ⁵⁄₁₆ inch in diameter to provide adequate holding power without cutting the face of the paper when the nail is dimpled. The heads of casing nails and common nails are too small in relation to the shank; they easily cut into the face paper and should not be used. Nail heads that are too large are also likely to cut the paper surface if the nail is driven incorrectly at a slight angle.

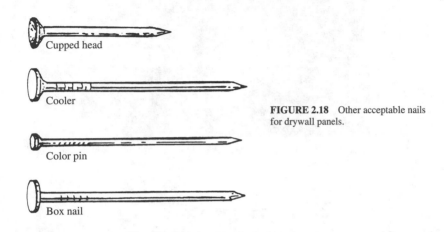

FIGURE 2.18   Other acceptable nails for drywall panels.

The nails used to attach prefinished wallboard are 1⅜ inches long and are provided by the wallboard manufacturer. These are the only mechanical fasteners that are provided by the manufacturer, and they should be driven with a plastic-headed hammer that does not mar the paint matching the wallboard. These nails are not dimpled; the underside of their heads should be just flush with the panel.

The tool for most drywall nails is a wallboard hammer (Figure 2.19). It has a slightly rounded head that is scored for accurate driving. Nails must be driven straight to a point just below the level of the wallboard's surface. This process is called *dimpling* (Figure 2.20). The rounded head of the wallboard hammer dimples the wallboard without breaking its surface paper; other tools do not.

Nails should be long enough to go through the wallboard layers and far enough into supporting construction to provide adequate holding power. Nail penetration into the framing member should be ⅞ inch for smooth shank nails, but only ¾ inch for annular ringed nails, which provide more withdrawal resistance. For fire-rated assemblies, greater penetration is required—generally 1⅛ inches to 1¼ inches for one-hour assemblies. Drywall panels are often double nailed (two nails) as shown in Figure 2.21.

Screws

Most drywall mechanics prefer screws to nails because they have a greater holding power and they are less likely to break the surface paper or crack the gypsum core. The best screw has a bugle head and alternately high and low threads. For greater holding power, the bugle head spins the face paper into the cavity under the head of the screw (Figures

FIGURE 2.19   Driving nails into the edge of a drywall panel with a drywall hammer.

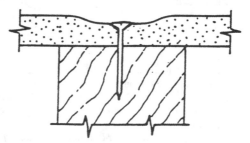

FIGURE 2.20   Properly shaped dimple.

2.22A through B). Defects associated with improper nail dimpling are eliminated. Other head types, such as pan head, are designed specifically for attaching metal to metal and installing wood and metal trim.

The following are the three types of drywall screws (Figure 2.23):

- Type-W gypsum drywall screws are designed for fastening gypsum board to wood framing or furring. Diamond-shaped points on type-W screws provide efficient drilling action through both gypsum and wood, and a specially designed thread gives quick penetration and increased holding power. Recommended minimum penetration into supporting construction is ⅝ inch. However, in two-ply construction where the face layer is screw-attached, additional holding power is developed in the base ply. This permits reduced penetration into supports to ½ inch. Type-S screws can be substituted for type W.

- Type-S gypsum drywall screws are designed for fastening gypsum board to steel studs or furring. They are self-drilling, have a self-tapping thread, and generally have a mill-slot or hardened drill point designed to easily penetrate metal. (Easy penetration is important because steel studs often are flexible and tend to bend away from the screws.)

- Type-G gypsum drywall screws are used for fastening gypsum board to gypsum backing or baseboards. Type-G are similar to type-W screws, but they have a deeper special thread design. They are generally 1½ inches long, but other lengths are available. Type-G gypsum drywall screws require penetration of at least ½ inch of the threaded portion into the supporting board. Type-G drywall screws should not be used to attach wallboard to ⅜-inch backing board because sufficient holding strength is not available. Nails or longer screws should be driven through both the surface layer and the ⅜-inch base ply to give the proper penetration in supporting wood or steel framing members. Type-S-12 screws are sometimes used to attach wallboard to heavier-gauge steel framing.

- Screws are generally installed using a power screwdriver with an adjustable clutch (Figure 2.24).

Staples

Staples are recommended only for attaching base ply to wood members in multi-ply construction. They should be 16-gauge, flattened, galvanized wire with a minimum ⁷⁄₁₆-inch-wide crown and spreading points (Figure 2.25). Staples should provide a minimum of ⅝-inch penetration into supports.

FIGURE 2.21   Double-nailing of a drywall panel.

FIGURE 2.22A   A bugle-head screw depresses the face paper of the gypsum panel without tearing. Threads cut into and deform the wood to hold tightly.

FIGURE 2.22B   A longer drywall nail grips with friction. The hold is loosened as the wood shrinks, which might pop the nail head above the surface to create a callback.

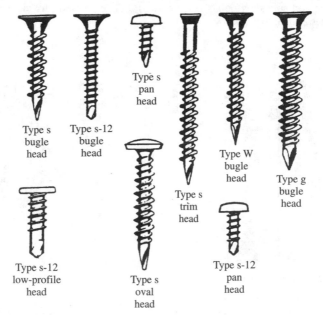

Type s
bugle
head

Type s-12
bugle
head

Type s
pan
head

Type W
bugle
head

Type g
bugle
head

Type s-12
low-profile
head

Type s
trim
head

Type s
oval
head

Type s-12
pan
head

FIGURE 2.23   Types of screws used in a drywall installation.

Adhesives

Adhesives can be used to bond single layers of gypsum board directly to framing, furring, masonry, or concrete. They can also be used to laminate gypsum board to base layer of backing board, sound-deadening board, rigid foam, or other rigid insulation boards. The recommendations of the adhesive manufacturer should be followed. They must be used in

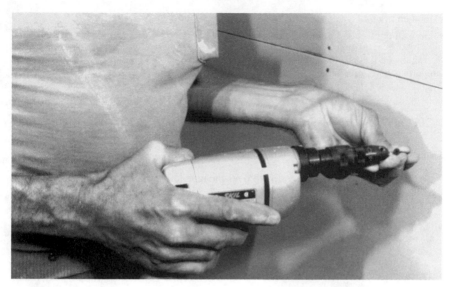

FIGURE 2.24   Adjusting the clutch on a power screwdriver to properly drive a screw.

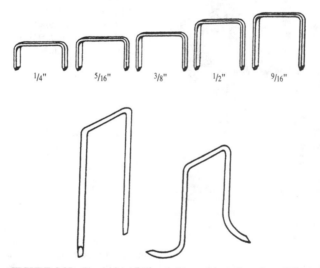

$^{1}/_{4}$" $^{5}/_{16}$" $^{3}/_{8}$" $^{1}/_{2}$" $^{9}/_{16}$"

FIGURE 2.25   Sizes of available staplers and how the points of the staples should react.

combination with nails, staples (in mobile homes), or screws that provide supplemental support. Adhesives for applying wallboard finishes are classed:

• Stud adhesive
• Laminating adhesive

- Joint compound adhesive
- Drywall contact and modified contact adhesive

Details on the use and application of these adhesives to fasten gypsum board panels to supports is given in chapters 5 and 6.

JOINT COMPOUNDS AND REINFORCING TAPES

Joint treatment compounds have three basic uses:

- To embed the joint tape and to finish over the tape, the corner bead, and nail or screw heads.
- To texture wallboard surfaces.
- To laminate wallboard to an existing surface such as old plaster, masonry, or a gypsum wallboard or backer board base.

FIGURE 2.26 Gypsum-board walls and ceilings usually have joints treated with tape and compound to give a smooth, monolithic appearance.

After the gypsum board is installed and secured with the proper fasteners, it is necessary to reinforce and conceal the joints, fasteners, and corner beads. Joint compound and reinforcing tape are used for this purpose to achieve the appearance of a monolithic surface as shown in Figure 2.26. Joint reinforcing compounds are of three basic types:

- A taping or bedding compound used to adhere the tape to the board.
- A finishing or topping compound used especially for finishing.
- An all-purpose compound to be used for both embedding and finishing.

Most joint compounds contain water-soluble, dispersible organic adhesives or synthetic resins. These products gain their strength and adhesion through drying (drying compounds). The loss of water is accompanied by shrinkage, which is overcome by several thin applications of the compound. Each application should be thoroughly dry before the next application is started. Synthetic resin compounds such as "vinyls" will keep longer than the organic, water-soluble types. Another family of joint compounds gains strength by setting. To meet varying job requirements, setting-type joint compounds are offered in a wide choice of setting times. The set might occur within 30 minutes or take as long as several hours. The quick-set type, having a shorter working time, must be used within the prescribed time limit. (Additional coats are possible before complete drying takes place.) It is common for setting compounds to be used for embedding the tape, and "nonsetting" types are used for the finishing operation.

Joint compounds of the premixed type are also available, and they come in two consistencies: one for hand application and the other for machine application. All compounds should be compatible. Do not mix different formulations unless this is recommended by the joint-compound manufacturer.

Joint tapes are designed for use with ready-mix or powder joint compounds to reinforce and finish the joints between adjacent gypsum panels. Precreased tape is available and should be applied in the corners of the walls and ceiling intersections. Exposed edges of the gypsum board might require some type of metal or plastic casing or appropriate trim.

Reinforcing tapes are usually of two types: paper tape or fiberglass tape. The paper type, approximately 2 to 2¼ inches wide, is the most commonly used. It usually comes with a crease down the middle to serve as a guide when folding it to make a corner joint. This type is also usually perforated with very tiny holes to increase gripping strength when the joint compound is forced through in the embedding process (Figure 2.27).

The fiberglass tape is also about 2 to 2¼ inches wide and is used where moisture resistance is important. It comes in a plain or open-weave (about 100-meshes-per-square-inch) configuration. The plain back is normally stapled in place, while the open weave generally comes with pressure adhesive backing that is pressed firmly against the joint with either a taping knife or a trowel. Use a corner trowel to press the tape into the inside corners. Do not apply one piece of tape on top of another or overlap them; the thickness of the tape makes the overlap too hard to conceal. Cover the tape with successive layers of joint compound. The adhesive backing on the fiberglass tape eliminates the need for an embedding coat of compound. Both types of fiberglass tape are much more expensive than the paper types of tape.

Complete details on the use and application of joint compounds and tape are given in chapter 10. Remember that a drywall joint treatment system (reinforcing tape and joint compound) must provide joints as strong as the gypsum board itself. Otherwise, normal structural movement in a wall or ceiling assembly can result in the development of cracks over the finished joint.

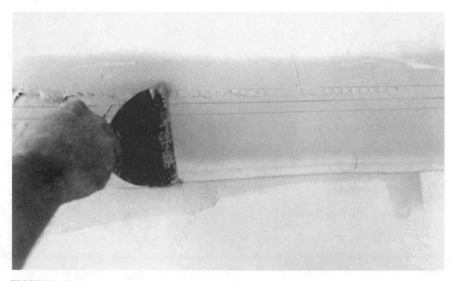

FIGURE 2.27   Embedding joint compound into reinforcing tape.

CHAPTER 3
TOOLS OF THE DRYWALL TRADE

Robert Scharff
Walls & Ceilings Magazine

As in any trade, suitably designed tools and their proper use are essential for high-quality drywall workmanship. Using the right tools for specific jobs can improve efficiency and reduce labor costs. This chapter contains an extensive sampling of tools designed to meet the needs of drywall, veneer, and plastering contractors. Some of the more commonly used hand tools can be found at building material dealers, hardware stores, and home centers.

When purchasing drywall tools, go for quality. Select tools made by companies with a good reputation within the building and drywall industry for making tools that will help to produce accurate, quality work for a long time. Bargain tools are available occasionally, but most bargains turn out to be a waste of money after they have been used for awhile.

So start with quality and maintain that quality with good care. Keep small tools in a sturdy toolbox with handles. Be sure that it is divided into compartments, and keep similar tools in the same compartment. Store sharp tools so that their edges are protected against nicks and bumps. Store flexible tools so that they will not bend out of shape as the toolbox is moved from place to place. The box should be strong, but it should not be so heavy that it is a chore to carry to and from the job.

Drywall tools can be divided into the following basic categories:

- Measuring tools
- Installation tools
- Attaching tools
- Finishing tools
- Miscellaneous drywall tools

MEASURING TOOLS

Accurate measurements are essential for proper fit when installing gypsum-drywall panels. There are, of course, two basic measuring systems in the world today: the U.S. Customary

System (USCS) or English system, which is most commonly used in the United States; and the International System of Units (SI), which is used in most other countries and is commonly referred to as the metric system. The United States, too, is now undergoing the process of converting to the metric system. The two systems are convertible; 1 meter equals 39.37 inches, and 1 inch equals 25.4 millimeters. In this book all dimensions are given in USCS units. The federal government has mandated that each federal agency make a transition to the use of metric units in all federal procurements, grants, and business-related activities. The leading gypsum-board manufacturers, in compliance with this order, already provide a full line of wallboard products in "hard" metric dimensions with regard to width and length. Standard board offerings are made in the width of 1200mm and a length of 3600mm. Job-size lengths are available on a special order basis requiring minimum order quantities and extended lead times. Full details on conversion between the two systems are given in appendix B.

Figure 3.1 shows most measuring rules and tapes used by drywall installers. The metal or wood folding rule might be used for certain measuring purposes. The simple folding rule is usually 2 feet long, while the multiple-folding or "zigzag" wood rule is 6 feet long. The sections are so hinged that it is 6 inches from the center of one hinge joint to the center of the next, which makes the sections roughly 8 inches in length. It is graduated in sixteenths of an inch. Some zigzag rules have a thin metal extension rule built into one of the end sections; it is particularly useful for inside measurements. The reading on the extension is simply added to the length of the opened rule.

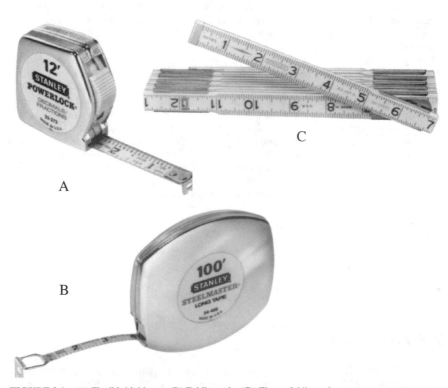

FIGURE 3.1   (A) Flexible/rigid tape. (B) Folding rule. (C) Zigzag folding rule.

FIGURE 3.2   Using a flexible/rigid tape.

Fiberglass or steel tapes are made from 6 to 100 feet in length. The shorter lengths are frequently made with a curved cross section so that they are flexible enough to roll up, but they remain rigid when extended. Long, flat tapes require support over their full length during measuring, or the natural sag will cause an error in the reading.

The flexible/rigid tapes are usually contained in metal cases into which they wind themselves when a button is pressed, or into which they can easily be pushed. A hook provided at one end can be hooked over the object being measured, so one person can handle the rule without assistance (Figure 3.2). On some models, the outside of the case can be used as one end of the tape for measuring inside dimensions. "Pull-push tapes," as this type is commonly called, usually come in lengths of 6 to 16 feet, graduated in feet, inches, and fractions of an inch down to $\frac{1}{16}$ inch.

The hand-held laser measuring tool shown in Figure 3.3 measures effectively from 10 inches up to 330 feet with accuracy to within ± $\frac{1}{8}$ inch. The digital display gives readings in both metric or English units. To get an accurate measurement, point the visible laser dot to the distant target and read the distance on the digital display.

FIGURE 3.3   Typical hand-held laser measuring tool.

Squares

These tools are used primarily for testing and checking the trueness of an angle or for laying out lines on materials. Most squares have a rule marked on their edge. As a result, they might also be used for measuring. There are three common squares used by the dry-wall mechanic or hanger:

- The framing or carpenter's steel square consists of a wide, long member, called the *tongue*, which forms a right angle with the blade (Figure 3.4). The outer corner, where the blade and tongue meet, is called the *heel*. The *face* of the square is the side one sees when the square is held with the blade in the left hand and the tongue in the right hand, with the heel pointed away from the body. The manufacturer's name is usually stamped on the face. The blade is usually 24 inches long and 2 inches wide. The tongue varies from 14 to 18 inches long and is 1½ inches wide, as measured from the heel.

- The try square (Figure 3.5) consists of two parts at right angles to each other: a thick wood or metal handle and a thin steel blade. Most try squares are made with the blades graduated in inches and fractions of an inch. The blade length varies from 3 to 12 inches. This square is used for testing the squareness of ends and edges of stock; held upside down on a flat surface, it can be used to check for warp; held against the inside corner of a workpiece, it can be used to check a right angle. It can also be used to measure sections (not exceeding the length of the blade) and to scribe across the face of the work.

- A 4-foot drywall T-square is an indispensable tool for making accurate cuts across the narrow dimension of gypsum board. Usually made of aluminum, it consists of a guide and a blade that come together in the shape of the letter "T" (Figure 3.6). They are available with or without a measuring scale printed on them. Details on the use of a drywall T-square can be found in chapter 5.

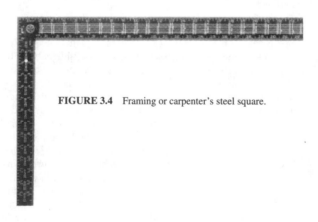

FIGURE 3.4   Framing or carpenter's steel square.

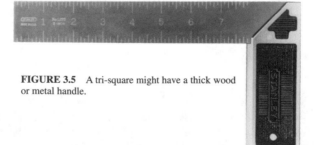

FIGURE 3.5   A tri-square might have a thick wood or metal handle.

FIGURE 3.6   A drywall T-square is used in the cutting of panels as described in chapter 5.

Marking gauges

Marking gauges are used to mark off guidelines parallel to an edge, end, or surface of a piece of wood, metal, or drywall panels. They are made of metal or wood and consist of a graduated beam about 8 inches long on which a head slides. The head can be fastened at any point on the beam by means of a thumbscrew. The thumbscrew presses a brass shoe tightly against the beam and locks it firmly in position. The steel pin or spur that does the marking projects from the beam about 1/16 inch.

To draw a line parallel to an edge with a marking gauge, first determine the required distance of the line from the edge of the stock. Adjust the marking gauge by setting the head the desired distance from the spur. Although the bar of a marking gauge is graduated in inches, the spur might work loose or bend. If this occurs, accurate measurements should be made with a rule between the head and spur (Figure 3.7A). To draw a line after setting

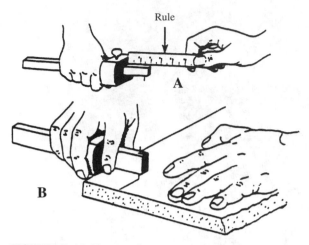

FIGURE 3.7   Marking gauge in use.

the gauge, grasp the head of the gauge with the palm and fingers as shown in Figure 3.7B; extend the thumb along the beam toward the spur. Press the head firmly against the edge of the work to be marked, and with a wrist motion, tip the gauge forward until the spur touches the work. Push the gauge along the edge to mark the work, keeping the head firmly against the edge of the work.

Chalk lines and plumb bobs

In some instances, using a chalk line to mark a straight line on a large surface is easier than using a straightedge. The line is first chalked by holding the chalk in the hand and drawing the line across it several times. The line is then tightly stretched between the points and snapped as shown in Figure 3.8. For an accurate line, never snap the chalk line for a distance greater than 20 feet. A less messy way of using a chalk line is to acquire a mechanical "chalk reel," which works much the same as a tape measure. The line is pulled from the housing and stretched across the surface that is to be marked, then snapped. The housing of the chalk reel has an opening that allows powdered chalk to be poured into it; once the chalk is in the housing, several vigorous shakes of the housing will coat the line with the chalk.

A *plumb bob* is a pointed, tapered brass or bronze weight that is suspended from a cord for determining the vertical or plumb line to or from a point on the floor. Gravity will hold the string perfectly vertical, as long as the bob is hanging free and is not moving. Common weights for plumb bobs used in drywall work are 5, 8, and 10 ounces (Figure 3.9).

A plumb bob is a precision instrument and must be cared for as such. If the tip becomes bent, the cord from which the bob is suspended will not show the true plumb line over the point indicated by the tip. Many plumb bobs have a detachable tip so that if the tip should become damaged, it can be renewed without replacing the entire instrument.

Levels

Levels are tools designed to determine whether a plane or surface is truly horizontal or vertical (Figure 3.10). Some precision spirit levels are calibrated so that they will indicate, in

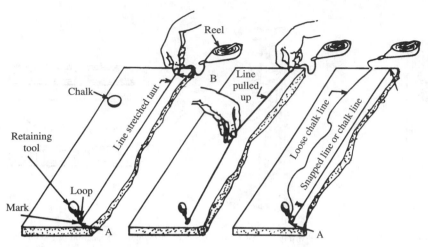

FIGURE 3.8 How to snap a simple chalk line.

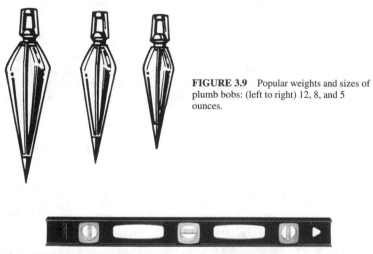

FIGURE 3.9 Popular weights and sizes of plumb bobs: (left to right) 12, 8, and 5 ounces.

FIGURE 3.10 Typical level used by a drywall hanger.

degrees, minutes, and seconds, the angle of inclination of a surface in relation to the horizontal or vertical. They are made in a variety of materials: aluminum, steel, plastic, hardwood, and softwood. Aluminum levels are lightweight, rustproof, and warp-proof; they are preferred for general drywall construction use.

The carpenter's level is usually either a 24-inch wood block or of metal I-beam construction with true surface edges (Figure 3.11). While this type of level might have two or more vials, there are two important bubble tubes in it. One is in the middle of one of the long edges. The other is at right angles to this, and parallel to the end of the level. The bubble tubes are glass vials nearly filled with alcohol, and they are slightly curved. As a bubble of air in such a tube will rise to the highest point, the bubble will be in the

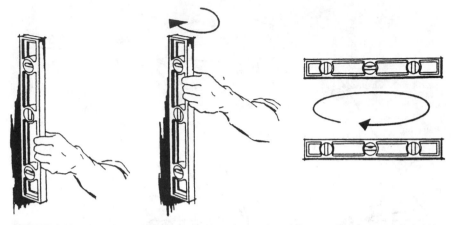

FIGURE 3.11 Place the level firmly against a surface and carefully note the location of the bubble. Then turn the level (end-for-end when checking the horizontal indicator, edge-for-edge keeping the same vial upright when checking the vertical). Place the level in exactly the same position. Any discrepancy between the two readings indicates a misalignment of the vial, nicks on the straightedge surface of the level, warpage, or some other problem that might be corrected or taken into consideration when using the level.

middle of the tube only when the tube is in a horizontal position. Scratch marks at equal distances from the middle of the tube mark the proper position of the bubble when the surface on which the tube rests is level. Incidentally, some I-beam levels feature a magnetic strip that holds the level fast to metal surfaces, leaving the user's hands free for work.

FIGURE 3.12 Typical laser alignment tool.

Laser alignment tool

Often called the "electronic level," this tool produces a 360° line of laser light that establishes horizontal or vertical reference planes to guide the drywall mechanic (Figure 3.12). It can be used in:

- Setting wall molding, main runners, and ceiling cross Ts.
- Checking for low-hanging ducts, sprinklers, and other obstructions.
- Layout of metal studs for drywall, overhead drop walls, and bulkheads.
- Transferring lines from walls to straight or sloping ceilings.
- Raised access floor layout and leveling.

(See Figures 3-13A through D.)

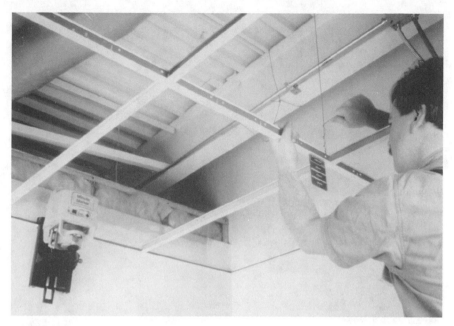

FIGURE 3.13A Operation of a laser alignment tool in a drywall installation. Leveling ceiling hangers.

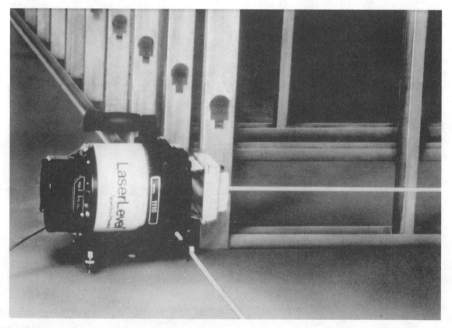

FIGURE 3.13B Setting runners and metal studs.

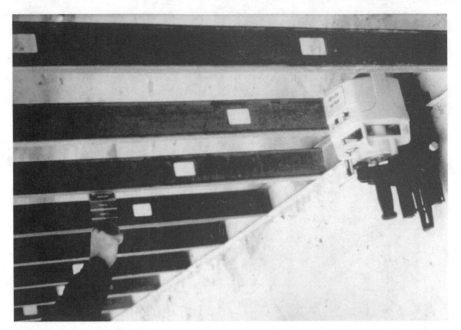

FIGURE 3.13C　Setting runners and metal studs.

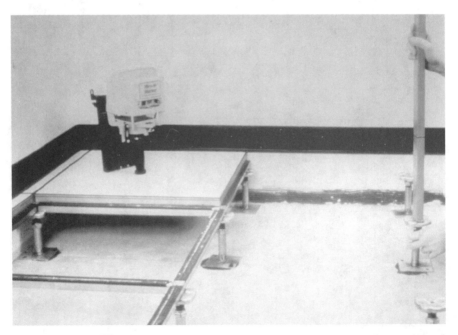

FIGURE 3.13D　Checking floor level.

INSTALLATION TOOLS

Installation tools are those tools required to cut and shape drywall gypsum panels and fasten them in place. These tools include knives, saws, rasping and sanding tools, hammers, staplers, and power screwdrivers.

Knives

The utility knife is the tool for cutting gypsum-board products (Figure 3.14A). The most satisfactory utility knife is one with a retractable blade and a button that prevents unintended sliding of the blade. The blade should be adjustable at two or more cutting positions so that a small cut or groove can be made without using the entire blade.

The hook-bill knife (also known as a linoleum knife) is useful for trimming gypsum board and for odd-shaped cuts (Figure 3.14B). Another valuable tool for making narrow cuts is the gypsum-board stripper. This tool has two cutting wheels that cut both sides of the panel simultaneously (Figure 3.15). The handle serves as an edge guide, and its position adjusts to make cuts up to 4½ inches wide.

Still another popular drywall cutting tool is the circle cutter (Figure 3.16). The calibrated steel shaft allows accurate cuts up to a 16-inch diameter. The cutter wheel and center pin are heat-treated.

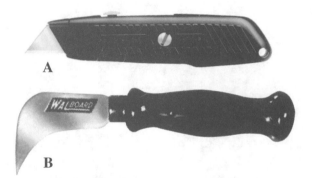

FIGURE 3.14   (A) Utility knife used to cut drywall, (B) Hook-bill knife used to cut drywall.

Stud crimper

The stud crimper (Figure 3.17) is used for setting and splicing metal studs, roughing-in door holders and window headers, setting electrical boxes, and punching hanger-wire holes in ceiling grids.

Saws

There are several types of saws used to cut gypsum board. The most common is possibly the drywall saw. It has a short blade and coarse teeth that avoid becoming clogged with gypsum as they make the cut (Figure 3.18). It should not be so coarse that it will leave the face-paper torn or ragged.

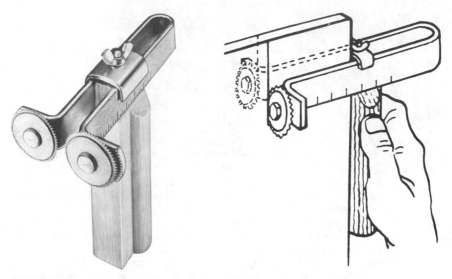

FIGURE 3.15   The tool shown above is used for making narrow cuts in gypsum panels. It has two cutting wheels that cut both sides of a panel simultaneously. The handle serves as an edge guide, and its position adjusts to make cuts up to 4½ inches wide.

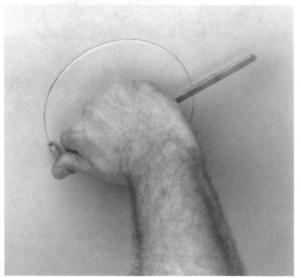

FIGURE 3.16   The calibrated steel shaft allows accurate cuts up to 16 inches in diameter.

The drywall keyhole saw is used for cutting small openings and making odd-shaped cuts (Figure 3.19). Its sharp point and stiff blade can be punched through the gypsum board for starting a cut.

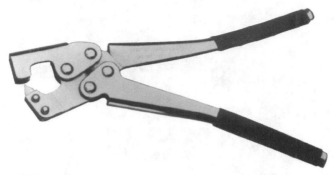

FIGURE 3.17 This tool is used for setting and splicing metal studs, roughing-in door holders and window headers, setting electrical boxes, and punching hanger-wire holes in ceiling grids.

FIGURE 3.18 The drywall short blade and coarse teeth cut gypsum boards quickly and easily.

FIGURE 3.19 A keyhole saw is used for cutting small openings and for making odd-shaped cuts. The sharp point and stiff blade can be punched through the board for starting cuts.

There are four basic types of power tools used by the drywall hanger for cutting:

- The saber or jigsaw can be used to make cutouts for outlets and switches in drywall (Figure 3.20). When making such cuts, the saw can be inserted directly into a panel or board; there is no need to drill a lead or pilot hole. Measure the cut and mark it clearly with a pencil. Next, tip the saw forward until the front end of the shoe sits firmly on the work surface. Switch the tool on, and allow it to attain maximum speed. Grip the handle firmly, and lower the back edge of the tool until the blade cuts smoothly into the material. Always be sure the blade reaches its complete depth, with the shoe flat against the work, before starting a forward cut. Saber-saw blades with medium-spaced teeth are usually recommended for most gypsum-board cuts. When cutting metal framing, use closely spaced teeth.

- The circular saw cuts steel studs, runners, and joists of various gauges with an appropriate blade (Figure 3.21). It can also be used to cut wood framing members. Hand-held and portable, the circular saw enables on-site cutting and trimming. Making a plunge

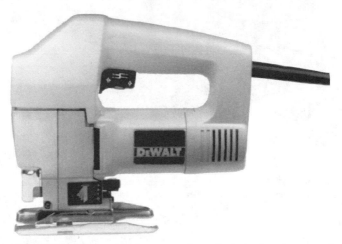

FIGURE 3.20   Jigsaws or saber saws can be used to make shaped cuts or end cuts.

FIGURE 3.21   Circular saws can cut both wood and steel framing members with appropriate blades.

cut into gypsum board with a circular saw is done by placing the front of the base on the board and the blade lifted about ½ inch away from the board (Figure 3.22). Start the motor, and after the saw has reached full speed, lower the rear end to let the blade enter the work. The front end of the foot resting on the work acts as a hinge point. When the foot rests flat on the work surface, proceed forward to the end of your cut. Release the switch, letting the saw come to a complete stop; then remove the saw from the work and start another cut. Never, under any circumstances, pull the saw backwards; the saw should be turned around, and the cut finished in the normal manner. Do the other three sides, and the pocket cut is complete. You might have to use a keyhole saw or handsaw

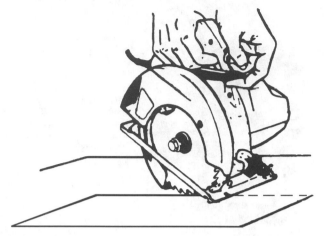

FIGURE 3.22 How a plunge or pocket cut is made with a circular saw.

to clean out the corners because the blade of the saw is round; if two cuts meet exactly at their tops, they will not meet at the bottom of the cut.

- The chop saw's abrasive wheel cuts all steel framing members. Its steel base can be placed on a bench, sawhorse, or floor for fast and efficient gang-cutting of metal framing members (Figure 3.23). Hand-held cut-off saws with abrasive wheels are available for on-site work with heavier-gauge steel framing members.

- The standard router shown in Figure 3.24 is used for irregular cuts and providing holes in gypsum board for electrical boxes, heating ducts and grilles, windows, and other openings. Some suitable routers are available that slip over the nosepiece of screw-guns and use the Phillips-head bit for power.

FIGURE 3.23 The chop saw's abrasive wheel cuts all types of metal framing members.

FIGURE 3.24   The standard router
can be used to make special-shaped
holes in drywall. In chapter 5, the
use of specially designed drywall
routers is described.

Other metal-framing cutting tools

Snips and shears are used for cutting metal framing. The metal or tin snips shown in
Figures 3.25A and 3.25B make straight and curved cuts in steel framing components.
Several sizes and styles are available. Most drywall mechanics prefer the straight-cut type
for general metal cutting. Do not attempt to cut heavier materials than those that the snips
are designed for. Never use tin snips to cut hardened steel wire or similar objects. Such use
will dent or nick the cutting edges of the blades.

   A metal channel-stud shear is frequently used to cut steel studs and runners quickly and
cleanly without deforming the work. The model shown in Figure 3.26 has fixed guides for
1⅝-inch, 2½-inch, and 3⅝-inch sizes and can be used with a maximum stud thickness of 20
gauge.

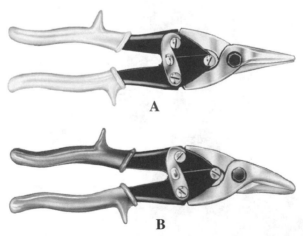

FIGURE 3.25   (A) Metal snips used to make a straight cut, (B) Metal
snips used to make a curved cut.

FIGURE 3.26   The channel-stud shear cuts steel studs and runners quickly and cleanly without deforming. It generally has fixed guides for 1⅝-inch, 2½-inch, and 3⅝-inch studs.

Hacksaws are hand-held tools used to cut metal framing that is too heavy for snips (Figure 3.27). Good work with a hacksaw depends not only upon the proper use of the saw, but also on proper selection of blades. For most metal frame cutting, a 24-tooth blade is recommended. For finer cuts, a 32-tooth blade can be used.

FIGURE 3.27   Hacksaws can be used to cut metal objects manually.

A variety of power band saw models are available for use in cutting steel framing members—both bench and floor models with wet or dry systems. Variable blade speeds and vertical cutting options provide on-site flexibility (Figure 3.28).

Electric shears (Figure 3.29) cut metal framing studs, runners, sheet metal, and cold-rolled steel up to 20 gauge. The cutting head on most shears rotate 180° for side and overhead work. Cutters are replaceable.

Rasps

The rasp is a quick and efficient means of shaping and smoothing rough-cut edges of gypsum boards. The manufactured rasp shown in Figure 3.30A features a replaceable blade and clean-cut slot to prevent clogging. The job-made model shown in Figure 3.30B consists of metal lath stapled to a 2-×-4-inch block. To use either rasp, run it along the cut edge several times until the edge is smooth.

FIGURE 3.28   A variety of power band sand saw models are available for use in cutting steel framing members, both bench and floor models with wet or dry systems.

FIGURE 3.29   The electric shear cuts steel studs, sheet metal, and cold-rolled steel up to 20 gauge.

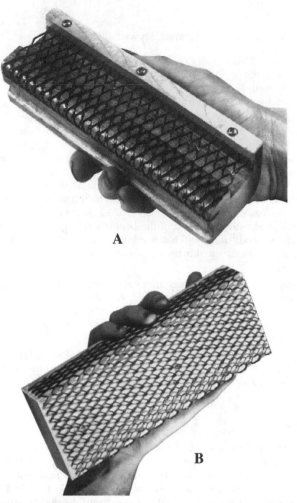

FIGURE 3.30 (A) This manufactured rasp features a replaceable blade and a clean-cut slot to prevent clogging when smoothing drywall panel edges, (B) This job-made rasp consists of metal lath stapled to a 2-×-4-inch wood block.

ATTACHING TOOLS

As stated in chapter 2, drywall gypsum board can be attached or fastened to wood and steel framing by several different methods: nails, screws, staples, or adhesive. Let's take a look at the tools used to attach drywall to supporting framing.

Nails

Four types of hammers are used to attach drywall to wood framing with nails. They are:

- Drywall hammer. This hammer (Figure 3.31) has a symmetrical convex face designed to compress gypsum panel face and leave the desired "dimple." The blade end is not for cutting but for wedging and prying a panel. It is not to be used for installing veneer plaster bases, which require a tool with a flatter head.
- Claw hammer. The primary use of the claw or carpenter's hammer is to drive or draw (pull) nails (Figure 3.32). The face of a nail hammer might be flat (plain-faced), or it might be slightly rounded, or convex (bell-faced). Handles might be hickory, tubular or solid steel, or fiberglass. Tubular-steel, solid-steel, and fiberglass handles are generally furnished with perforated, neoprene-rubber-type grips that are occasionally also used on hickory handles. These grips are more comfortable and seem to absorb the shock better than plain handles. Remember that the type of hammer handle affects the way it feels in the hand, as well as its balance. (The balance of a hammer depends on the weight of the head as compared with the weight of the handle.) When rested on a narrow board, a hammer with a wood handle will balance fairly close to the head. Those with tubular steel or fiberglass handles will balance somewhere in between the head and the end of the handle.
- Soft-face hammers. These hammers are made of various nonferrous materials (wood, rawhide, rubber, plastic, copper, brass, lead, etc.) Their heads are cylindrical with two flat striking faces (Figure 3.33). Their handles are usually hickory or fiberglass. Soft-face hammers are intended for striking blows where steel hammers would mar or damage the surface of the gypsum board.
- Magnetic hammer. The magnetic head of this hammer (Figure 3.34) holds the nails to speed attachment of floor and ceiling runners. The magnetic portion of the hammer head is replaceable because it will eventually lose its magnetism.

Stud drivers

Stud drivers are used to drive fasteners (studs) into concrete and other masonry surfaces for the attachment of metal runners (Figure 3.35). The power-actuated stud driver uses .22-cartridge loads to literally "fire" the stud fasteners into the concrete or masonry. Operational instructions for the so-called "velocity" stud driver are in the applications manual that comes with the tool. Be sure to follow these instructions closely at all times.

Screwdrivers

While manual screwdrivers can be used to install drywall screws, a power screwdriver is generally always used. The power screwdriver (Figure 3.36) most preferred by drywall hangers has a magnetic Phillips bit. It also has an adjustable depth control and a positive clutch. These last two features let the drywall mechanic drive screws to the same depth as nails—just below the original surface of the wallboard—but not farther. When the desired depth is reached, the clutch disengages the bit.

Cordless electric screwdrivers are available (Figure 3.37), but when using them, be sure to have an extra power pack available in case the battery goes dead in the middle of a job. The dead battery pack can be recharged in as little as an hour, depending on the type of battery and charger.

FIGURE 3.31   The typical drywall hammer has a symmetrical convex face that is designed to compress the gypsum panel face and leave the desired "dimple."

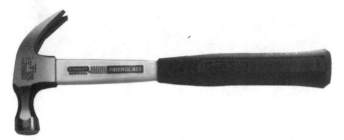

FIGURE 3.32   A typical clawhammer.

FIGURE 3.33   Soft-faced hammers are used to provide striking blows without damaging the surface of the gypsum board.

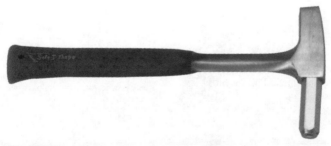

FIGURE 3.34   The magnetic head of this hammer holds the nail to be driven. The head is usually replaceable.

FIGURE 3.35   The stud driver is used to drive fasteners in concrete.

FIGURE 3.36   A typical screw gun with clutch.

FIGURE 3.37   A cordless screw gun operates with power from a battery pack, which recharges in one hour.

Staplers

Mechanical and power staplers are sometimes used in drywall applications. As shown in Figures 3.38A, 3.38B, and 3.38C, there are three basic stapling tools used in drywall fastening. To load a typical staple or tacker gun, proceed as follows (Figure 3.39):

1. With the operating lever or handle locked, hold the gun in the normal firing position. Push the loading latches forward on both sides simultaneously, and pull out on the staple channel with the other hand.
2. Holding the staple gun upside down, pull back on the staple channel until the spring pulls the feeding bar completely back. Then put the staples in the staple pocket with the legs pointing up.
3. Lower the staple channel, pull back on the loading latches, push the channel securely into place, and release the latches, making sure the channel is secure.
4. When you are ready to use the gun, release the handle lock and allow the handle to open. Your staple gun is now ready to fire when you depress the handle. This procedure might vary slightly with different makes of guns.

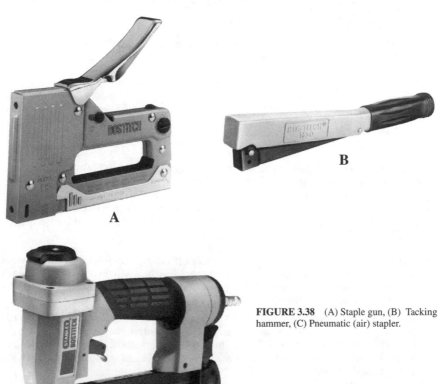

FIGURE 3.38 (A) Staple gun, (B) Tacking hammer, (C) Pneumatic (air) stapler.

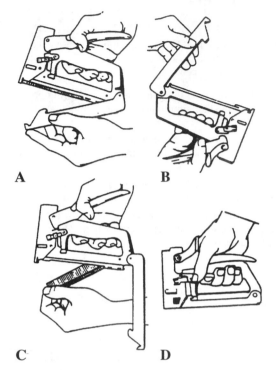

A   B

FIGURE 3.39   Loading a typical staple gun.

C   D

The hammer tacker is used in the way its name implies. Swing it like a hammer; when it hits the surface, it automatically drives a staple. Loaded much the same as described previously, the hammer tacker is an efficient stapler.

Air-powered (pneumatic) staplers can be used to do the same jobs as the mechanical or electric staplers, but in one-fourth less time. Normal operation of an air stapler can usually be accomplished in one of two ways:

1. Squeeze the trigger and keep it in the squeezed position, then fully depress the work contacting element (safety) against the workpiece. The tool will drive one fastener each time the work contacting element (safety) is depressed against the workpiece and released. This method is called *touch trip*.

2. Depress the work contacting element (safety) against the board and keep it in the depressed position, then squeeze the trigger. The tool will drive one fastener each time the trigger is squeezed and released. This is the single-cycle method. If the tool drives more than one fastener (double-cycle), you are applying too much force in holding down the tool against the board.

The pneumatic nailer and bradder load and operate in much the same manner as the air stapler, except they drive nails and brads respectively (Figure 3.40). The jobs that all of these staplers, nailers, and bradders are used for include installing insulation blankets to wood frames and to the inner face of the gypsum boards in both wood- and steel-frame assemblies. Also, they are used to attach corner beads and reinforcing tape.

FIGURE 3.40   Pneumatic nailer at work.

Caulking and adhesive

Both manual and power equipment are available for the application of adhesives and acoustical sealants: Manual equipment is illustrated in Figure 3.41.

- Cartridge-type hand gun: Used with 30-ounce cartridges, bead size is determined by how much of the nozzle is cut off. This gun aids the uniform application of adhesive. Applicator capacity: $\frac{1}{10}$ gallon, 1 quart.
- Bulk-type hand gun: Has a trigger mechanism and withstands rough usage while offering minimum resistance to large bulk loads of adhesive. Applicator has a 1-quart capacity and might be filled using a loader pump.
- Loader pump: Clamps on a 5-gallon container to mechanically load bulk-type adhesive into hand guns. Eliminates waste of hand and paddle loading.
- Air-powered caulking and adhesive guns: A typical pneumatic caulking gun and adhesive applicator (Figure 3.42) is easy to use and applies material quickly.
- Pumping equipment. Because of their higher volume of output, pumping machines provide greater efficiency and production in the transfer, flow, and spray of adhesives (Figure 3.43). Nail and screw attachments are supplemented or replaced by this type of adhesive application equipment in many building operations such as flooring, partitions, and ceilings (see chapters 5 and 6). Large pumping equipment permits purchasing in bulk and enables high-volume application; this contributes to job economy by reducing waste and application time. Most machine dispensing systems are available with a selection of pumps, flow valves, nozzles, and accessories. Equipment manufacturers offer a wide choice of components to provide the exact system for the job.

- Pail extruder: For high-volume extrusion of adhesives from pails. Air power depends on viscosity of the material (low, medium, or high). Offered in portable or mobile units with pump, air regulators and gauge, pail ram, adapter, and hose.
- Drum extruder: Comparable to a pail extruder. Used for high-ratio extrusion of adhesive from bulk containers.

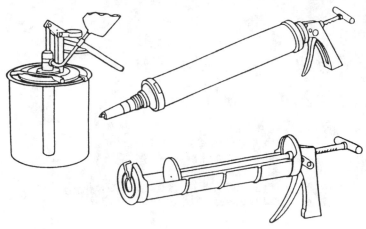

FIGURE 3.41   Types of caulking guns and loader pump.

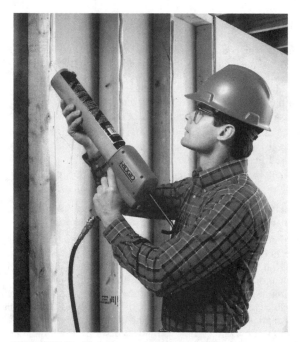

FIGURE 3.42   Typical pneumatic adhesive (caulking) gun.

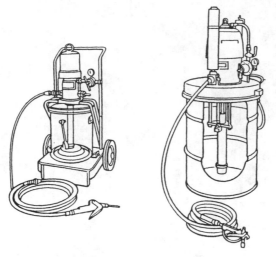

FIGURE 3.43 Pumping equipment shown here provides greater ease and production in the transfer and flow of adhesive.

Joint compound and adhesive spreaders

Made either commercially or by the applicator, joint compound and adhesive spreaders are used by applying joint compound in laminated gypsum-board assemblies (see chapter 6). The spreader shown in Figure 3.44A is easily made on the job. Stainless or galvanized sheet steel make the best spreaders. Other materials usually are not satisfactory because compound tends to accumulate and dry in the notches. A good spreader blade has about the same stiffness as a plasterer's trowel. Notches should be an inverted "V" shape, ½ inch deep, ⅜ inch wide at the base, and spaced 1½ inches O.C. A piece of wood dowel or window stop attached near the top edge of the blade provides a grip. A ready-made spreader is shown in Figure 3.44B. The spreader shown in Figure 3.45 is a laminating spreader that applies properly sized beads of adhesive at correct spacings.

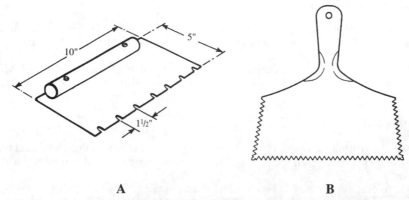

A   B

FIGURE 3.44 Joint compound and adhesive spreaders can be job-made of stainless or galvanized sheet steel (A) or purchased commercially (B).

FIGURE 3.45   The laminating spreader applies the proper size bead of adhesive at the desired spacing.

FINISHING TOOLS

The finishing tools, as the name implies, are those that the drywall installer uses for taping and applying compound (Figure 3.46) so that the other finishing trades—painters, wallpaper hangers, etc.—can do their work. Because this is a specialized part of the drywall trade, the tools employed are covered in chapter 10.

MISCELLANEOUS DRYWALL TOOLS

There are several drywall tools that the drywall applicator should be aware of. These tools make gypsum-board application easier. For instance:

Gypsum-panel lifters

There are several different types of drywall gypsum-panel lifters. The device shown in Figure 3.47 is designed to move the panel forward as it lifts. It can be used for panels applied either perpendicularly or parallel.

The cradle lifter allows one-person application of drywall to the sidewalls, sloped ceilings, and level ceilings (Figure 3.48). The tripod base has rollers for easy movement.

Scaffolding

The midget scaffold shown in Figure 3.49 is portable and easy to set up. It is ideal for jobs that do not require full scaffolding. Of course, there are jobs that require full scaffolding.

The folding trestle shown in Figure 3.50 has a top surface of 9½-x-48 inches, providing a work surface or a standard platform. The legs adjust from 18 to 32 inches in 2-inch increments. For high-ceiling work, aerial platforms are often used (Figure 3.51).

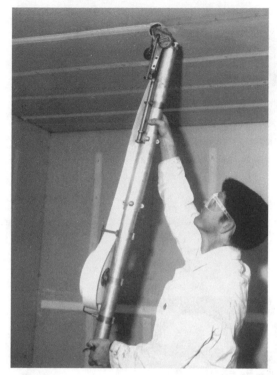

FIGURE 3.46   Mechanical taper at work.

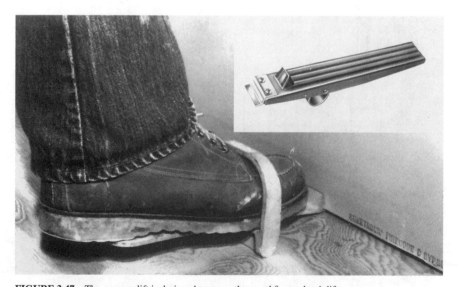

FIGURE 3.47   The gypsum lift is designed to move the panel forward as it lifts.

FIGURE 3.48 A cradle-type lifter allows one-person application of drywall panels to sidewalls and sloped ceilings as well as level ceilings. The tripod base with rollers permits easy movement.

FIGURE 3.49 A folding trestle provides a work platform.

FIGURE 3.50 The portable midget scaffold is good for jobs that do not require full scaffolding.

FIGURE 3.51   Using aerial work platforms for ceiling work.

Stilts

These eliminate the need for scaffolding or trestles on most drywall jobs, while giving the applicator full mobility plus the height needed for ceiling work. Some stilts have articulated joints to flex with ankle movement. They are available in fixed-height and adjustable-height types. (An adjustable, articulated model is shown in Figure 3.52.) Stilts are not legal in some states.

Gypsum-board dolly

Gypsum-board dollies are designed for the efficient transport of gypsum boards around the floor of a building (Figure 3.53). The load, centered over large side wheels, is easily steered and moved by one worker.

Tool pouch

Available in a variety of styles, tool pouches are designed to carry all of the hand tools needed by the gypsum drywall installer (Figure 3.54). Nail bags are worn on the belt to

FIGURE 3.52   Stilts eliminate the need for scaffolding on most drywall jobs.

FIGURE 3.53   A gypsum-board dolly is an efficient way to transport panels around the floor of a building. The board, centered over the large-size wheels, is easily steered and moved by one worker.

keep nails or screws within easy reach. The tool pouch is also available with a hammer loop and extra pockets for small tools.

SAFETY

When using any of the tools described in this chapter, uppermost in the mind of the drywall mechanic or applicator must be safety. When using power-actuated tools, always fol-

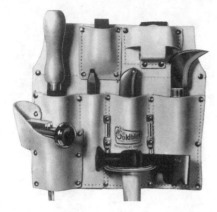

FIGURE 3.54 A tool pouch or holder is designed to carry all the common hand-tools needed by the drywall installer.

low the manufacturer's instruction to the letter. Hand tools can be very dangerous if not used properly. Remember that bad cuts, smashed extremities, and serious injuries (even death) can occur when drywall tools are misused.

The drywall applicator must also dress safely. Wear the proper eye protection (safety glasses with side shields or wraparound safety goggles) and heavy work gloves. Head protection (a hard hat) is usually required on most construction sites. Wear proper nonslip work shoes, not sneakers. When sanding or cutting gypsum board, be sure to wear a dust mask (Figure 3.55). Do not wear loose clothing or jewelry that can get caught in a power tool. Whenever using a power tool or in the presence of other tradespeople who are using power tools, proper ear protection should be used; many different styles of ear plugs and ear muffs are available for this purpose.

FIGURE 3.55 How a dust mask is worn.

CHAPTER 4
JOB PLANNING

Robert Scharff
Walls & Ceilings Magazine

Advance planning by the wall and ceiling drywall installer or mechanic can mean savings in time and material costs and can result in a better-appearing job. Proper planning achieves the most effective use of materials, elimination of unnecessary joints, and the placement of necessary joints in the least-conspicuous locations. One gypsum board should span the entire length or width of the wall or ceiling, if possible. By using the longest available board lengths wherever possible, end joints are kept to a minimum. Where they do occur, end joints should be staggered. In double-layer construction, end joints in the face layer must be offset at least 10 inches from parallel joints in the base layer. Layout of the base layer must be planned to accommodate this offset and still provide optimum joint-finishing conditions and efficient use of materials in the face layer.

The general contractor is usually in charge of the actual building of a structure. It is his/her job to follow the architect's or designer's plan and specifications and the owner's desires. Generally, the general contractor will subcontract the work to a drywall contractor or hangers. It is the responsibility of the drywall contractor to follow the plans and specifications as far as they concern the application of gypsum board. Failure to do so can result in callbacks and financial loss to the drywall contractor.

Many of the problems described in association with drywall installations are not the result of any failures by the drywall contractor, the general contractor, or even the architect. For instance, movement in structures can cause cracks in the drywall hanger's finished job. Structural movement and most cracking problems are caused by deflection under load, physical change in materials due to temperature and humidity changes, seismic forces, or a combination of these factors. The major factors are:

- Wind and seismic forces cause a cyclical shearing action on the building framework, which distorts the rectangular shape to an angled parallelogram. This distortion, called *racking*, can result in cracking and crushing of partitions adjacent to columns, floors, and structural ceilings.

- All materials expand and contract with increases and decreases in temperature. In tall concrete or steel-frame buildings, thermal expansion and contraction might cause cracking problems resulting from racking when exterior columns and beams are exposed or partially exposed to exterior temperatures. Since interior columns remain at a uniform temperature, they do not change in length.

- Many building materials absorb moisture from the surrounding air during periods of high humidity and expand; they contract during periods of low humidity. Gypsum, wood, and paper products are more readily affected by hygrometric changes than are steel and reinforced concrete.

Materials that come into contact with each other must be compatible. Differences in thermal or hygrometric expansion, strength of substrate or plies in relation to finish, thermal conductivity and galvanic action are common problem-causing situations. The subject is too complex to be covered in detail in this book. The architect or designer usually contacts specific manufacturers for recommendations should questions arise. Following are some precautions of this kind associated with gypsum construction:

- Gypsum surfaces should be isolated with control joints or other means where necessary to abut other materials and isolate structural movements, changes in shape, and gross area limits.
- Due to expansion differences, the application of high-pressure plastic laminates to gypsum panels is generally not satisfactory.
- Standard gypsum panels do not provide sufficient moisture resistance as a base for adhesive application of ceramic tile. Use water-resistant MR or WR board or cement tile backer board.
- Install resilient thermal gaskets around metal window frames to keep condensation from damaging wall surface materials. The gasket might also reduce galvanic action and resultant corrosion, which occurs when two dissimilar metals contact each other in the presence of moisture.

With the increased use of thermal insulation brought about by the need for energy conservation, the use and proper placement of vapor retarders is extremely important in modern construction. Inattention to proper placement or omission of a vapor retarder with thermal insulation might result in condensation in the exterior wall-stud cavities. Cold climates require a vapor retarder on the warm interior side of the wall. A vapor retarder might be required on the outside of the exterior wall for air-conditioned buildings in climates having sustained high outside temperatures and humidity. A qualified mechanical engineer should determine the location of the vapor retarder.

Two vapor retarders or barriers on opposite sides of a single wall can trap water vapor between them and create moisture-related problems in the core materials. When a polyethylene vapor-retarding film is installed on ceilings behind gypsum panels under cold conditions, it is recommended that ceiling insulation (batts or blankets) be installed before the board. Also, the plenum or attic space should be properly vented. Failure to follow this procedure can result in moisture condensation in the back side of the gypsum panels, causing board sag.

ESTIMATING MATERIALS

In this chapter, only methods of estimating the amount of material required to complete a drywall construction job are addressed. This includes the essential drywall components, the gypsum panels, joint tape, corner beading, fasteners, and compound.

To determine the materials needed to complete a drywall installation, the information needed can be found by reading the plans (blueprints) and specifications of the job. If the structure is already framed, the necessary information can be taken from actual room measurements themselves.

A general contractor uses a set of plans or drawings to guide the building of a structure. These plans and specifications contain the graphic and written information that will indicate the type of framing, finish material, and all other necessary information needed by tradespeople working on the structure, including the drywall contractor or mechanic. In effect, they tell what, where, and how to use the various materials of construction. They are the main source of information for those responsible for the actual work. For drywall contractors or hangers, the major concerns are interior room dimensions (Figure 4.1).

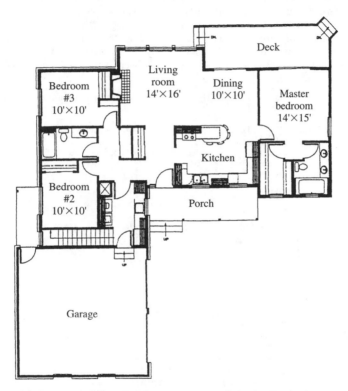

FIGURE 4.1   The sketch here was redrawn from the architect's drawings to simplify the interior rooms for easy estimating of the number of panels required.

Drywall panels

From practical experience, professional estimators have developed methods for determining footage required to complete various types of jobs. Basically, these methods stem from the simple principle of "scaling a plan" and determining the length and width and ceiling height of each room on the plan. Frequently, door and window openings are "figured solid," with no openings considered. Exceptions might be large picture windows and large door openings. From these dimensions the estimator determines the square footage of each room. The square footage of each room is added to determine total square footage needed. From these figures the number of drywall boards needed can be calculated. (Refer to chapter 2 for available lengths and widths of each panel.)

Based on rectangular rooms with 8-foot ceilings, the room measurement given in Table 4.1 allows the drywall contractor to determine quickly the combined wall and ceiling areas of the job. For example, a 12-×-16-×-18-foot room contains a wall/ceiling area of 640 square feet. Measure or scale door and window areas, and if larger than 4 × 4 feet, subtract their square footage from the 640 to obtain net room area. Use the net area figure in the panel coverage shown in Table 4.2 to locate the number of drywall panels required for the room.

One of the easiest methods of estimating the number of panels for a given job is to find the square footage of each room or area. To make a "take-off" of the number of panels needed for the living room in the three-bedroom home shown in Figure 4.1, the ceiling area is 14 × 16 feet or 224 square feet (room length times width). If 4-×-8-foot panels are used, each panel will cover 32 square feet. To find out the number of panels needed for this living room ceiling, divide 224 square feet by 32. The ceiling of this room would require 7 panels (Figure 4.2A). If 14-by-4-foot panels were being used, only 4 panels would be needed (Figure 4.2B).

TABLE 4.1   The Perimeter Method of Estimating Panel Needs

Perimeter	Number of 4'-×-8' panels needed
36 feet	9
40 feet	10
44 feet	11
48 feet	12
52 feet	13
56 feet	14
60 feet	15
64 feet	16
68 feet	17
72 feet	18
92 feet	23

For example, if the room's walls measured 14 feet + 14 feet + 16 feet + 16 feet (Figure 4.1) the room's perimeter would equal 60 feet and would require 15 panels. To allow for areas such as fireplaces, doors, windows, etc., use the following deductions:

Door	½ panel
Window	¼ panel
Fireplace	½ panel

Thus, the actual number of gypsum panels for this room would be 13 pieces (15 pieces minus 2 total deductions). If the perimeter of the room falls in between the figures in the table, use the next highest number to determine the panels required. These figures are for rooms with 8-foot ceiling heights or less. For walls over 8 feet high, select a paneling that has V grooves and that will "stack," allowing panel grooves to line up perfectly from floor to ceiling.

TABLE 4.2 Drywall Conversion Chart

NO. OF PIECES	SIZE (Areas in Square Feet)				NO. OF PIECES	SIZE (Areas in Square Feet)			
	4″ × 8″	4″ × 10″	4″ × 12″	4″ × 14″		4″ × 8″	4″ × 10″	4″ × 12″	4″ × 14″
10	320	400	480	560					
11	352	440	528	616	36	1152	1440	1728	2016
12	384	480	576	672	37	1184	1480	1776	2072
13	416	520	624	728	38	1216	1520	1824	2128
14	448	560	672	784	39	1248	1560	1872	2184
15	480	600	720	840	40	1280	1600	1920	2240
16	512	640	768	896	41	1312	1640	1968	2296
17	544	680	816	952	42	1344	1680	2016	2352
18	576	720	864	1008	43	1376	1720	2064	2408
19	608	760	912	1064	44	1408	1760	2112	2464
20	640	800	960	1120	45	1440	1800	2160	2520
21	672	840	1008	1176	46	1472	1840	2208	2576
22	704	880	1056	1232	47	1504	1880	2256	2632
23	736	920	1104	1288	48	1536	1920	2304	2688
24	768	960	1152	1344	49	1568	1960	2352	2744
25	800	1000	1200	1400	50	1600	2000	2400	2800
26	832	1040	1248	1456	51	1632	2040	2448	2856
27	864	1080	1296	1512	52	1664	2080	2496	2912
28	896	1120	1344	1568	53	1696	2120	2544	2968
29	928	1160	1392	1624	54	1728	2160	2592	3024
30	960	1200	1440	1680	55	1760	2200	2640	3080
31	992	1240	1488	1736	56	1792	2240	2688	3136
32	1024	1280	1536	1792	57	1824	2280	2736	3192
33	1056	1320	1584	1848	58	1856	2320	2784	3248
34	1088	1360	1632	1904	59	1888	2360	2832	3304
35	1120	1400	1680	1960	60	1920	2400	2880	3360

Looking at the walls for the living room, we find that the main wall has floor-to-ceiling picture-window units. The opposite kitchen/living-room wall can use two 4-×-6 panels. The remaining living room walls require 128 square feet of panel. Another panel would be required for filler applications. The square footage of the walls and ceiling would equal 384 square feet or 12 panels (4 × 8 feet).

As stated previously, gypsum drywall panels can be applied horizontally (long edges of the board at right angles to the framing members) or vertically (long edges parallel to the framing). Fire-rated partitions might require vertical or parallel application (see chapter 9 for information on fire-rated systems).

Horizontal drywall application is generally preferred because it offers the following advantages:

- Reduces the lineal footage of joints to be treated up to 25 percent.
- Strongest dimension of board runs across framing members.
- Bridges irregularities in alignment and spacing of frame members.
- Better bracing strength. Each board ties more frame members together than do parallel applications.
- Horizontal joints on wall are at a convenient height for finishing.
- Applied vertically, each sheet covers three stud spaces when studs are spaced 16 inches on center, and each sheet covers two spaces when stud spacing is 24 inches. Edges should be centered on studs, and only moderate contact should be made between edges of sheets.

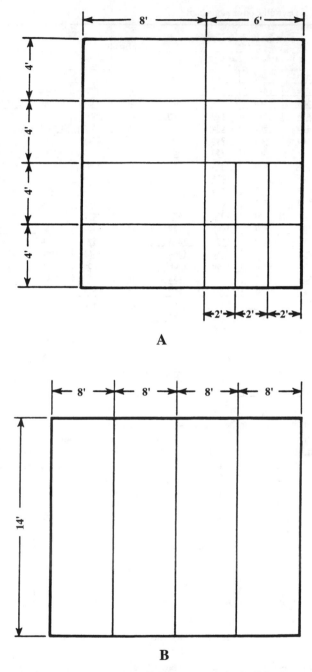

FIGURE 4.2 Two methods of laying out panels for the living-room ceiling shown in Figure 4.1.

For wall applications, if the ceiling height is 8 feet 1 inch or less, horizontal application results in fewer joints, easier handling, and less cutting. If the ceiling height is greater than 8 feet 1 inch or the wall is 1 foot wide or less, vertical or parallel application is more practical. For ceiling application, use whichever method results in the fewest joints or is required by frame-spacing limitations.

For double-layer ceiling application, apply base-layer boards perpendicular to frame members; apply the face layer parallel to framing with joints offset. On the wall, apply the base layer parallel with long edges centered on framing; apply the face layer perpendicular. An exception is when using predecorated panels for the face layer. In that case, apply the base-layer boards at right angles to the studs. Of course, the extra panels required for double-layer must be considered in the estimate.

Although long panels are priced slightly higher than those 8 feet long, it is wise to order the longest panel you can use; the difference in price is worth it because the panel covers a larger area with less time and reduces the number of joints that must be taped. (But remember that smaller boards are much easier for one person to handle.) If, for instance, the wall to be wallboarded is 21 feet long, it would be better to use one 4-x-12 panel and one 4-x-10 panel rather than three 4-x-8 panels for each horizontal course. Not only would there be a smaller amount of waste, there would also be one less joint to tape. In such a case, the little extra cost of the large sheets and the effort needed to handle them would be justified in the time saved and neatness of the finished job.

Fasteners

Once the number of gypsum panels has been calculated, estimate the amount of the other drywall components needed. For example, the number of fasteners used to install gypsum board varies with framing spacing, fastener spacing, panel orientation, and panel size.

Screws

For single-layer wall application to 16 inches O.C. (on center), approximately 1,000 type W screws for wood studs or type S for steel framing are required per 1,000 square feet of gypsum board. For 24-inch O.C. wall-framing installation, approximately 850 screws are needed.

For ceilings, screw spacing varies. With joists spaced 16 inches O.C. with perpendicular panel installation, for example, each 8-foot panel is screwed for 7 joists. There are 5 screws per joist, or 35 screws per ceiling panel. Table 4.3 shows estimated screw usage per thousand square feet of gypsum board for both horizontal and vertical board attachment. Allowance should be made for loss.

Nails

When using ring-shank nails on walls, the nail spacing is usually 8 inches O.C. for 16-inch O.C. studs. Ceiling installation spacing for ½-inch-board 16-inch O.C. joints is 7 inches. Usage for other nail installations are given in Table 4.4.

Adhesive coverage

To help determine how much drywall adhesive is needed for a given project, Table 4.5 gives the bead length in feet as related to the bead size in diameter. The bead size is determined by the drywall application (see chapters 5 and 6). Other quantities of fasteners needed for various other types of gypsum board installation are given in chapters 5 to 8.

TABLE 4.3 Screw Usage

Frame spacing	Screw Spacing (inches)			
	8	12	16	24
Horizontal Board Attachment				
4'-×–8' Board				
8"	2844	2031	1625	1219
12"	1969	1406	1125	844
16"	1531	1094	875	656
24"	1094	781	625	469
4'-×–10' Board				
8"	2800	2000	1600	1200
12"	1925	1375	1100	825
16"	1488	1063	850	638
24"	1050	750	600	450
4'-×–12' Board				
8"	2780	1980	1590	1190
12"	1900	1360	1090	820
16"	1460	1050	840	630
24"	1030	730	590	440
Vertical Board Attachment				
4'-×–8' Board				
8"	2844	1969	1531	1094
12"	2031	1406	1094	781
16"	1625	1125	875	625
24"	1219	844	656	469
4'×10' Board				
8"	2800	1925	1488	1050
12"	2000	1375	1063	750
16"	1600	1100	850	600
24"	1200	825	638	450
4'×12' Board				
8"	2771	1896	1458	1021
12"	1979	1354	1042	729
16"	1583	1083	833	583
24"	1188	813	625	438

Other drywall components

The number of feet of outside corner bead needed to reinforce this joint can be calculated by the number of joints in the room multiplied by their height. Outside corners are not always on walls. Corners might be in the form of skylight openings or attic ladders.

TABLE 4.4 Selector Guide for Gypsum-Board Nails[1]

fastener description(2)	fastener length		total thickness of surfacing materials(3)										approx. usage	
			In	1/4	3/8	1/2	5/8	3/4	7/8	1	1-1/4	1-3/8		
	In	mm	mm	6.4	9.5	12.7	15.9	19.1	22.2	25.4	31.8	34.9	lb/1,000 ft²	kg/100m²
Annular Ring Drywall Nail 12½ ga. (2.50 mm) ¼" (6.35 mm) diam. head, med. diamond point	1¼	31.8		X	X	X							4.50	2.20
	1⅜	34.9					X						5.00	2.44
	1½	38.1						X					5.25	2.56
	1⅝	41.3							X				5.75	2.81
Same as above except 19/64" (7.54 mm) diam. head	1¼	31.8		X	X	X							4.50	2.20
	1⅜	34.9					X						5.00	2.44
	1½	38.1						X					5.25	2.56
	1⅝	41.3							X				5.75	2.81
	1¾	44.5								X			6.00	2.93
	2	50.8									X		7.00	3.42
12½ ga. (2.50 mm) 19/64" (7.54 mm) diam. head	1¼	31.8		X	X	X							4.50	2.20
	1⅜	34.9					X						5.00	2.44
	1½	38.1						X					5.25	2.56
	1⅝	41.3							X				5.75	2.81

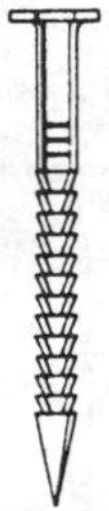

TABLE 4.4 Selector Guide for Gypsum-Board Nails[1] (Continued)

fastener description[2]	fastener length In	fastener length mm	1/4 6.4	3/8 9.5	1/2 12.7	5/8 15.9	3/4 19.1	7/8 22.2	1 25.4	1-1/4 31.8	1-3/8 34.9	lb/1,000 ft²	kg/100m²
Same as above except 1/4" (6.35 mm) diam. head													
14 ga. (2.03 mm)	1⅜ (4d)	34.9				X						3.50	1.71
13½ ga. (2.18 mm)	1⅝ (5d)	41.3					X					4.50	2.20
13 ga. (2.32 mm)	1⅞ (6d)	47.6							X			5.75	2.81
13½ ga. (2.18 mm)	2⅛ (7d)	54.0									X	7.50	3.66
Color Nails for Vinyl Panels													
15½ ga. (1.71 mm)	1⅜	34.9			X	X						2.00	0.98
³⁄₃₂" (2.36 mm) diam. head													

(In column refers to total thickness of surfacing materials[3]; mm values given below each fraction.)

(1) For wood framing 16" o.c., nails 8" o.c. for walls, 7" o.c. for ceilings.
(2) All nails treated to prevent rust with joint compounds or veneer finishes. Fire-rated assemblies generally require greater nail penetration; therefore, for fire-rated assemblies, use exact nail length and diameter specified for rated assembly (see Fire Test Report).
(3) In laminated double-layer construction, base layer is attached in same manner as single layer.

TABLE 4.5 Adhesive Coverage

Volume	Bead Diameter Size In Inches				
	⅛"	³⁄₁₆"	¼"	⁵⁄₁₆"	⅜"
	Lineal feet of extruded adhesive (length)				
Small cartridge (11 fluid ounces)	135'	60'	34'	21½'	15'
Large cartridge (29 fluid ounces)	355'	158'	89'	57'	39'
1 gallon (128 fluid ounces)	1,569'	697'	392'	251'	174'

In round figures, 1000' of adhesive bead will require: ⅔ gallon at ⅛" diameter bead, 2½ gallons at ¼" diameter bead, 5¾ gallons at ⅜" diameter bead.

To determine the amount of joint compound and tape required, use the drywall layout employed when calculating the number of panels needed. But keep in mind:

- Unless noted in the specifications, most edges of panels of walls are not taped or filled.
- Do not double count the perimeter joints. For example, the joint between the ceiling and wall should be counted as either a ceiling or a wall joint, but not two joints to be taped and filled. To estimate the joint compound and tape needed for a job, check the component chart given in Table 4.6.

TABLE 4.6 Typical Compound/Tape Calculator

With this amount of square footage	Use this amount of mixed compound in pounds	Or this amount of total joint compound in gallons	And this amount of joint tape in feet
100	14	0.9	37
200	28	1.9	74
300	41	2.8	111
400	55	3.8	148
500	69	4.7	185
600	83	5.6	222
700	97	6.6	259
800	110	7.5	296
900	124	8.5	333
1000	138	9.4	370

* Coverage figures shown here approximate the amount of joint compound needed to treat the flat joints, internal corners, and external corners using metal corner bead, in a "typical room." Coverage can vary widely depending upon factors such as condition of substrate, tools used, application methods, and other job factors.

ESTIMATING LABOR COSTS

To properly estimate labor costs on a drywall installation job, there are two components that must be considered:

- Work-hours required to perform the installation work.
- Taxes and insurance costs associated with the total work-hours allocated to the job.

Let's first consider estimating work-hours required to perform the drywall installation. All segments of the installation should be estimated separately. Ceilings, walls, and finish work are the easiest segments of the job to remember to include in estimates, but any and all work required to correct any framing imperfections must be included as well. Before estimating labor for the installation of the drywall panels, carefully inspect the framing and make allowances for any labor costs necessary to correct framing problems. Correcting problems to ensure that the framing is plumb and level can require as many (if not more) work-hours as the installation of the drywall panels themselves. To calculate the labor costs of installing gypsum drywall panels, a simple formula to use is the following: the labor rate per hour multiplied by the total number of work-hours equals the total labor cost.

At this point, the definition of the term work-hours should be clearly understood. For example, if two people require 10 minutes to install a 4-×-8 ceiling panel (including fasteners but not including taping and finishing), and the ceiling requires 3 panels, the total labor time equals 1 work-hour (10 minutes multiplied by 3 panels = 30 minutes, multiplied by 2 people = 60 minutes = 1 work-hour).

Once the total number of work-hours has been calculated, multiplying that figure by the labor rate per hour will result in the labor estimate to complete the basic installation for that segment of the job. With this formula, and the materials estimate, calculations can be completed for each individual segment of the job.

WALLS

Once estimates have been completed for ceiling areas, the same estimating procedure should be used for the wall segments of the job. Unless otherwise specified by the general contractor, architect, or owner of the property, the drywall contractor has the option of using either nails or screws for the installation of gypsum board panels over wood framing. If screws are to be used, less labor will be required because fewer fasteners are needed per panel. But the cost of screws is greater than the cost of nails, so a portion of the savings in labor costs is absorbed by higher material costs. However, a factor that must be considered is that although screws have a higher initial cost, they also have much greater holding power than nails. Consequently, by absorbing higher material costs up front, the contractor might very well reduce his/her overall expenses that result from repairing loose panels caused by nail pops and fastener failure during construction or in the future. The expense of repairing loose panels due to fastener failure is, of course, a variable cost that the drywall contractor will have to judge using past experience as a guide.

If nails are used, the initial material costs will be less, but labor costs will be higher because more nails than screws are required per panel. The variable cost of repairing loose panels due to fastener failure must again be considered. If gypsum-board panels are being applied over metal framing, no choice of fasteners exists. Screws must be used.

Cutouts and corners

Another consideration in estimating labor costs for wall applications is the number and size of window, door, electrical outlet, and switch openings that must be cut into the gypsum board. Each of these openings must be cut precisely, and this requires additional time to ensure a quality job. Be sure to take an accurate count of the number and type of openings that need to be cut, and add these costs to the total labor estimate.

The installation of corner bead is another component of the drywalling job that adds additional labor time and expense. A careful study of the job specifications needs to be made to calculate the appropriate linear footage of corner bead to be installed.

Gypsum-drywall finishing

Taping and filling the joints, spotting the fastener heads, and applying texturing or other finishing material to the gypsum boards are all activities that fall into the category of finishing labor. The drywall contractor's familiarity with his/her crews and accurate records of the amount of time each crew required to perform these tasks on previous installations will enable the drywall contractor to properly estimate the number of work-hours needed for this step of the job.

Scheduling and avoiding downtime

Whenever joint compound is applied during the application of gypsum-drywall panels, work on that section of the job must be stopped until the joint compound is completely dry. This work stoppage, known as "downtime," can result in additional expenses to the drywall contractor if he/she has to pull crews off the site and move to another job before returning to finish the first job. To avoid this situation, plan to have different rooms at different stages of completion throughout the installation process. A crew should be able to embed reinforcing tape, spot fastener heads, or apply texturing in one room, and while waiting for the joint compound or texturing to dry, move into other rooms to fasten panels onto framing and ceilings or apply successive coats of joint compound or texturing. Once the panels are up, joints are taped, fastener heads spotted, etc., the crews should be able to move back to the first room(s) to apply any necessary successive coatings of joint compound or texturing. No matter how well the work is sequenced to minimize downtime, some period of downtime will most likely be experienced. Make sure to inform the customer of the reason for this downtime so that he/she will not fall under the misconception that he/she is being neglected simply because the drywall crew is not on site.

Taxes and insurance costs

As mentioned earlier in this chapter, labor costs are actually composed of two sets of costs. In addition to the work-hour costs already discussed, another factor referred to as "labor burden" must now be added in order to calculate total labor costs. On average, labor burden will increase labor costs by 25 to 30 percent on each drywall job. This labor burden is the percentage of payroll dollars the drywall contractor is compelled to pay to government agencies in the form of taxes and in the form of premiums paid to insurance companies. The following taxes and insurance are examples of the components that make up the labor burden:

- Unemployment insurance: All states levy an unemployment insurance tax on employers, based on total payroll for each calendar quarter. The actual amount assessed will vary on the history of unemployment claims filed by employees of the company. This tax might range from 1 to 4 percent of payroll dollars.
- FUTA: This is the federal government's unemployment tax. This tax has averaged 0.8 percent of payroll dollars per employee up to a maximum dollar amount per year. The tax is periodically set by law.
- Social Security and Medicare (FICA): The federal government also requires FICA payments averaging 7½ percent of payroll dollars per employee up to a maximum dollar amount per year that is prescribed by law.
- Workers' Compensation insurance: All states require that this insurance be carried by employers to cover employees in the event of a job-related injury. The cost of this insurance is a percentage of payroll dollars based on the occupation of the employee. Secretarial jobs have a rate that is low compared to higher-risk jobs (such as construction jobs). They carry a rate that is usually between 5 and 10 percent of payroll dollars.
- Liability insurance: This insurance protects the drywall contractor in the event of an accident. Most general contractors will require that a certificate of insurance be presented by subcontractors prior to beginning work. The cost of this insurance is based on total payroll and is dependent on the location of the company (and the work), history of claims by the company, and the liability limits needed.

From these examples it is clear why the labor burden must be included in every labor-cost estimate. Each state and local government passes its own laws and sets its own percentages for these taxes, and individual companies regulate their own insurance rates. So frequent updating of information pertaining to these taxes and insurance costs must be made to avoid underpricing jobs, reducing profit margins, and perhaps even losing money.

A computer, plus the proper software, is a very handy tool for drywall take-offs (Figure 4.3). It can also be used for estimating labor and material costs. Software is available to make estimates for residences, offices, apartment buildings, shopping malls, and other commercial structures.

HANDLING AND STORING DRYWALL

Even quality products can contribute to problems during application and can cause job failures if they are not protected from damage and improper handling. Generally, gypsum products should be stored inside at temperatures above freezing. They should be protected from moisture and external damage and used promptly after delivery.

Safety tips for handling drywall panels

Stacks of gypsum board are very heavy and can become unstable if proper stacking and handling procedures are not followed. Workers must always be extremely careful when stacking or working in an area where gypsum board is stacked. A 4-foot-wide by 12-foot-long by ½-inch-thick gypsum board can weigh more than 80 pounds. This means a stack of only 25 boards weighs more than a ton. Heavy equipment is frequently used to move, stack, load, stock, or otherwise handle gypsum board. This equipment, such as lift and boom trucks, can create dangerous situations if proper safety precautions are ignored.

FIGURE 4.3 A computer with the proper software makes estimating materials needs and labor costs an easy task.

Only trained, qualified, and properly certified drivers should operate this equipment. Suitable safety measures must always be followed when operating or working around these machines.

Workers who are inexperienced in using any of the tools or equipment in the procedures described, or are uncertain about the safety of these procedures for a particular activity or undertaking, must consult with someone who is skilled or certified in this area of work before beginning. Seeking help from a more experienced worker or supervisor when uncertain about proper safety measures can safeguard against possible injury. Time, material, property, and equipment can also be preserved. Safe work practices can make the job easier and more enjoyable and help prevent harmful and costly accidents. Remember and follow these safety tips while handling gypsum board:

- Work in pairs whenever possible (Figure 4.4).
- Lift carefully with good techniques by using the legs, not the back.
- Always stack gypsum board flat—never on edge.
- Wear a dust mask when conditions warrant.
- Ground electrical power tools properly.
- Select and use the correct tool for each job.
- Ensure that all tools are in good repair.
- Protect eyes with safety glasses or goggles when necessary (Figure 4.5).
- Proceed at a deliberate but steady pace.
- Always take precautions and time to make sure the work is done safely.
- Wear other personal protective devices and clothing such as a hard hat, gloves, safety shoes, etc.

FIGURE 4.4 Handling large gypsum-board panels is usually a two-person job.

FIGURE 4.5 Protect eyes with safety glasses or goggles.

Inspect on delivery

Products should be inspected for proper quantity and possible damage when delivered on the job. Incorrect quantities might result in job delays due to shortages or extra cost for overages that are wasted. Be sure to check products for such physical damage. For example, look for broken corners or scuffed edges on gypsum board and wet board, and check for bent or corroded steel studs and runners. Look for damaged or torn bags that could result in waste or lumpy joint-finishing compound. Report any damaged material or shortages immediately.

If possible, gypsum-drywall construction materials should be ordered for delivery to the job just before application. Materials might become damaged by abuse if stored for long periods. Many installation and callback problems can be directly traced to unfavorable job conditions. These problems might occur during product application, or they might not appear until long after job completion. Recommendations for proper job conditions, given in the appropriate product application chapters of this book, should be closely followed. If job conditions are unfavorable, correct them before product installation.

Storage

Enclosed protection from the weather is required for the stored panels. That is, the boards should be stored in a warehouse or other suitable structure where it will not be exposed to inclement weather or to temperatures that frequently exceed 125°F. Stacks of gypsum board should be stored supported evenly on a firm, dry, level, and structurally sound floor. Gypsum board should not be stored in areas of excessive humidity, nor should it be stored beneath overhead equipment that might have a tendency to drip grease, oil, or water. Gypsum board should not be left in heavy traffic areas or where it can be damaged by lift trucks and other warehouse equipment, nor should it be stored at aisle intersections. If board is stored at aisle junctions because of absolute necessity, corner protectors constructed of sheet metal or similar suitable materials must be used.

Though not recommended by most manufacturers, outdoor storage for up to one month is permissible if products are stored above ground and completely covered. Boards stored outside should be arranged so that individual storage units are covered with watertight material. Several inches of space should be left at ground level to permit air circulation within the unit. The first row of risers in contact with the floor of the storage area should be wood or plastic, not gypsum, and the risers should be placed no more than 28 inches apart. To prevent lifting and ripping of the covering material, horizontal tie ropes or bands should be used around the bottom of the units.

Gypsum board should always be stored flat. Placing it vertically on edge for an extended period might damage the edges and can also cause the board to warp. Also, board stacked on edge can easily become unstable and accidentally fall over. Stacking gypsum board flat will lower the potential for a safety hazard.

One of the most common problems created by improper storage is sagging. Careful placement of risers (Figure 4.6) will help minimize this problem. As a general rule, do not store gypsum board on gypsum risers. Use wood risers to prevent moisture from wicking up and wetting material. Various problems can result when these products get wet or are exposed to direct sunlight for extended periods.

Figure 4.7 shows how sagging might result when risers are placed improperly. When boards are stored on wood risers, the risers should be at least 2⅞ inches wide and placed directly under each other vertically within 2 inches of board ends and no greater than 28 inches apart for 14-foot board, 23 inches apart for 12-foot board, 24 inches apart for 10-foot board, 21 inches apart for 9-foot board, and 25 inches apart for 8-foot board.

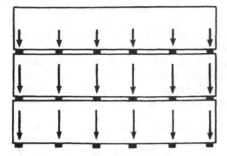

FIGURE 4.6   Proper placement of risers.

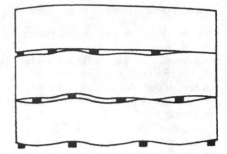

FIGURE 4.7   Sagging will result if panels are improperly stacked.

Good stock rotation and inventory control systems will help avoid minor sagging problems. However, if minor sagging occurs, the gypsum board can be straightened by one of the following methods.

- Restack the board and move the risers about 4 to 6 inches closer together than the recommended interval shown in Figure 4.8. Add evenly spaced risers as necessary to ensure that the entire stack is adequately supported. The sagging should be minimized within several days.
- Restack the board without using risers on a flat, dry, interior floor. Evenly distribute the weight on the top of the board stack. The sagging should be minimized quickly.
- If gypsum board must be restacked from vertical to horizontal, stand each board vertically on its side as close to the edge of the pile as possible (Figure 4.9). Tilt the board slightly toward the stack, and let the board drop freely on top of the stack. Take proper precaution to ensure that the remaining vertically positioned boards do not become unstable and topple on someone while restacking.

Minor adjustment in the location of the risers might be required to adapt to spacing of lift-truck forks. When absolutely necessary, risers can be moved a few inches in either direction if the number of risers is not reduced and vertical alignment between stacks is maintained.

Locate stored stock of gypsum board away from heavy-traffic areas to prevent damage from other trades. To protect them from dirt, corrosion, and distortion, keep materials in their packages or containers until ready for use. Damaged board edges are more susceptible to ridging after joint treatment. Boards with rough ends will require remedial action before installation. Otherwise, deformation or blistering might occur at end joints.

Be sure to stack bagged goods and metal components on planks or platforms away from damp floors and walls. Corrosion on corner bead, trim, and fasteners might bleed through finishing materials. Ready-mixed joint compounds that have been repeatedly frozen and thawed lose strength, which might weaken the bond.

Handling of gypsum board

Gypsum panels should always be handled carefully. When the board is moved manually, it should be supported by the edges and must never be carried flat nor dragged or slid on its ends, edges, or face. Major job-site stocking efforts nearly always require at least three

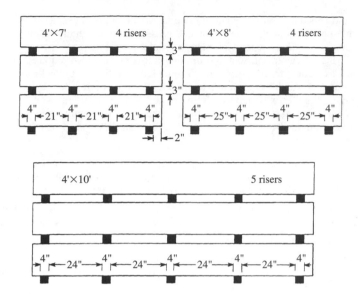

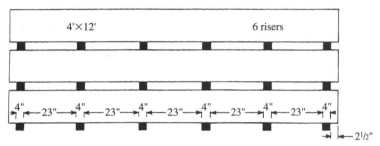

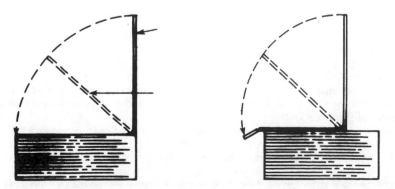

FIGURE 4.8   Restacking of gypsum-board panels.

FIGURE 4.9   Restacking from vertical to horizontal position.

people, and depending on the quantity to be stocked in a given period of time, might require additional personnel. If the customer's personnel help with unloading and stocking, make sure the unloading supervisor makes them follow safety precautions.

Delivering a large quantity of gypsum board to a job site also requires special equipment such as a boom truck specifically designed to expedite the unloading process. Only trained operators should be permitted to operate the boom during the off-loading process. The operator must be extremely careful with the boom to ensure that it does not come in contact with electrical or other utility lines or otherwise inflict damage in the area.

Everyone should always be aware of and observe the following when stocking gypsum board on the job site.

- Gypsum board, as already stated, should be delivered as near to the time it will be used as possible, especially in commercial construction because the walls might be left open and the board exposed to the weather if stocked prematurely.

- Gypsum board delivered to a job site must be placed under cover immediately and not exposed to outside elements such as rain, snow, or other high-moisture conditions.

- At least two people should always be used to handle the board while stocking.

- Gypsum board should always be stacked flat—never on edge. Board stacked on edge can easily become unstable, and the entire stack can become a serious hazard in the workplace should it accidentally topple.

- Board placed on a job site should be separated by:
  ~ Type. (Place the type of board near areas where it will be installed, e.g., type X, regular board, moisture-resistant, etc. This system of placement reduces the chance that the wrong type of board will be installed and applicators/hangers will have easy access to the stocked gypsum board.)
  ~ Size. (Do not place longer-length boards on top of shorter lengths.)

- The board must be stocked out of the way of construction traffic.

- Special care should be taken to ensure that the board does not damage the exposed studs, windows, door frames, etc.

- Board should be stocked so as not to hinder the work of construction workers such as electricians and plumbers.

- Gypsum board stocked on a job site should never have any other materials stored or stacked on top of it.

- The board should be stocked so that its weight is evenly distributed and the floor is not overloaded.

Because of the bulky and heavy nature of gypsum board, it is almost always handled mechanically in warehouses, staging areas, storage, etc. Lift trucks are typically used to move stacks of gypsum board, and boom trucks are normally used to deliver gypsum board (Figure 4.10). Although any lift truck in good condition can be used to move gypsum board, lift trucks with appropriate weight-capacity ratings must always be used to move units of board. A lift truck with a minimum of 15,000 pounds of capacity is preferred for handling gypsum board.

Special forks are available to minimize the possibility of damage caused by a fork that contacts the bottom sheet of a stack of gypsum board. These forks feature rounded or beveled edges and a slightly exaggerated taper to the tip of the fork. Cushioning material applied to the load-face of the forks will minimize damage to the edge of the board. Nonmarking rubber or polyethylene backing pads installed on the back of the forks are recommended to absorb the impact between the fork uprights and the load. Cushioning the load face will reduce the incidence of board edges being crushed or marred by the fork up-

FIGURE 4.10   Using a boom truck to unload drywall panels at the site.

rights. Side shifting forks might be less likely to damage units of board and help prevent
shifting or "interleafing" during transit.

Fork spacing must be adequate for the length of board being carried. If only one length
of gypsum board is handled, lift trucks with nonadjustable forks might be suitable.
However, for maximum flexibility in handling gypsum board of varying lengths, forks
should be mounted on carriages, which permit operators to adjust the distance between
forks. Fork spacing should be about ½ the length of the board being handled so that a maximum of 4 feet of board extends beyond the forks on either end. A carriage spread in the
range of 46 to 84 inches is suitable for carrying the most common lengths of gypsum board.

Forklift operators can load orders alone, if necessary, by using a wooden or plastic
wedge (Figure 4.11). Two or even three persons might be needed to stage, load, and fill orders if wedges are not used. When wedges are used that are properly designed and constructed, risers can be omitted between units of stacked board. Stacking is simplified, and
less waste is generated when riser/spacers are not used.

STOCKING GYPSUM BOARD ON JOB SITES

When drywall construction moved into high-rise buildings, it brought with it the new chal-
lenge of moving large gypsum boards from the ground to many stories above the ground.
Inefficient materials handling at the job site can add cost and reduce profit. Time and
money savings can be substantial when correct handling procedures are used. As already
stated, gypsum board:

- Should not be stacked high enough to pose a danger from toppling.
- Should be placed far enough inside an unenclosed building so that it is not exposed to
  inclement weather (i.e., blowing rain or snow).

- Should be handled with extreme care when being stocked on upper floors of open buildings during periods of high wind to ensure that the board and the handler(s) are not accidentally blown out of the building.

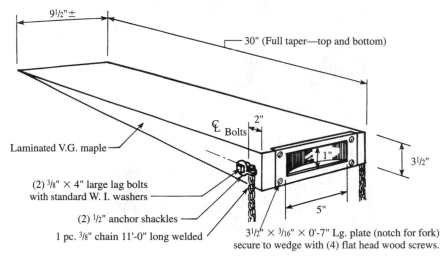

FIGURE 4.11   Typical wood wedge.

JOB CONDITIONS

Many problems can be directly traced to unfavorable job conditions. These problems might occur during product application, or they might not appear until long after completion. The following environmental factors can present problems in drywall construction.

Temperature

Install gypsum panels and joint compound at temperatures above 50°F. In cold weather, provide controlled, well-distributed heat to keep the temperature above minimum levels. For example, if gypsum board is installed at a temperature of 28°F, it expands at the rate of ½ inch for every 100 linear feet when the temperature is raised to 70°F. Joint compounds and textures are negatively affected by low temperatures. Loss of strength and bond occur from freezing after application and might require replacement. Repeated freezing and thawing of ready-mixed compounds causes them to lose their workability and might render them useless. Even temperatures should be maintained to avoid cracking from the thermal shock caused by sudden changes in temperature.

Humidity and moisture

Water vapor is absorbed by gypsum board. This causes the core to soften and the paper to expand, ultimately causing the panel to sag between ceiling supports. Consistent high humidity, whether from atmospheric conditions or the installation of moisture-laden construction products such as concrete, stucco, plaster, or spray fireproofing, gives the galvanized steel components of the panels more opportunity to rust, especially if the humidity comes from salt water. Job delays might result from high moisture content in the air due to extended drying time between coats of joint compound.

Warmer temperatures combined with sufficient airflow and low humidity will accelerate drying. Faster drying time might result in dry-out of the joint compound and edge cracking. Extremely hot and dry conditions will result in checking, cracking, and crusting of fresh compound. Under these conditions, the board must be handled carefully during erection to prevent core damage and cracking.

Wind-blown rain and standing water on floors increase the humidity in a structure and might cause the problems previously described. Water-soaked gypsum board has less structural strength and might sag and deform easily. Their surfaces, when damp, are extremely vulnerable to scuffing and mildew. A device such as the one shown in Figure 4.12 can be used to check for the presence of moisture.

Two other environmental factors that must be constantly monitored and controlled are:

- Sunlight: Exposure to strong sunlight for long periods of time will cause discoloration of the panels and make decoration difficult. If the normally light-green face paper on MR panels appears gray or tan in color, it has been exposed to too much ultraviolet light.

- Ventilation: Ventilation should be provided to remove excess moisture, permit proper drying of joint compounds, and prevent problems associated with high-humidity conditions.

FIGURE 4.12   Typical moisture-indicating meter.

CHAPTER 5

WORKING WITH GYPSUM-BOARD PANELS

Robert Scharff
Walls & Ceilings Magazine

As stated earlier, drywall gypsum panels can be hung on wood or metal framing and fastened with screws, nails, or adhesive. This chapter will cover the steps necessary to prepare for the actual installation of gypsum drywall on wood and metal framing.

MEASUREMENTS

To achieve the desired effects of good drywall installation, measurements must be taken accurately at correct ceiling or wall locations for each edge or end of the panel. Make two measurements as a check. This procedure will usually ward off partitions or door openings that are out of plumb or out of square. That is, accurate measuring will usually reveal irregularities in framing and furring so that corrective allowances can be made in cutting. Poorly aligned framing should be corrected before the board is hung.

As mentioned in chapter 3, a 12-foot to 25-foot flexible/rigid steel power tape is the handiest measuring tool for making most drywall installation measurements. It is generally used in conjunction with a chalk line. Measure the first dimension on the surface being covered. Then transfer this measurement to the surface of the gypsum board, near one edge (Figure 5.1). After marking this point with a pencil, move the tape to the opposite edge of the board and measure the same distance, making another pencil mark. Then snap a chalk line between the two marks as described in chapter 3. This chalked line that is left on the board is the cut line.

CUTTING DRYWALL PANELS

Drywall gypsum panels can be cut by scoring and breaking (the preferred method) or by sawing, working from the face-paper side. Using a T-square or straightedge and a wallboard (utility) knife, score the face paper of the gypsum board completely to the core

FIGURE 5.1 Accurate measurements are a must before undertaking any cutting procedures.

(Figure 5.2A). Then use firm, even pressure to snap the board back away from the cut face (Figure 5.2B). The back paper should be broken by snapping the gypsum board in the reverse direction (Figure 5.2C) or preferably by cutting the back paper (Figure 5.2D). Smooth any rough edges with either a rasp or sandpaper (Figure 5.3).

For cuts along the long length of the board, use a steel tape with an adjustable edge guide and a tip that accepts the utility knife blade. With this tape the edge guide is set for the desired width and placed against the board edge. The knife blade is then inserted into the slotted tape tip, and by moving both hands together the tool is drawn down the full length of the board to make a smooth and accurate cut.

Cut and fit the drywall panels for pipes, electrical outlet boxes, medicine cabinets, and similar openings. Holes for electrical outlet boxes can be made with a special outlet-box cutting tool. When cutting an outlet hole with this tool, the cut is made without any damage to the surrounding gypsum paper facing or core. Another method of accomplishing this is to carefully measure for the exact location, score the outline of the box, and score diagonally (Figure 5.4). Then strike a sharp hammer blow to the "X" and cut away the back paper.

An adjustable cutting tool makes quick work of cutting circular holes (Figures 5.5A and 5.5B). Set the radius of the hole's diameter on the calibrated shaft. Set the center pin on the board and rotate the shaft to make the circular cut. Edges can be trimmed with a utility knife.

Keyhole or drywall saws can be used for any type of cutout that does not extend to the edge of a panel (Figure 5.6). To use a keyhole or drywall saw, first bore a starter hole at one corner or point of the cutout. Insert the keyhole saw into the hole and start the cut, working slowly and carefully with a minimum of pressure. A power saber saw can be used in the same manner. The saber or jigsaw can also be used to trim off drywall at doorways and windows. Where two cuts join, one cut must be made with a saw; the other cut can be made by scoring and snapping (Figure 5.7). Cuts like this are usually required around door and window openings.

A

FIGURE 5.2   (A) The gypsum board is cut by scoring it with a utility knife against a T-square, (B) Snapping back, (C) Cut the back paper with the same knife and separate the sections.

B

C

D

FIGURE 5.2   Snapping a gypsum for a clear break.

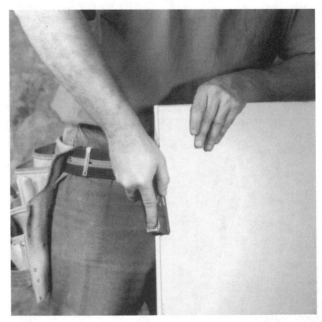

FIGURE 5.3   The cut edges of the board are smoothed with a rasp or with coarse sandpaper.

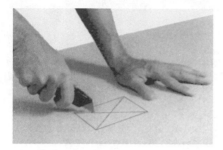

FIGURE 5.4 Making an electrical-outlet-box cut.

A

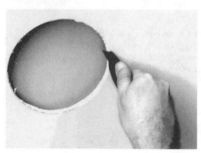

B

FIGURE 5.5 (A) An adjustable cutting tool makes quick work of circular holes, as the cutter wheel on a calibrated shaft rotates from a center pin. (B) Edges are trimmed with a hook-bill knife.

FIGURE 5.6 Circular cuts can also be made with a keyhole saw.

FIGURE 5.7 Where two cuts join, one cut must be made with a saw and the other by scoring and snapping.

Power electric routers (shown in Figure 5.8) can also be used for irregular cuts and for providing holes in gypsum drywall for electrical boxes, heating and air conditioning ducts, grilles, and other small openings. But, regardless of how the openings are made, all cut edges of the gypsum boards should be smoothed where necessary with a rasp or sandpaper to obtain neat fitting joints when the panel is installed (Figure 5.9). Where gypsum board meets projecting surfaces, it should be scribed and neatly cut.

FIGURE 5.8 A typical electric drywall router used for irregular cuts and providing holes in gypsum board for electrical boxes, heating ducts and grills, and other small openings.

FASTENERS

At one time in the history of drywall construction, the only method of fastening gypsum board was with nails. Today, drywall installers and mechanics still use nails, but they also employ screws and adhesives, and in some cases staples.

Screw attachment

As mentioned in chapter 2, screws are excellent insurance against fastener pops caused by loosely attached board. Screws are recommended for wood frame attachment, and they are

FIGURE 5.9   Regardless of the type of cut, the edges must be smoothed with a rasp or sandpaper.

required for attachment to steel framing and resilient channels. When mounting to resilient channels, take care not to locate screws directly over studs (Figure 5.10), thereby "shorting out" or negating the resiliency (see chapter 9).

Because fewer fasteners are required when screws are used to attach gypsum board, the number to be treated is reduced and possible application defects minimized. Generally,

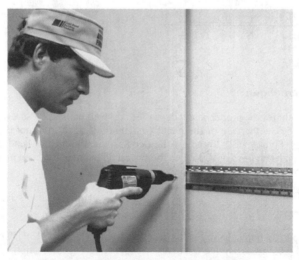

FIGURE 5.10   Installing resilient channel using a screw gun.

screws should be spaced not to exceed 12 inches O.C. on ceilings and 16 inches O.C. on walls where framing members are 16 inches O.C. (Figure 5.11). Screws should be spaced a maximum of 12 inches O.C. on walls and ceilings where framing members are 24 inches O.C. For more information about the type and size of screws used in drywall construction, see chapter 2.

Screws are applied as previously mentioned with a positive-clutch electric power tool, commonly called an *electric screw gun*, equipped with adjustable screw-depth control head and a Phillips bit. The use of screws provides a positive mechanical attachment of gypsum board to either wood or steel framing.

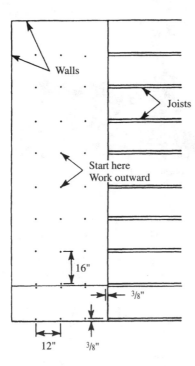

FIGURE 5.11   Proper screw placement.

Adjust the screw gun

Set the adjustment for the proper screw depth. For drywall panels, the screw head must be driven slightly below the face of the panel (maximum ½ inch), but not deep enough to break the paper (Figure 5.12). To adjust the depth, rotate the control head to provide the proper screw depth (Figure 5.13A). When the proper adjustment has been made, secure the control head to maintain the adjustment.

Place the screw

The Phillips-head tip holds the drywall screw for driving (Figure 5.13B). The bit tip does not rotate until pressure is applied to the drywall panel during application.

Screw head

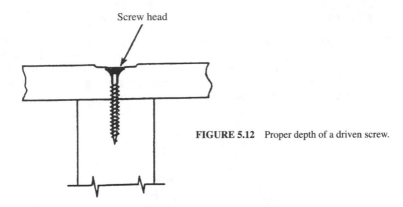

FIGURE 5.12   Proper depth of a driven screw.

A   **FIGURE 5.13**   (A) Adjust the screw gun. (B) Place the screw.

B

Start the screw straight

A firm grip on the electric screw gun is important for a straight line of entry. To avoid stress on the wrist, hold the gun as shown in Figure 5.13C, by the pistol grip. The screw must enter perpendicular to the board face for proper performance. Drive the screws at least ¾ inch from the edges or ends of the board. Screw types and spacing are given in chapters 2 and 4 and in Tables 5.1A and 5.1B.

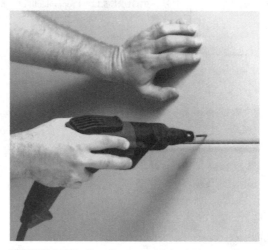

FIGURE 5.13C   Start the screw straight.

Staple applications

Staples are recommended only for attaching the base-layer boards to wood framing in double-layer assemblies. The staples should be 16-gauge, flat-head galvanized wire with ¹⁄₁₆-inch-wide crown divergent points and leg lengths to provide a minimum ⅝-inch penetration into the supports. Drive the staples with the crown perpendicular to the gypsum-board edges, except where edges fall on supports. Drive staples so the crown bears tightly against the board but does not cut the paper. Spacing of staples is shown in Figure 5.14.

Nail applications

Nails are employed only when the supporting members are wood. Gypsum drywall can be attached by either a single-nailing or double-nailing method. Double-nailing produces a tighter board-to-stud contact. Wherever fire-resistive construction is required, nail spacing specified in the fire test should be followed.

TABLE 5.1 (A) Selector Guide for USG Screws (B) Basic Types of Screws

fastening application	fastener used	fig[2]
GYPSUM PANELS TO 12-GA. (MAX.) STEEL FRAMING		
½" and ⅝" panels and gypsum sheathing to steel studs and runners; specify Cadmium-Plated screws for exterior curtain wall applications	1" Type S-12 Bugle Head	3
Self-Furring Metal Lath and brick wall ties through gypsum sheathing to steel studs and runners; specify Cadmium-Plated screws for exterior curtain wall applications	1¼" Type S-12 Bugle Head 1¼" Type S-12 Pancake Head	4 13
½" and ⅝" double-layer gypsum panels to steel studs and runners	1⅝" Type S-12 Bugle Head	4
Multilayer gypsum panels and other materials to steel studs and runners	1⅞", 2", 2⅜", 2⅝", 3" Type S-12 Bugle Head	4
RIGID FOAM INSULATION TO STEEL FRAMING		
Rigid foam insulation panels to steel studs and runners; Type R for 20 and 25-ga. steel	1½", 2", 2½", 3" Type S-12 or R Wafer Head	15
ALUMINUM TRIM TO STEEL FRAMING		
Trim and door hinges to steel studs and runners (screw matches hardware and trim)	⅞" Type S-18 Oval Head Cadmium-Plated	7
Batten strips to steel studs in Demountable partitions	1⅛" Type S Bugle Head	1
Aluminum trim to steel framing in Demountable partitions	1¼" Type S Bugle Head Cadmium-Plated	1
GYPSUM PANELS TO WOOD FRAMING		
⅜", ½" and ⅝" single-layer panels to wood studs, joists	1¼" Type W Bugle Head	8
RC-1 RESILIENT CHANNELS TO WOOD FRAMING		
Screw attachment required for both ceilings, and partitions	1¼" Type W Bugle Head 1¼" Type S Bugle Head	8 1
For fire-rated construction	1¼" Type S Bugle Head	1
GYPSUM PANELS TO GYPSUM PANELS		
Multilayer adhesively laminated gypsum-to-gypsum partitions (not recommended for double-layer ⅜" panels)	1½" Type G Bugle Head	8
PLYWOOD TO STEEL JOISTS		
⅝" to ¾" plywood to steel joists (penetrates double thickness 14-ga.)	1 15/16" Type S-12 Bugle Head, Pilot Point	16
STEEL TO POURED CONCRETE OR BLOCK		
Attachment of steel framing components to poured concrete and concrete block surfaces	3/16" × 1¾" Acorn Slotted Anchor	14

fastening application	fastener used	fig[2]
GYPSUM PANELS TO STEEL FRAMING[1]		
½" single-layer panels to steel studs, runners, channels	1" Type S Bugle Head	1
⅝" single-layer panels to steel studs, runners, channels	1" Type S Bugle Head 1⅛" Type S Bugle Head	1 1
1" coreboard to metal angle runners in solid partitions	1¼" Type S Bugle Head	1
½" double-layer panels to steel studs, runners, channels	1⅝" Type S Bugle Head	2
⅝" double-layer panels to steel studs, runners, channels	1⅝" Type S Bugle Head	2
½" panels through coreboard to metal angle runners in solid partitions	1⅞" Type S Bugle Head	2
⅝" panels through coreboard to metal angle runners in solid partitions	2¼" Type S Bugle Head 3" Type S Bugle Head	2 2
1" double-layer coreboard to steel studs, runners	2⅝" Type S Bugle Head	2
WOOD TO STEEL FRAMING		
Wood trim over single-layer panels to steel studs, runners	1" Type S or S-12 Trim Head 1⅝" Type S or S-12 Trim Head	5 5
Wood trim over double-layer panels to steel studs, runners	2¼" Type S or S-12 Trim Head	5
Steel cabinets, brackets through single-layer panels to steel studs	1¼" Type S Oval Head	6
Wood cabinets through single-layer panels to steel studs	1⅝" Type S Oval Head	6
Wood cabinets through double-layer panels to steel studs	2¼", 2⅞", 3¾", Type S Oval Head	6
STEEL STUDS TO DOOR FRAMES, RUNNERS		
Steel studs to runners	⅜" Type S Pan Head	9
Steel studs to runners Steel studs to door frame jamb anchors Other metal-to-metal attachment (12-ga. max.)	⅜" Type S-12 Pan Head ⅝" Type S-12 Low-Profile Head	10 11
Steel studs to door frame jamb anchors (heavier shank assures entry in anchors of hard steel)	½" Type S-12 Pan Head ⅝" Type S-12 Low-Profile Head	10 11
Strut studs to door frame anchors, rails, other attachments in movable partitions	½" Type S-16 Pan Head Cadmium-Plated	10
Metal-to-metal connections up to double thickness of 12-ga. steel	¾" S-4 Hex Washer Head Cadmium-Plated	12

Notes: [1]Includes Steel Studs and Runners, Metal Angles; Metal Furring Channels; and RC-1 Resilient Channels. If channel resiliency makes screw penetration difficult, use screws ⅛" longer than shown to attach panels to RC-1 channels. For other gauges of studs and runners, always use Type S-12 screws. For steel applications not shown, select a screw length which is at least ⅜" longer than total thickness of materials to be fastened. Use cadmium-plated screws for exterior applications.
[2]Figures refer to following screw illustrations.

A

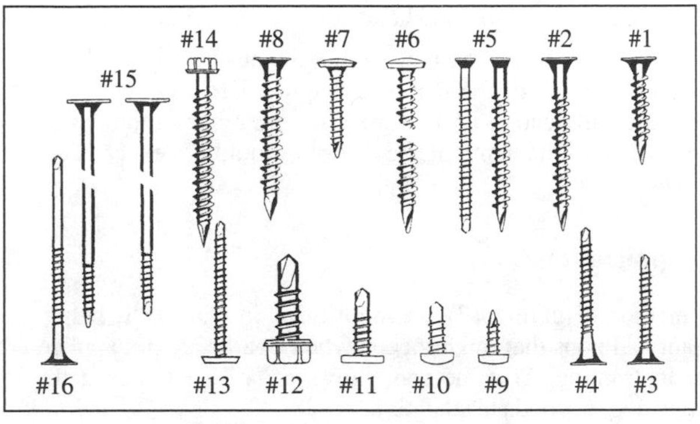
#14
#8
#7
#6
#5
#2
#1
#15
#16
#13
#12
#11
#10
#9
#4
#3

B

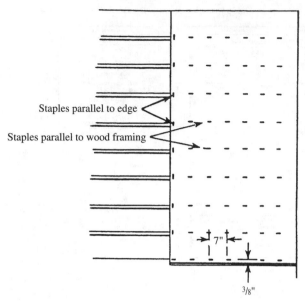

FIGURE 5.14 Proper staple placement.

Single-nailing application

When applying drywall using the single-nailing method (Figure 5.15), proceed as follows:

1. Begin the nailing from the abutting edge of the board and proceed toward the opposite ends or edges. Do not nail the perimeter before nailing the field of the board. Ceiling application might cause the board to deflect or sag in the center and prevent a firm fastening.
2. Position the nails on the adjacent ends or edges opposite each other.
3. Drive the nails at least ⅜ inch from the ends or edges of the board.
4. To ensure that the board is in tight contact with the framing member, apply hand pressure on the board adjacent to the nail being driven.
5. Drive the nails with the shank perpendicular to the face of the board.
6. Use a drywall hammer with a crowned head for gypsum panels.
7. For gypsum-drywall panels, seat the nail so that the head is in a shallow, uniform dimple formed by the last blow of the hammer (Figure 5.16). Do not break the paper or crush the core at the nail head or around the circumference of the dimple by overdriving. Never use a nail set. The depth of the dimple should not exceed ½₂ inch.

Double-nailing applications

This application method (Figure 5.17), as mentioned in chapter 1, helps prevent loose boards and resultant nail pops that might occur when boards are not applied correctly and are drawn tightly to framing. This method, however, will not reduce the incidence or severity of nail pops due to wood shrinkage.

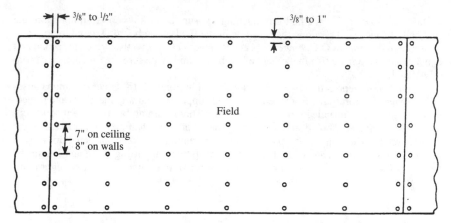

FIGURE 5.15 In a single-nailed gypsum board, the nails are spread 7 to 8 inches apart along the supports and are not less than ⅜ inch from the edges and ends. Nails are first driven in the middle area of the board and then out toward the edges and ends.

FIGURE 5.16 A properly driven nail.

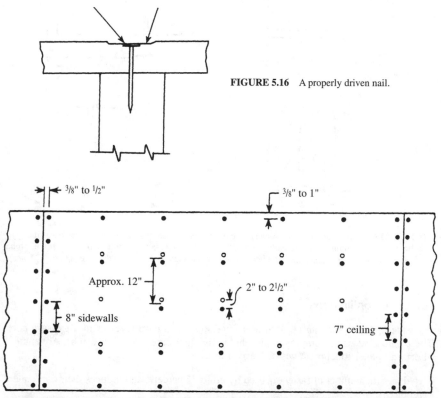

FIGURE 5.17 In double nailing, the first nails, represented here by black dots, are driven in the middle area of the board and then out toward the edges and ends. The second nails, represented here by circles, are driven in the same sequence.

In the double-nailing method for attaching gypsum board to wood framing space the first nails 12 inches O.C. along the supports in the field of the board. Around the perimeter, space nails 7 inches O.C. for ceilings and 8 inches O.C. for walls. Drive the second nail about 2 inches from the first in the field of the board, and make sure the first nails are properly seated.

Examples of incorrectly driven nails are shown in Figure 5.18. Other common causes of face-paper fractures are misaligned or twisted supporting framing members and projections of improperly installed blocking or bracing. These framing faults prevent solid contact between gypsum board and supporting members, and hammer impact causes the board to rebound and rupture the paper. Defective framing should be corrected prior to application of gypsum board (see chapter 6). Protruding supporting members should be trimmed or reinstalled. The use of screws, adhesives, or two-ply construction might minimize problems resulting from these defects.

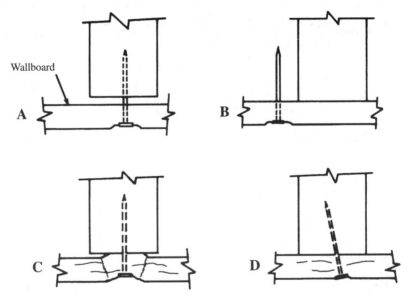

FIGURE 5.18   Incorrectly driven nails can cause problems. (A) Loose nails are caused by poor fit of gypsum board to the framing, or (B) by nails missing the framing. (C) Nails driven in loose boards will probably fracture the board core and paper. (D) Nails driven on an angle also fracture the face paper.

Adhesive applications

Construction adhesive can be used to secure studs to a base layer or to a gypsum core. These adhesives can be employed just about anywhere screws or nails can be. Advantages of drywall panel attachment with adhesives are:

- Reduces the number of fasteners used by up to 75 percent, and reduces their consequent problems.
- Stronger than conventional nail application. Up to 100 percent more tensile strength, and up to 50 percent more sheer strength.

- Unaffected by moisture, high or low temperature, and is vermin-resistant.
- Fewer loose panels caused by improper fastening.
- Bridges minor framing irregularities.
- Will not stain or bleed through most finishes.

Using adhesives in applications

While there are several types of adhesives that can be used to fasten gypsum panels, they fall into two basic categories: stud adhesive or laminating adhesives, either of joint compound or contact types. In this chapter we will concern ourselves with stud adhesive, which forms a bond between wood studs and the boards. While many of the precautions given in this chapter hold true when laminating two boards to form a multi-ply panel, the complete use of laminating adhesive is covered in chapter 6.

When using stud or construction type adhesive, keep the following instructions and recommendations in mind in order to obtain a quality finished job.

1. Select the proper adhesive for specific job requirements. Read container directions carefully and follow the instructions to the letter. Different stud adhesives are needed for different framing situations.

2. Make sure that all substrate is clean, sound, and free from oil, dirt, or contamination so that the adhesive sticks firmly.

3. A foil surface of a foil-backed gypsum board is not recommended for adhesive lamination to any surface.

4. Prefinished gypsum-board application is not usually recommended for ceilings.

5. In cold weather, maintain a room temperature between 50°F and 70°F for 48 hours prior to application and continuously thereafter until the adhesive is completely dry. Never let the adhesive freeze.

6. In hot weather, the room temperature during installation and curing time should never reach 100°F. Extremely high temperatures cause solvent-based products to evaporate rapidly, shortening the open time and damping the bonding characteristics as described later in this chapter.

7. Adequate heat and ventilation must be provided to ensure complete drying of the adhesive within 72 hours.

8. Adequate cross-ventilation must be provided, and proper precautions against sparks and open flame must be taken when using adhesives containing flammable solvents.

9. Keep the container closed whenever adhesive is not in use. Evaporation of solvent or vehicle affects the adhesive's wetting, bonding, and application characteristics.

10. Never exceed the open time given by the manufacturer. Disregarding these directions might cause poor bonding, as noted later in this chapter.

11. Follow the manufacturer's recommendations concerning the proper amounts of adhesive to be applied. Too small or too large a bead will lead to performance problems or waste. Also apply the adhesive with the proper tools and as recommended by the manufacturer.

12. Allow the adhesive to dry for at least 48 hours before treating the drywall joints.

Cartridge preparation

Cut the ridge tip in two different ways (Figure 5.19): For walls, make a chevron or "V" cut in order to produce a round, uniform bead. The cut edge of the nozzle then rides along the stud easily. For ceilings, use a single, angled slash across the nozzle. This gives a wipe-on effect on the ceiling joint to minimize dripping. If any adhesive is left in the cartridge, it can be saved by inserting a screw or bolt into the end of the cartridge to seal it.

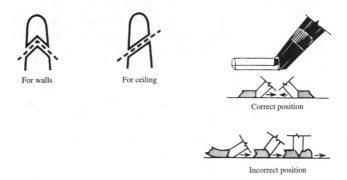

For walls   For ceiling

Correct position

Incorrect position

FIGURE 5.19   (Left) Proper nozzle cut and (right) proper opening and gun position.

Applying the adhesive

The proper nozzle opening and gun position are required to obtain the right size and shape of the bead to produce satisfactory results. For most wall and ceiling drywall panel installations, the initial height of the bead over the framing should be ⅜ inch and of sufficient volume to provide a ¹⁄₁₆-inch thickness of adhesive over the entire support when compressed.

Apply adhesive in a continuous ⅜-inch bead in the center of the attachment face and to within 6 inches of the ends of all framing members (Figure 5.20A). A zigzag pattern such as shown in Figure 5.20B can also be employed. Where the two gypsum boards meet on a framing member, apply two continuous ⅜-inch beads to the framing members at the extreme edges of the face to ensure adequate contact with the paper on the back of the board (Figure 5.20C). Do not apply the adhesive to the members (such as bridging, diagonal bracing, etc.) into which no supplemental fasteners will be driven. Adhesive usually is not required at the inside corners, top and bottom plates, bracing, or fire stops, and adhesive is not ordinarily used in closets.

In a typical adhesive nail-on or screw-on installation, position the gypsum-drywall panel against the framing shortly after adhesive is applied, and fasten immediately, using proper screws or nails. Adhesive should be applied to no greater an area than can be covered with gypsum board within the open time of the adhesive. Remember that all adhesives have an open time limit. Once the applied adhesive begins to dry, it forms a skin as it sets up. It is important to apply the drywall panels before the adhesive sets up. Once a skin forms, the sticking power of the adhesive is decreased and the bond will not be as strong.

Position the gypsum board to provide a tight fit at the abutting ends or edges. Do not slide the board. If the properties of the adhesive are such as to assure bridging between the gypsum board and the wood framing, no nailing is required in the field of the board on walls. In such cases, perimeter nailing might be used, as required. If properties of the adhesive are such that there is no positive bridging between the board and the wood framing,

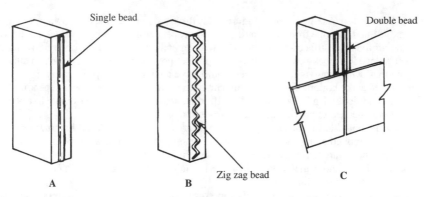

FIGURE 5.20   Three methods of applying adhesive to studs.

either temporary field nailing or temporary bracing might be required to ensure the contact between the board, adhesive, and stud face until the adhesive develops adequate bond strength. Unless otherwise recommended by the manufacturer of the gypsum board or the adhesive, fasteners should be spaced in accordance with Table 5.2.

Temporary fastening or bracing must be used to supplement permanent fastening where visual inspection shows the need to assure positive bonding or to maintain flush panel joints. Temporary fasteners might be double-headed nails, common nails driven at an angle, or drywall screws that might or might not be removed after adhesion is complete.

When fasteners at the vertical joints are objectionable (such as with predecorated panels) the boards might be prebowed and adhesively attached with fasteners at top and bottom. Predecorated panels must be warped or bowed to give pressure at the center of the board during adhesive applications. If the boards were not bowed, temporary bracing

TABLE 5.2   Maximum Fastener Spacing for Base Ply in Multi-Ply Construction

Base-ply fastener	Face-ply fastening method	Application	Maximum spacing for base-ply fasteners (O.C.)
Nails	Laminated face ply	Ceilings	7"
		Walls	8"
	Nailed face ply	Ceilings	16"
		Walls	16"
Screws	Laminated face ply (framing 16" O.C.)	Ceilings	16"
		Walls	16"
	Laminated face ply (framing 24" O.C.)	Ceilings	12"
		Walls	12"
	Screwed face ply	Ceilings	24"
		Walls	24"
Staples	Laminated face ply	Ceilings	7"
		Walls	7"
	Nailed or screwed face ply	Ceilings	16"
		Walls	16"

would be required. As illustrated in Figure 5.21, there are two methods of bowing. Be sure to remove bundling tape from the boards. Cut to proper ceiling height, and stack as shown with all prefinished surfaces facing up or down, depending on which method of bowing is used. Use padded blocks cut from 2-×-4s to protect prefinished surfaces. Stack in such a manner that, when applying, each panel would have a tendency to spring away at the top when nailed at the bottom. Proper bowing can take from one to several days depending on weather conditions. (Under very humid conditions, boards might be too flexible to assume the stiff bow needed to provide adequate pressure against the framing.)

After the board has been set in place, impact by hand or a soft-faced hammer (Figure 5.22) can be applied along each stud or joist to ensure good contact at all points. To assist in cleanup, make sure to remove excess adhesive from the boards and tools before it dries. Use a solvent-based cleaner, and follow the manufacturer's instructions and safety precautions printed on the container.

Predecorated panels are not the only type of gypsum board that can be prebowed. For instance, when installing gypsum-drywall panels on curved surfaces (such as a curved staircase) or entry-wall partitions, the panels can be prebowed to curve them gently. More information on curved drywall surfaces can be found in chapter 8.

Special adhesives and stud adhesives are suitable for attaching gypsum board directly to concrete and masonry. However, adhesive manufacturers' recommendations can vary and should be reviewed to ensure proper selection and application. Supplemental fastening, bracing, or shoring is required while the adhesive develops bond strength. Actually, some stud adhesives (such as those used with metal framing) require fasteners on intermediate supports as well as at the perimeter of gypsum board. Fastener spacing varies according to type of fastener, support spacing, and load-bearing condition. Always check the adhesive manufacturer's recommendations.

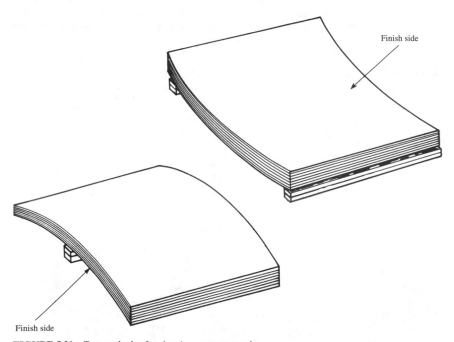

Finish side

Finish side

FIGURE 5.21   Two methods of prebowing gypsum panels.

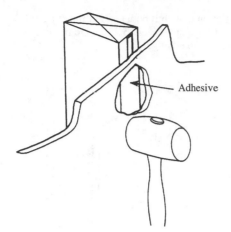

FIGURE 5.22   To be sure a panel is firmly set, tap it in place with a soft-faced hammer.

Edge-grip clips

Special edge-grip clips are available that provide mechanical attachments of drywall panels over steel or wood framing, over steel or wood furring on concrete block, or on any other sound, level wall surface. Used primarily for predecorated drywall installations, it can be used in standard gypsum-board installations as well.

The edge-grip clip is positioned on the back of the board and tapped in place, using the installation tool (Figure 5.23). The prongs are driven into the board edges. The leading edge of each clip along one edge of the board is screw/nail-attached to the studs, furring, or other wall surface. For clips on succeeding panels, slip under the previously applied panels. Top and bottom edges must be fastened to the framing, furring, or wall (Figure 5.24). The edge-grip clips hold the board firmly in place. When using 4-foot-wide panels, use adhesive along intermediate studs.

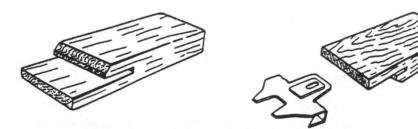

FIGURE 5.23   How a clip is held in an installation tool.

The clips should be installed into the edge of the gypsum board with the wooden tool included in each box of clips. To use the installation, proceed as follows:

1. Place the clip into the slot of the tool, as shown in Figure 5.25A. Make sure the back edges of the teeth are against the wood.

2. Position the clip and tool against the back surface of the board so that the clip is flat to the back and perpendicular to the edge of the panel.

3. Using a hammer, tap the end of the installation tool until both teeth of the clip are fully inserted and the back legs are tight against the edge (Figure 5.25B). Do not overdrive the clips, as this can cause deformation of the board edge.

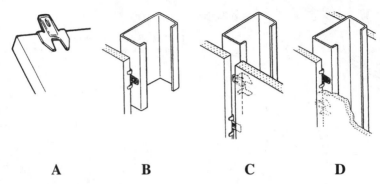

A   B   C   D

FIGURE 5.24   Applications of gypsum-board clips.

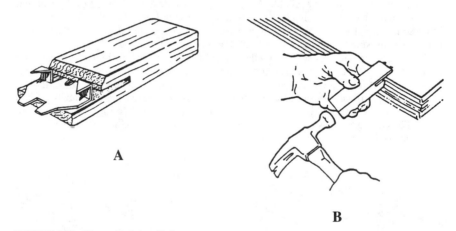

A

B

FIGURE 5.25   How a clip is installed.

Apply clips to the leading edge of the panel 16 inches O.C., starting 16 inches down from the top. Clips on the trailing edge of the next panel are also spaced 16 inches O.C. but are about 2 inches from those on the first panel's leading edge. If greater rigidity is desired, clip spacing can be reduced. All panels require clips along both edges, except when panels abut doors, windows, intersections, or corners, in which case one edge of the panel will be directly fastened with nails or screws.

Position the first panel, aligning the uncut edge at the center of the framing member, plumb, and attach it top and bottom as well as directly to the starting stud. Attach the top and bottom with fasteners 1 inch from each panel edge and 12 inches O.C. between. Fasten the clips to the steel studs with the screws provided. Fasten the clips to wood studs with

1-inch nails or 1¼ type-W screws through the hole in the clip. Do not fasten clips before securing the top and bottom of this first panel.

On all intermediate framing, apply ¼-inch-diameter beads of drywall stud adhesive. In fixed-wood or furred-wall construction, the adhesive must be applied progressively with the drywall panel application. In a steel stud system, adhesive need not be applied until the opposite face of the partition is finished. Intermediate studs are rotated back into position. This procedure allows the intermediate studs, which are the joint studs on the opposite face, to be adjusted as necessary when the second side panels are erected. Apply the base trim at the bottom of the partition. Install the snap-on accessories at the inside corners, outside corners and the wall-ceiling juncture if desired (see chapters 8 and 10).

GENERAL DRYWALL APPLICATION RECOMMENDATIONS

The following general recommendations for gypsum-drywall panels apply to wood and steel framing and should be kept in mind:

- In most applications, gypsum board should be applied first to ceilings, at right angles to the framing members. Next the top panel on the wall is hung, followed by the bottom sheet (Figure 5.26).
- Cut the drywall panels so that they fit easily into place without force.
- Whenever possible, match similar edges and ends, i.e., tapered to tapered, square-cut ends to square-cut ends.

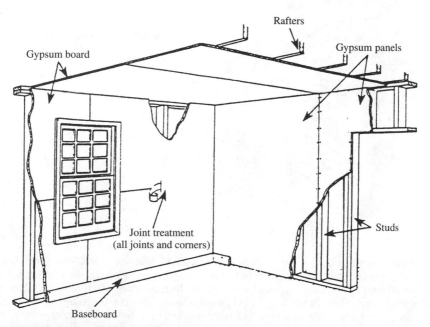

FIGURE 5.26 Installation of drywall panels.

- Plan to span the entire length of the ceiling or wall with single boards if possible to reduce the number of butt joints, which are more difficult to finish. Stagger butt joints and locate them as far from the center of the wall and ceiling as possible so they will be inconspicuous.

- Drywall joints at openings should be located so that no end joint will align with edges of openings unless control joints will be installed at these points. End joints should be staggered, and joints on opposite sides of a partition should not occur on the same stud.

- Gypsum-drywall board should be held in firm contact with the framing member while fasteners are being driven (Figure 5.27). Fastening should proceed from the center portion of the wallboard toward the edges and ends. Fasteners should be set with the heads slightly below the surface of the wallboard in a dimple formed by the hammer or power screwdriver. Care should be taken to avoid breaking the face paper of the wallboard. Improperly driven nails or screws should be replaced.

FIGURE 5.27   Be sure that there is firm contact with the framing member when driving a fastener.

- Fasteners, when used at the edges or ends, should be spaced not less than ⅜ inch from the edges and ends of gypsum board (Figure 5.28). Fasteners used at the edges or at the board ends in horizontal application should not be more than 1 inch from the edges or ends, except when the floating-angle method is used. Perimeter fastening into the partition plate or sole at the top and bottom is not required or recommended except where fire rating, structural performance, or other special conditions require such fastening (see chapter 8).

FIGURE 5.28   Space fasteners not less than ⅜ inch from the edges and ends of the gypsum board.

- To ensure level surfaces at the joints, arrange board application so that the leading edge of each board is attached to the open or unsupported edge of a steel stud flange on the metal framing. To do this, all studs must be placed so that their flanges point in the same direction. Board application is then planned to advance in the direction opposite to the flange direction. When this simple procedure is followed, attachment of each board holds the stud flange of the metal framing at the joint in a rigid position for the attachment of the next board.

- If gypsum-drywall ceiling panels are nailed to cross furring, these members should have a minimum cross section of 2-×-2 inches (nominal) with the same spacing limitations as previously discussed. With screws, nominal 1-×-2-inch furring can be used. Spacing of the framing members to receive the furring must not exceed 24 inches O.C.

- Corner bead should be nailed with annular ring nails, spaced no greater than 9 inches on each flange of the framing, with the nails opposite. In lieu of nailing, corner bead can be crimp-applied 6 inches O.C. with a special stud-crimping tool (see chapter 3). Some corner bead is available that is self-crimping.

- Mechanical and electrical equipment should be installed to allow for the gypsum-drywall panel thickness when applying the trim components such as cover plates, registers, and grilles. The depth of electrical boxes should not exceed the framing depth, and boxes on opposite sides of a wall should not be placed in the same stud-cavity space. Electrical boxes, cabinets, and other devices preferably should not penetrate completely through walls. This can be detrimental to sound and fire resistance.

- Lighting and other fixtures should be supported by framing (see chapter 8). Do not use gypsum wallboard to support them.

CHAPTER 6

INSTALLING DRYWALL
OVER WOOD FRAMING

Robert Scharff
Walls & Ceilings Magazine

As stated in previous chapters, gypsum drywall can be installed over wood or steel framing. While providing the support for the drywall can be done by carpenters, metal workers, masons, and other tradespeople, the drywall contractor or installer must know how the support or framing has been done. This is necessary so that the drywall contractor can select the correct installation procedures.

WOOD FRAMING AND FURRING

In this chapter, the emphasis will be placed on the installation of gypsum drywall when wood framing has been used. Fastening drywall to wood studs and joists is still the most common method of installation for residential jobs (Figure 6.1).

In wood-frame construction, one of the most expensive problems encountered in drywall surfaces, in terms of callbacks, is fastener pops, which is often caused by lumber shrinkage. Shrinkage occurs as lumber dries. Even "kiln-dried" lumber can shrink, warp, bow, and twist, causing boards to loosen and fasteners to fail. Gypsum surfaces can also crack, buckle, or develop joint deformations when attached across the wide dimension of large wood-framing members such as joists. Typically, this installation occurs in stairwells and high wall surfaces where the gypsum finish passes over midheight floor framing, as in split-level houses.

To obtain a quality gypsum drywall finish, the wood framing must meet the following minimum requirements:

- The wood framework should meet the minimum requirements of all applicable building codes.
- All framing lumber should be of the correct grade for the intended use, bear the grade mark of a recognized inspection agency, and be of 2-×-4 nominal size or larger.
- All framing lumber should have a moisture content not in excess of 19 percent at the time of gypsum-board application.

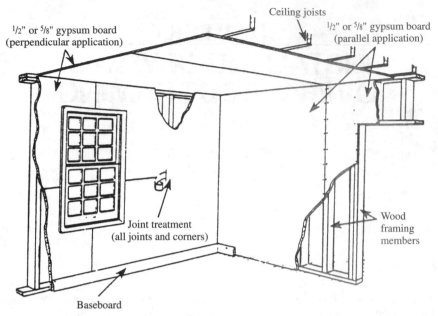

FIGURE 6.1   Drywall panels installed on wood framing supports.

Framing lumber, as commonly used, has a moisture content of 15 to 19 percent. After installation, the lumber loses about 10 percent of this moisture content and consequently shrinks, particularly during the first heating season. Remember that wood shrinks most in the direction of the growth rings (flat grain), somewhat less across the growth rings (edge grain), and very little along the grain (longitudinally). Shrinkage tends to be most pronounced away from outside edges and toward the center of the member. When nails are driven toward the central axis, shrinkage leaves a space between the board and the nailing surface.

The moisture content of the wood framing should be allowed to adjust as closely as possible to the level it will reach in service before gypsum-panel application begins. After the building is enclosed, delay the drywall installation for as long as possible (consistent with schedule requirements) to allow this moisture-content adjustment to take place.

Framing should be designed to accommodate shrinkage in wide dimensional lumber such as is used for floor joists or headers. As shrinkage occurs, gypsum-wallboard surfaces can buckle or crack if firmly anchored across the flat grain of these wide wood members. With high, uninterrupted walls such as those that are a part of cathedral ceiling designs or in two-story stairwells, regular or modified balloon framing can minimize the problem. Do not fasten the gypsum boards to heavy timber framing. When the panel must span headers or other wide timbers, the board should not be attached to these framing members. Instead, attach the boards to the edges of the framing members that are next to the headers and timbers. As heavy timbers age, they will shrink, pulling the drywall with it and leaving an uneven finished surface.

Based on experiments conducted by the Forest Products Laboratory and Purdue University, the use of shorter nails results in less space left between the board and nail-

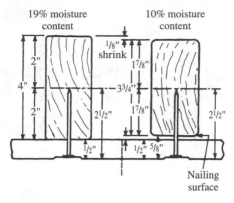

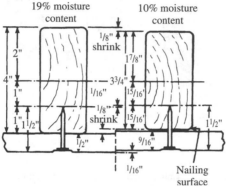

FIGURE 6.2   Shrinkage and nail penetration. Effects on holding ability.

ing surface after shrinkage (shown in Figure 6.2). Using the shortest nail possible with adequate holding power will result in less popping due to shrinkage. Longer nails, however, usually are required for fire-rated construction. Choose the proper nail length from the selector guide for gypsum-board nails given earlier in chapter 5. The annular drywall nail, with an overall length of 1¼ inches, has equivalent holding power to a 1⅜-inch coated cooler-type nail, but the shorter length of the nail lessens the chances for nail popping due to lumber shrinkage.

Wood framing members must be straight, true, and of uniform dimensions. All wood framing and furring must be accurately aligned in the same plane so that the gypsum board fits flat against it at all points (Figure 6.3). The fastening surface of any framing or furring member should not vary more than ⅛ inch from the plane of faces of adjacent framing, bridging, or furring members. Furthermore, the spacing of framing should not exceed the maximum recommended for the gypsum-board thickness, as shown in Table 6.1 for single-ply and in Tables 6.2 and 6.3 for multi-ply construction. Avoid placing and stapling paper flanges of insulation batts over framing faces because the paper might cause eventual nail problems and ridging problems. Remember that a gypsum-board installation cannot compensate for improper or misaligned framing.

Improper
framing

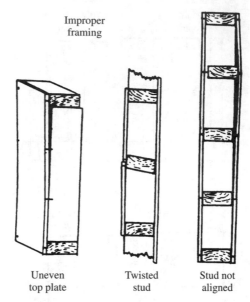

| Uneven top plate | Twisted stud | Stud not aligned |

FIGURE 6.3 Framing that is not accurately aligned can cause loose board attachment and problems in finished surfaces.

TABLE 6.1 Maximum Framing Spacing Single-Ply Application

Single-ply gypsum board (thickness) in inches	Application to framing	Maximum O.C. spacing of framing in inches
Ceilings:		
** ⅜	*perpendicular	16
½	perpendicular	16
½	*parallel	16
⅝	parallel	16
½	*perpendicular	24
⅝	perpendicular	24
Sidewalls		
⅜	perpendicular or parallel	16
½	perpendicular or parallel	24
⅝	perpendicular or parallel	24

** Should not support thermal insulation.

* On ceilings to receive a water-based textural material, either hand or spray applied, install gypsum board perpendicularly to framing and increase board thickness from ⅜" to ½" for 16" O.C. framing and from ½" to ⅝" for 24" O.C. framing.

TABLE 6.2 Two-Ply Application without Adhesive between Plies

Gypsum board (thickness in inches)		Application to framing		Maximum O.C. spacing of framing in inches
BASE	FACE	BASE	FACE	
Ceilings				
⅜	⅜	perpendicular	perpendicular*	16
½	⅜	parallel	perpendicular*	16
½	½	parallel	perpendicular*	16
½	½	perpendicular	perpendicular*	24
⅝	½	perpendicular	perpendicular*	24
⅝	⅝	perpendicular	perpendicular*	24

Sidewalls:

For two-ply application with no adhesive between plies, ⅜-, ½-, or ⅝-inch-thick gypsum board may be applied perpendicularly or parallel to framing, spaced a maximum of 24 inches O.C. Maximum spacing should be 16 inches O.C. when ⅜-inch-thick board is used as face ply.

* On ceilings to receive a water -based textural material, either hand - or spray-applied, install gypsum board perpendicularly to framing and increase board thickness from ⅜" to ½" for 16" O.C. framing and from ½ " to ⅝" for 24" O.C. framing.

TABLE 6.3 Two-Ply Application with Adhesive between Plies*

Gypsum board Thickness in inches		Application to framing		Maximum O.C. spacing of framing in inches
BASE	FACE	BASE	FACE	
Ceilings:				
⅜	⅜	perpendicular	perpendicular or parallel	16
½	⅜	perpendicular or parallel	perpendicular or parallel	16
½	½	perpendicular or parallel	perpendicular or parallel	16
⅝	½	parallel	perpendicular or parallel	24
⅝	⅝	perpendicular or parallel	perpendicular or parallel	24

Sidewalls:

For two-ply applications with adhesive between plies, ⅜-, ½-, or ⅝-inch-thick gypsum board may be applied perpendicularly or parallel to framing, spaced a maximum of 24 inches O.C.

* Adhesive between plies should be dried or cured prior to any decorative treatment. This is especially important when water -based textural material (hand or spray applied) is to be used.

Wood studs in load-bearing partitions are usually nominal 2-×-4 or larger (can be 2-×-3 in double wall). In nonload-bearing, single-row stud, or staggered-stud partitions, 2-×-3 wood studs can be used (Figure 6.4). Backup framing or special clips should be provided at all interior corners for support or as a nailing base for the gypsum board.

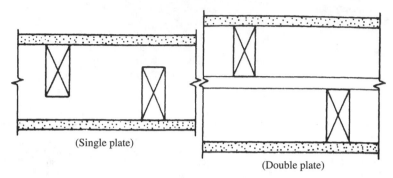

(Single plate)

(Double plate)

FIGURE 6.4   Staggered-stud partition.

Ceiling joists should be evenly spaced, with faces aligned in a level plane. Excessively bowed or crooked joists should not be used. Joists with a slight crown can be used if they are installed with the crown up. Slightly crooked or bowed joists can sometimes be aligned by nailing bracing members (strong-back or leveling plates) across the joists approximately at midspan (Figure 6.5). These 2-×-6-inch strong-backs are attached perpendicularly to, and across from, the top of the ceiling joists. Toe-nailing into the joists pulls the framing into a true horizontal alignment and ensures a smooth, level ceiling surface.

Wood trusses, to which a ceiling is to be attached, might have irregularities in spacing and leveling. When wide variances are found, cross furring is recommended to provide a level surface to support the gypsum board. When trusses change direction in the middle of a room, proper blocking should be installed so that maximum spacing of framing does not exceed requirements indicated in Tables 6.1, 6.2, and 6.3 with regard to board direction.

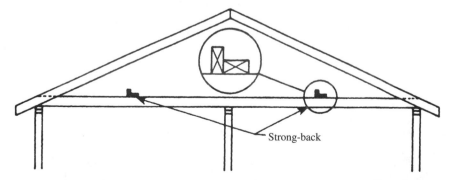

Strong-back

FIGURE 6.5   Slightly crooked or bowed joists or truss chords can be corrected by nailing stringers approximately at the midspans. These strong-backs are made by laying a 2-×-4 stringer flat and setting another 2-×-4 on the edge as illustrated.

With truss roof construction, the exterior walls and ceilings often are finished before interior partitions are erected and finished. When this method is used, the roofing and all other construction elements that increase roof loads should be installed before interior partitions are erected. If substantial roof loads are introduced after partitions are installed, the ceiling might be forced down against the partitions and might be distorted as the roof trusses deflect (Figure 6.6). Actually, with any roof design, it is wise not to install either ceiling or walls until the roof has been loaded. The roof finishing materials should be placed and spaced evenly on the roof surface, even if they have not been installed yet. Roof materials are heavy, and this additional weight can affect the structure of the building, compressing the framing slightly. While gypsum drywall can take some compression without showing the effects, too great a shifting of weight could show up as stress cracks in the finished job. For this reason, the drywall installation should not be started until the roof is fully loaded.

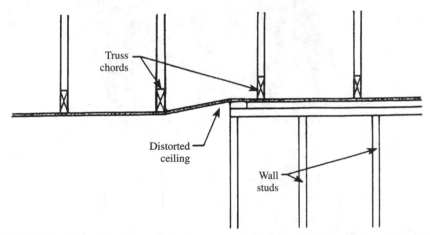

FIGURE 6.6   Ceiling distortion can result under truss roofs where the weight of the roof forces the ceiling down while the interior partitions remain firmly in place. Nonload-bearing partitions should be installed only after truss roofs and ceilings are completed and the roof covering is finished.

Warped or bowed studs in nonload-bearing partitions can often be straightened by sawing the hollow sides at the middle of the bow, pulling the stud back into line, and inserting a wedge into the saw kerf to fill the void (Figure 6.7). Reinforcement of the stud is accomplished by securely nailing 1-×-4-inch wood strips or "scabs" on each side of the cut (Figure 6.8).

Cross furring or blocking should be used to correct surface unevenness in the existing framing. The fastening surface of wood furring strips must be no less than 1½ inches actual dimension. In general, wood furring should not be less than nominal 2-×-2 to provide a rigid support during nailing when the wood furring strips are directly attached to the underlying framing. Where wood furring strips are attached to concrete or masonry walls and where screws are used to attach the gypsum board, wood furring can be nominal 1-×-3 (¾-inch minimum thickness). The maximum spacing between furring strips should be the same as for framing members. In wood-framed construction where a higher degree of sound control is desired, gypsum board can be screw-attached to resilient metal furring channels, laminated, or attached as specified in specific sound-control assemblies, as described in chapter 9.

FIGURE 6.7   Nailing of a "scab" will often straighten a warped wood stud.

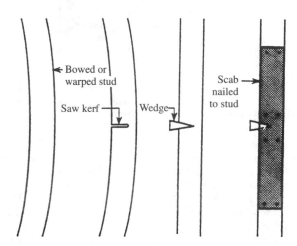

FIGURE 6.8   Position of a scab.

As stated earlier, the drywall contractor usually is not responsible for the framing installation. However, the drywall contractor is responsible for the finished drywall job. Therefore, if a very careful inspection by the drywall contractor of the job done by the subcontractor responsible for the framing uncovers less-than-acceptable work, he/she should report it to the general contractor, architect, or owner of the structure. Only when the proper framing practices are followed can a firm, even drywall ceiling or wall job be obtained. Headers or lintels should be provided over the opening to support structural loads, and special construction should be provided where required to support wall-hung equipment and fixtures. The bath and shower areas are examples where special framing must be provided for grab bars and heavy fixtures. Provision should also be made for support of cabinets or wall-hung appliances. If warped or crooked studs and joists have been used, they should be replaced with straight lumber. Remember that gypsum board cannot compensate for improper or misaligned framing.

METHODS OF APPLYING DRYWALL

As stated in chapter 1, gypsum-drywall panels can be applied in one or two layers (or plies) directly to wood framing members.

Single-ply application

The quality of single-ply surfaces is dependent on accurately aligned framing supports. Before a single-ply application of gypsum board is made, the framing or furring members should be checked for firmness and alignment. As described in chapter 5, gypsum board is generally attached to framing through the use of nails, screws, staples, or adhesives. Nails are the most commonly used, either in single- or double-nailing systems.

Screws are now being used more often than nails in wood construction because screws are applied with automatic screw guns, have excellent holding qualities, and reduce the possibility of nail pops. A combination of nails and screws can also be used, with nails along edges and screws in the field. Staples are used because they are economical and can be quickly applied with staple guns; however, their application is limited to the base-ply of two layers or for gypsum sheathing over wood framing. Stud-type adhesives, which are applied with a caulking gun, are becoming popular for use with single-panel installations, especially predecorated gypsum panels (Figure 6.9).

FIGURE 6.9 Applying adhesive to a stud with an adhesive caulking gun.

Multi-ply applications

Multi-ply or double-layer construction consists of a face layer (or ply) applied over a base ply of gypsum board. The plies can be nailed or screwed together, or an adhesive can be used to laminate the panels (Figure 6.10).

Double-ply gypsum drywall application over wood framing is recommended for the ultimate in wall surfacing and in areas where increased fire protection and better sound insulation are desired between rooms. Custom-built homes, commercial buildings, and party walls between apartments should be considered appropriate areas for double-layer (or multi-ply) application.

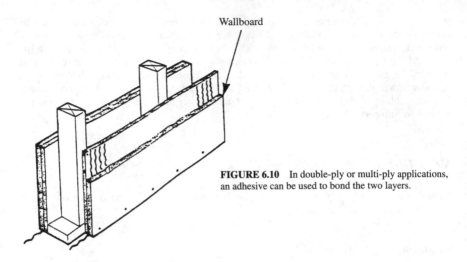

Wallboard

FIGURE 6.10 In double-ply or multi-ply applications, an adhesive can be used to bond the two layers.

Multi-ply without adhesive

When adhesive is not used between plies, the gypsum board should be applied as indicated in Table 6.4. The face layer should be applied with spacing of nails or screws required for normal single-ply applications. Nails used for the base and face layers should be long enough to penetrate at least ⅞ inch into the wood framing members. The screw length should be long enough to penetrate at least ⅝ inch into the wood. The face layer joints that are parallel to the framing should fall over the framing members and be offset from the base-layer joints.

TABLE 6.4 Two-Ply Application without Adhesive between Plies

Gypsum board thickness in inches		Application to framing		Maximum O.C. spacing of framing
Base	Face	Base	Face	
Ceilings:				
⅜	⅜	perpendicular	perpendicular*	16
½	⅜	parallel	perpendicular*	16
½	½	parallel	perpendicular*	16
½	½	perpendicular	perpendicular*	24
⅝	½	perpendicular	perpendicular*	24
⅝	⅝	perpendicular	perpendicular*	24

Sidewalls:

For two-ply application with no adhesive between plies, ⅜-, ½-, or ⅝-inch-thick gypsum board may be applied perpendicularly or parallel to framing, spaced a maximum of 24" O.C. Maximum spacing should be 16" O.C. when ⅜" thick board is used as face ply.

* On ceilings to receive a water-based textural material, either hand- or spray-applied, install gypsum board perpendicularly to framing and increase board thickness from ⅜" to ½" for 16" O.C. framing and from ½" to ⅝" for 24" O.C. framing.

Multi-ply with adhesive

When an adhesive is used between the plies, the two layers should be applied as indicated in Table 6.3. The first layer is hung in the same manner as a single-ply application, except that the fasteners should be driven with the board surface, and the joints should not be treated. The application of the base ply might have the long edges either parallel or perpendicular to the wood framing. Plan the layout of the face ply so that all joints are offset a minimum of 10 inches from parallel base-ply joints. It is preferable to apply the face ply perpendicularly to the base layer. At the inside vertical angles, only the overlapping base ply should be attached to the framing to provide a floating corner. Omit all the face-layer fasteners within 8 inches of the vertical angles. The base plies should not be secured to the framing with clips.

Sidewalls

For two-ply application with adhesive between plies, ⅜-inch, ½-inch, or ⅝-inch-thick gypsum board can be applied perpendicularly or parallel to framing spaced a maximum of 24 inches O.C. Adhesive between plies should be dried or cured prior to any decorative treatment. This is especially important when water-based textured material (hand or spray applied) is to be used.

Application of joint compound as an adhesive

Use either a setting-type joint compound or a ready-mix compound. With the latter, use the compound at package consistency for best leveling action. If a thinner adhesive is desired, add cool water in half-pint increments to avoid overthinning. Remix lightly with a potato-masher-type mixer and test apply after each water addition. If the compound becomes too thin, add thicker compound from the container and remix.

Setting-type joint compound should be mixed according to bag directions. Mix only as much adhesive as can be used within the working time specified by the manufacturer. Water, when used, should be at room temperature and should be clean enough to drink.

Cut and fit the board prior to the compound application. Spread the compound over the entire back surface of the face ply (Figure 6.11). It can be applied in parallel ribbons (Figure 6.12) or in a pattern of spots as recommended by the manufacturer. For most applications, use a metal spreader blade having ⅜-inch-wide-×-½-inch-high minimum size notches spaced 1½ to 2 inches O.C. A mechanical tool can be employed to spread laminating adhesive in parallel ribbon strips.

Immediately after the compound is applied, position the face plies and fasten with a sufficient number of nails or screws to hold the gypsum boards in place until the adhesive develops adequate bond strength. Unless otherwise recommended by the gypsum-board manufacturer, permanent, rather than temporary, mechanical fasteners should be used on ceilings, spaced 12 inches O.C. around the perimeter and 16 inches O.C. in the field. In lieu of mechanical fastening, a second ply of gypsum board applied on sidewalls can be held in position by shoring with props and headers or other temporary supports to ensure adequate pressure for bonding. Unless otherwise recommended by the gypsum-board manufacturer, permanent fasteners should be used on the top and bottom of the wall 16 inches O.C. maximum. Nails or screws used to hold the gypsum-board face ply should penetrate into the framing and be finished in the same manner as for single-ply gypsum-board applications.

FIGURE 6.11   In sheet or panel laminations, a notched spreader can be used to spread the compound over the entire back surface of the face-layer boards.

FIGURE 6.12   In strip lamination of vertical sidewall boards, the adhesive can be applied with a mechanical laminating spreader to either the base surface or face board.

For temporary nailing, use double-headed scaffold nails driven through the wood or gypsum-board scraps so that the nail penetrates the framing a minimum of ¾ inch. To permanently attach the face ply with screws, drive type-G screws (see chapter 2) into the base layer (if ½-inch or thicker gypsum board is used). Avoid the framing. Apply the compound just prior to the face-ply erection to prevent wetting of the base layer, which would reduce the holding power of the screws. Press the face ply against the base layer when driving the screws. The compound should be thin enough to spread as the screw is driven.

When joint compound or any water-thinned adhesive is used, the base or the finish layer must be a nonvapor retarder to allow proper drying of the adhesive. (Aluminum foil, vinyl plastic, and painted surfaces are considered vapor retarders.) If a vapor-retarding material is used for both faces of a partition, there must be an airspace or cavity within the partition.

For vertical face ply on sidewalls only, strip laminations can be used. This method is often preferred because it requires less compound and improves sound attenuation. Apply the strips (four beads, each ⅜ inch wide × ½ inch high, spaced 1½ inches O.C.). The strips should be 24 inches O.C. maximum at each end of the face ply. Drive type G screws as shown in Figure 6.13.

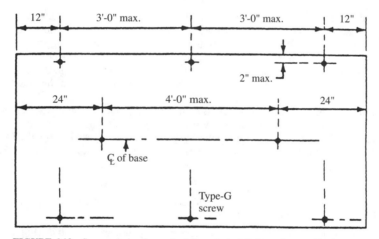

FIGURE 6.13   Screw spacing for vertical face-ply installation using an adhesive.

Application of drywall contact and modified contact adhesive

These adhesives generally require permanent mechanical fasteners at least at the perimeter of the boards that are applied to walls, ceilings, and soffits. If used to apply predecorated gypsum board vertically on sidewalls, permanent mechanical fasteners are required only at the top and bottom of the boards, where they will be concealed by base and ceiling moldings or other decorative trim. On ceilings, fasteners should be no farther apart than 24 inches O.C., regardless of the type of adhesive used. Contact adhesives can be used to laminate gypsum boards to each other or to steel studs. The adhesive is applied by roller, spray gun, or brush in a thin, uniform coating to both surfaces to be bonded. Some drying time is usually required for most contact adhesives before the surfaces can be joined and a bond can develop. To assure proper adhesion between mating surfaces, the face board should be impacted over its entire surface with a suitable tool such as a rubber or plastic mallet.

While a contact adhesive sets and the bond forms, no temporary supports are needed, unless recommended by the adhesive manufacturer. One disadvantage of contact adhesives is their inability to fill in irregularities between surfaces, which leaves areas without adhesive bond. Another disadvantage is that most of these adhesives do not permit moving the boards once contact has been made. Extra care should be taken when contact adhesives are used, and manufacturer's recommendations should be followed.

Modified contact adhesives provide a longer placement time. They have an open time of up to ½ hour during which the board can be repositioned if necessary. They combine good long-term strength with sufficient immediate bond to permit erection with a minimum of temporary fasteners. In addition, the adhesive has bridging ability. Modified contact adhesive is intended for attaching wallboard to all kinds of supporting construction, including solid walls, other gypsum board, and various insulating boards, including some types of rigid foam insulation. Stud and construction adhesive described in chapter 5 can also be used for laminating gypsum-board panels together.

CEILING INSTALLATION

Apply the gypsum panels to the ceiling first. This will permit the wall boards to be butted up against the ceiling panels, giving the best possible joint between the ceiling and walls. Apply the gypsum panels so that the ends and edges occur over the framing members, except when joists are at right angles to the framing members, as in perpendicular applications, or when the end joints are to be back-blocked as described later in this chapter. Fit the ends and edges closely, but do not force the boards into place. Cut the boards accurately to fit around the pipes and fixtures.

To minimize the end joints, use panels of maximum practical lengths. When the end joints occur, they should be staggered. Arrange the joints on the sides of a partition so they occur on different studs. If foil-backed gypsum boards are used, apply the foil side against the framing. Installing ceiling panels usually will require two people (Figure 6.14). If a one-person ceiling installation is necessary, there are three possible solutions:

• Several types of lifting devices are available that will lift the ceiling panels up into position for attaching to the joists (Figure 6.15).

• Using a temporary wood support, nail a piece of scrap lumber to the studs (Figure 6.16). Rest one end of the panel on the "shelf," then raise the other end into position for fastening. A level should be used to check the shelf.

• A T-shaped brace and a step ladder can be used to hoist a panel into place for fastening. Place one end of one panel on the top of the step ladder. Then lift the other end to a point where the T-brace can fit under the board, and wedge the panel against the joists (Figure 6.17). The major disadvantage with this method is that it is difficult to position the panel precisely and to keep the free end in place (Figure 6.18). Incidentally, the T-brace can also be useful when employing the second method.

To prevent objectionable sag in new gypsum-panel ceilings, the weight of overlaid unsupported insulation should not exceed 1.3 pounds per square foot (psf) for ½-inch-thick panels with framing spaced 24 inches O.C., 2.2 psf for ½-inch panels on 16-inch framing, and ⅝-inch panels on 24 inch O.C. Three-eighths-inch panels should not be overlaid with unsupported insulation. A vapor retarder or barrier should be installed in exterior ceilings, and the plenum or attic space to prevent condensation.

FIGURE 6.14   Ceiling installation is usually a two-person job.

FIGURE 6.15   Mechanical lifters are ideal for holding panels for fastening.

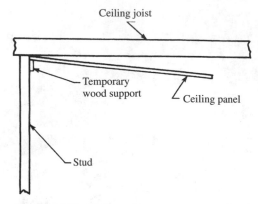

FIGURE 6.16 The use of temporary support when installing a ceiling.

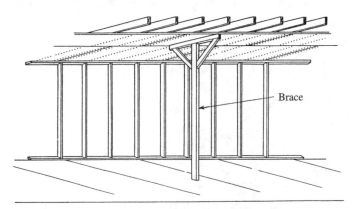

FIGURE 6.17 A T-brace ceiling installation.

FIGURE 6.18 The T-brace in use.

During periods of cold or damp weather when a polyethylene vapor retarder is installed on ceilings behind the gypsum board, it is important to install the ceiling insulation before or immediately after installing the ceiling board. Failure to follow this procedure might result in condensation on the back side of the gypsum board, causing the board to sag. Also, water-based textures, interior finishing materials, and high ambient humidity conditions can produce sag in gypsum ceiling panels if adequate vapor and moisture control is not provided. The following precautions must be observed to minimize sagging of ceiling panels:

- Where vapor retarders are required in cold weather, the temperature of the gypsum ceiling panels and vapor retarder must remain above the interior dew point during and after the installation of panels and finishing materials.
- The interior space must be adequately ventilated, and air circulation must be provided to remove water vapor from the structure.

Most sag problems are caused by the condensation of water within the gypsum panel. The placement of vapor retarders, insulation levels, and ventilation requirements will vary by location and climate and should be reviewed by a qualified engineer if in question.

To help prevent panel bowing and associated problems, start the fastener installation in the center of the board and work out toward the edges. Do not start the perimeter fastening before fastening the field. While the fasteners are being driven, the panels must be held in firm contact with the joists. When single fasteners are used, attach boards to the joists with screws or nails spaced as given in Table 6.1. In single nailing, space the nails no more than 7 inches apart and no closer than ⅜ inch to any edge and the ends of the boards. If the fasteners are located any closer than that, the edges might break or crumble. Remember that there must be enough board surrounding the fastener to provide a good bearing surface for the fastener head.

When double nailing, begin nailing in the middle of the panel 12 inches O.C. Then drive the second set of nails 2 to 2½ inches from the first set after the panel is in place (Figure 6.19). At the ends, space nails 7 inches O.C. Most manufacturers recommend that nails be omitted at the edges along walls. Instead, nail about 8 inches away (Figure 6.20) and let the edges float. They are supported on the wall panels anyway. This method reduces stresses in

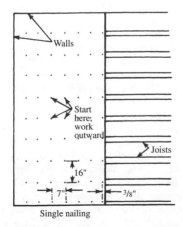

Single nailing

FIGURE 6.19 In ceilings, installation of a single set of nails is made as shown.

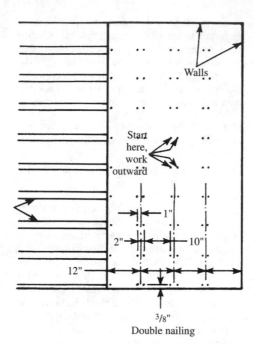

FIGURE 6.20   The location of the second set of nails in a double-nailed application.

corners created by structural movement. If screws are used instead of nails, drive them 12 inches O.C. into all structural members (Figure 6.21). Wallboard should not be attached to any blocking or any member that is not part of the ceiling frame itself.

For ceiling application of a stud adhesive to joists, supplemental fasteners are required in the perimeter of the gypsum board and in the field 24 inches O.C. (Figure 6.22). Adhesive is not required at inside corners, top or bottom plates, bridging, bracing, or fire stops.

When a multi-ply system with a laminated face ply is used over wood ceiling joists, the base ply should be fastened as recommended for single-ply construction. Double nailing is not needed because the fasteners used on a two-ply application will produce a firmly fastened system. The base ply can be applied with long edges perpendicular or parallel to framing members. End joints can occur on or between framing members. Face-ply joints, however, should occur over framing and be offset from base-ply joints. When both layers of a double-layer ceiling run in the same directions, edges must be offset at least 10 inches (Figure 6.23). This adds ceiling strength because every joint will have a solid gypsum board overlapping it. If the base ply is foil-backed board, apply the foil side against the joists. The installation of a suspended ceiling is covered in chapter 8.

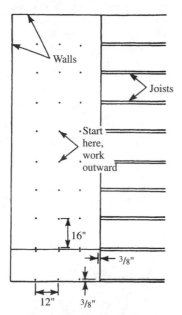

FIGURE 6.21   Screw spacing on a ceiling.

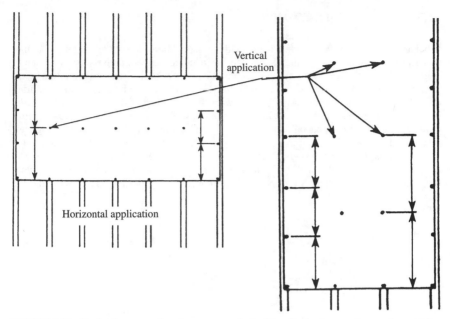

FIGURE 6.22 Single-ply gypsum-board systems attached with stud adhesives require supplemental fasteners on the perimeter. Spacing is the same whether board edges are perpendicular or parallel to supports. Ceiling installations require supplemental fasteners in the field as well as on the perimeter.

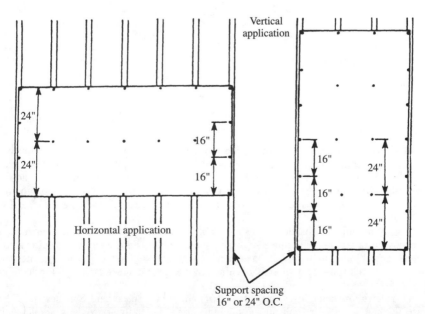

FIGURE 6.23 When both layers of a double-layer ceiling (or wall) run in the same direction, edges must be offset at least 10 inches.

SIDEWALL INSTALLATION

When the single-layer is used, the 4-foot-wide gypsum sheets are usually applied parallel (vertically) to the studs, but the sheets can be installed perpendicularly or horizontally (Figure 6.24) on the walls after the ceiling has been covered. The horizontal method of application is best adapted to rooms in which full-length sheets can be used, as it minimizes the number of vertical joints. Also, plan to work from the top of the room down, i.e., the ceiling and/or top half of the walls, in that order. On walls, this approach provides a better joint, and panels already installed are less likely to be marred by other panels being handled. Where joints are necessary, they should be made at windows or doors. End joints over openings should be on studs. When ceiling heights are over 8 feet 1 inch, or when this horizontal method results in more waste or joint treatment, the vertical method of application should be used. Where 8-foot ceilings are required, consider the use of 54-inch-wide panels (see chapter 2).

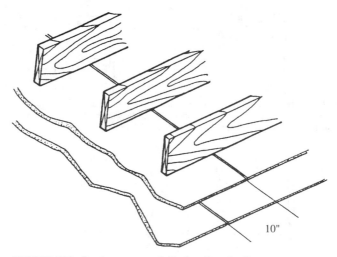

10"

FIGURE 6.24   Panel arrangement for both walls and ceilings.

Wherever possible, use a board of sufficient length to span wall areas. If the joints occur near an opening, apply boards so vertical joints are centered, if possible, over the opening. Keep vertical joints at least 8 inches away from external corners of windows, doors, or similar openings except at interior or exterior angles within the room or when control joints are used as described later in this chapter. This practice reduces the need for narrow strips of gypsum board.

Rough framing for most door and window openings follows conventional construction methods. Install additional cripple studs above the header and ½ inch from bearing studs where control joints are required. Do not anchor a cripple stud in the bearing stud, header, or plate. In long runs, treat window openings in the same manner as shown for doors in Figure 6.25.

On sidewall installations, space screws 16 inches O.C.; space nails 8 inches O.C. The base ply on double-layer applications should be applied with the long edges parallel with the framing members, unless otherwise specified. When predecorated gypsum board is to

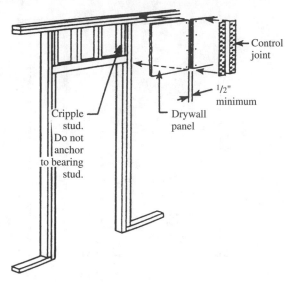

FIGURE 6.25 Door-framing installation.

be used, the base ply should be applied perpendicularly to the framing. (See chapter 8 for complete details for installing predecorated gypsum board.) At inside corners, it is recommended that only the overlapping base-board end be nailed or screwed and that fasteners be omitted from the face ply. The floating-corner treatment, described later in this chapter, is better able to resist structural stresses.

The adhesive nail-on or screw-on installations described in chapter 5 are good for the gypsum-board-to-sidewall framing. The advantages of this system are that the number of nails can be reduced by 50 percent or more, a continuous bond between the gypsum board and the framing is provided, and a stronger assembly with fewer fasteners is the result. The adhesive also serves to bridge minor framing irregularities. In the nail-on adhesive system, supplemental fasteners should be spaced 16 inches O.C. along the edges or ends that fall on parallel supports, and at each point where edges or ends cross perpendicular supports.

Staples used to fasten base plies should be driven with the crown perpendicular to the edges of the board. Where edges fall over supports, staples should be driven parallel with the edges (Figure 6.26). Crowns of driven staples should bear tightly against the board without breaking the face paper.

After installation of either single- or multi-ply applications, exert hand pressure against wall and ceiling surfaces to detect loose fasteners. If loose fasteners are found, drive them tight. Whenever nails or screws have punctured paper, hold the board tight against the framing and install another fastener properly, about 1½ inches from the screw or nail head that punctured the paper. Remove the faulty fastener. When nailing boards to the second side of a partition, check the opposite side for nails loosened by pounding, and drive them tight again.

The application of gypsum panels over an insulating blanket that has first been installed continuously across the face of the framing members is not recommended. Blankets should be recessed and blanket flanges attached to sides of studs or joists (Figure 6.27). In addition, precautions should be taken against creating a double vapor retarder. Use gypsum panels as a base for highly water-vapor-resistant coverings when the wall al-

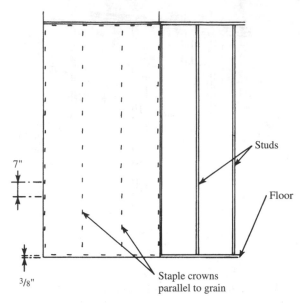

7"

3/8"

Studs

Floor

Staple crowns
parallel to grain

FIGURE 6.26   Spacing of staples for backer-board installations.

FIGURE 6.27   Staple insulation blanket flanges on the sides of the studs.

ready contains a vapor retarder. Moreover, do not create a vapor retarder by such wall coverings on the interior side of exterior walls of air-conditioned buildings in hot, humid climates where conditions dictate a vapor retarder location near the exterior side of the wall. Such conditions require assessment by a qualified mechanical engineer.

CONTROL JOINTS

To allow for the natural expansion and contraction of the board surfaces, a control joint must be used in any situation where large expanses of drywall are involved. The control joint, sometimes called an *expansion joint,* allows the wall surface to move and thus prevents cracking and buckling of the gypsum panel.

Control joints, such as the typical zinc metal preformed expansion joint shown in Figure 6.28, should be installed in ceilings exceeding 2500 square feet in area and in partition, wall, and wall furring runs exceeding 30 feet. The distance between ceiling control joints should not exceed 50 feet in either direction, and a control joint should be installed where the ceiling framing or furring changes direction. Distance between the control joints in walls or wall furring should not exceed 30 feet, and a control joint should be installed where an expansion joint occurs in the base exterior wall. Ceiling-height door frames can be used as vertical control joints for partitions; however, door frames of lesser height can only be used as control joints if standard control joints extend to the ceiling from both corners of the top of the door frame. When planning locations for control joints in the ceiling, it is recommended that they be located in such a way as to intersect column penetrations, since movement of columns can impose stresses on the ceiling membrane. For this same reason, control joints should be positioned so that they intersect with light fixtures, air diffusers, and other areas of stress concentrations. Whenever possible, drywall control joints should coincide with any other building-control or expansion joints.

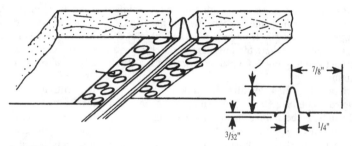

FIGURE 6.28 Typical control-joint strip.

Apply the control joint over the face of the gypsum board where indicated. Cut the metal control joint to length with a fine-toothed hacksaw (32 teeth per inch). Cut the end joints square, butt them together, and align to provide a neat fit. Attach the control joint to the gypsum board with ⁹⁄₁₆-inch staples (Figure 6.29), or a nail using a maximum 6-inch O.C. spacing along each flange. Finish with joint compound as described in chapter 10.

FLOATING-INTERIOR-ANGLE CONSTRUCTION

To minimize fastener popping in areas adjacent to wall and ceiling intersections, the floating-interior-angle method of construction is often recommended for use with either single- or double-layer applications of gypsum-drywall board to wood framing. This method is applicable where single nailing, double nailing, or screw attachments are used.

FIGURE 6.29   Fastening a control-joint strip.

In floating-interior-angle construction where the ceiling framing members are perpendicular to the wall/ceiling intersection, the ceiling fasteners should be located 7 inches from the intersection for single nailing and 11 to 12 inches for double nailing or screw applications. On ceilings, where the joists are parallel to the intersection with a wall, nailing should start at the intersection. Gypsum drywall board should be applied to the ceiling first and then to the walls.

Gypsum board on the sidewalls should be applied to provide a firm, level support for the floating edges of the ceiling board. The top attachment into each stud should be located 8 inches down from the ceiling intersection for single nailing, and 11 to 12 inches for double nailing or screw applications (Figures 6.30A and 6-30B). At vertical angles (Figure 6.30C), apply the overlapping board firmly against the underlying board into firm contact with the face of the framing member behind it. The overlapping board should be nailed or screwed and fasteners omitted from the underlying board at the vertical intersection. As shown in Figure 6.31, floating-angle construction for multiple systems has the overlapping side of the base layer nailed only at the interior corner.

The edge-grip clips described in chapter 5 can be used to support the gypsum-drywall panels at the wall corners; wall/ceiling intersections can be used where approved (Figure 6.32). These clips are used to replace one of the two conventional "backup" studs or blocking used to provide support at such locations. Clip spacing varies according to the type of clips.

BACK-BLOCKING APPLICATIONS

Back-blocking is a system designed to minimize an inherent joint deformation (ridging) in single-ply gypsum-board construction, which sometimes occurs under a combination of adverse job and weather conditions. It consists of laminating cut-to-size pieces of gypsum

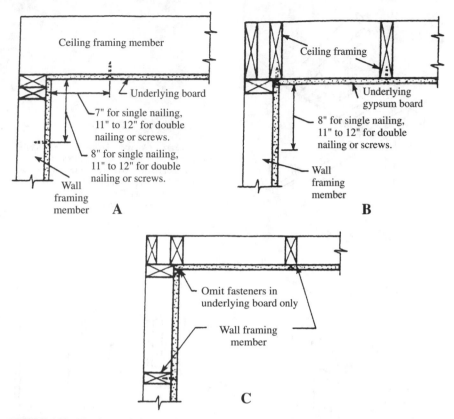

FIGURE 6.30 Floating-angle construction. (A) Vertical section, ceiling framing perpendicular to the wall. (B) Vertical section, ceiling framing parallel to the wall. (C) Cross section through the interior vertical angle.

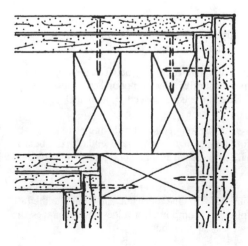

FIGURE 6.31 Floating-angle construction for the multi-ply system has the overlapping side of the base ply nailed only at the interior corner.

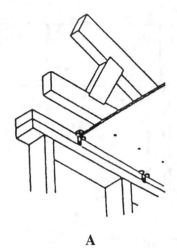

A

FIGURE 6.32 (A) Special clips used in lieu of floating angles when joists are parallel to the intersection of a wall. (B) Special clips used at the interior eliminates a backup stud. (C) Use of special clips allows a full insulation and eliminates cutting of insulation.

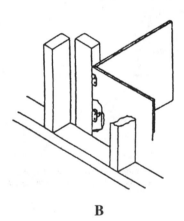

B

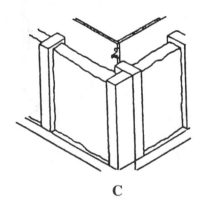

C

board to the back surface of the boards directly behind the joints, thus providing resistance to rigidity. Back-blocking is accomplished in the following manner:

1. Blocking blocks, 8 inches wide and long enough to fit loosely between the framing, are spread with joint compound or all-purpose adhesive. The compound or adhesive is applied in beads ½ inch high and ⅜ inch wide at the base, spaced 1½ inches O.C. (Figure 6.33A).

2. Apply the gypsum boards horizontally with the long edges at right angles to the joists. Place the backing blocks along the full length of the edges and ends of the boards (Figure 6.33B). Floating end joints make it easier to form a good joint over a twisted stud or joist.

3. Immediately after all the blocks are in place, erect the next board, which has been previously cut. Butt the ends loosely (Figure 6.33C). One mechanic can complete the fastening of the board while another applies the compound or adhesive and places the blocks along the long edges of the previously applied board.

4. The cross-section drawing (Figure 6.33D) shows how the floated end joint can be tapered with back-blocking. A brace is temporarily nailed over the wood strip, which depresses the ends of the panels. When the strips are removed, the tapered formation remains.

5. The sidewall blocks should be flush with or slightly behind the stud faces. To hold the blocks in place, install gypsum strips along the sides of the studs and set back from the stud faces enough to accommodate the block thickness (Figure 6. 33E).

6. After the gypsum board is nailed in place, immediately butt the adjacent board over the backing blocks. Stagger the end joints between the upper and lower courses of the board as shown in Figure 6.33F.

Back-blocking the long edge joints on sidewalls is less important, but floating and back-blocking of all end joints on both sidewalls and ceilings is recommended. At the discretion of the owners or general contractor, end joints on both the sidewall and ceiling can be tapered for gypsum-panel construction by the back-blocking method.

FIGURE 6.33A Back-blocked joints fall between the framing members. The blocks create a tapered joint that is easier to finish than a butt joint. The compound or adhesive is applied in beads ½ inch high and ⅜ inch wide at the base, spaced 1½ inches O.C.

FIGURE 6.33B   Place the backing blocks along the full length of the edges and ends of the boards.

FIGURE 6.33C   Butt the ends loosely.

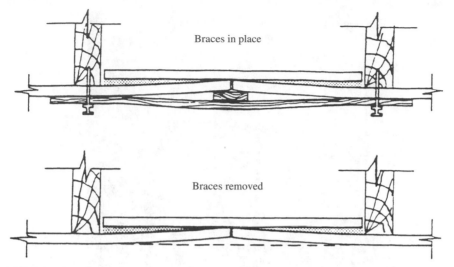

Braces in place

Braces removed

FIGURE 6.33D The floated end joint can be tapered with back-blocking.

FIGURE 6.33E To hold the blocks in place, install gypsum strips along the sides of the studs and set back from the stud faces enough to accommodate the block thickness.

FIGURE 6.33F   Stagger the end joints between the upper and lower courses of the board.

CHAPTER 7
INSTALLING DRYWALL OVER METAL FRAMING

Robert Scharff
Walls & Ceilings Magazine

In this day of widely fluctuating lumber prices and environmental consciousness, many builders are looking very closely at light steel framing as a cost-saving alternative to traditional wood construction. Due to this growing trend, especially with the residential construction segment, the drywall contractor and installer must become familiar with the procedures for applying gypsum panels over steel framing systems (Figure 7.1).

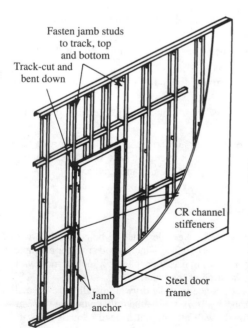

FIGURE 7.1 Gypsum drywall over steel metal framing.

Fasten jamb studs to track, top and bottom

Track-cut and bent down

CR channel stiffeners

Steel door frame

Jamb anchor

ADVANTAGES OF STEEL CONSTRUCTION

Steel framing has long been known for its strength, insect-resistance, and fire-protection qualities in commercial construction. It also enables home builders to design homes with large, open floor plans, straighter walls, quieter partitions, and easier electrical and mechanical installations than with wood framing. And because steel framing is made from an abundant supply of recycled steel, it is not subject to the same pricing fluctuations that have become common with lumber.

Construction workers, including drywall installers, who have made the transition from wood to steel have discovered the significant decrease in effort when assembling a partition wall with a screw gun and hand snips rather than a hammer and saw. Mistakes in assembly are easier to adjust, and finished walls require fewer fasteners than wood. Plus, the light weight of steel framing makes handling the material and completed assemblies much easier.

Steel framing components are precision manufactured in a controlled environment (Figures 7.2A and 7.2B), and they provide other advantages that home owners, builders, and construction workers all enjoy:

- Screw-attached components eliminate squeaks, nail pops, and resulting callbacks for repairs.
- Corrosion-resistant members will not shrink, warp, rot, or split.
- Consistent dimensions mean straighter, stronger walls and floors.
- Superior strength enables longer floor spans and higher walls.
- Cut-to-length material reduces costly labor time for in-field cutting and reduces up to 75 percent of the waste resulting from on-site cutting.
- Engineered performance produces materials designed to withstand hurricane and earthquake forces.
- Openings provided throughout the length of the metal studs permit the horizontal routing of water, gas, and electrical conduit.
- The resilient nature of steel studs (sometimes called "screwstuds") helps walls absorb sound.
- The material itself is noncombustible (improving fire safety) and will not support termites or other insects or vermin.
- Environmentally, steel is easier to recycle or reuse, thus saving trees and preserving wildlife areas.
- Steel-stud systems are generally simpler to erect, and errors are easier to correct than with wood systems. Once construction crews become experienced with steel framing, labor time and costs, compared to wood framing, are significantly reduced.

Wood and steel framing compatibility

Since the advent of steel framing, the components were designed to be compatible with wood framing materials. The standard dimensions of a 2-×-4-inch wood stud, for example, is now 1½-×-3½ inches (formerly 1⅝-×-3⅝ inches). In use, there can be ⅛ inch or more variation for saw cut differences, warping, or twisting of the wood.

As with wood framing, the major areas of concern of the drywall installer are the ceiling, nonload-bearing walls, and load-bearing walls. Actually, the only change in these areas in most cases is the use of screws for drywall attachment instead of nails. Top and

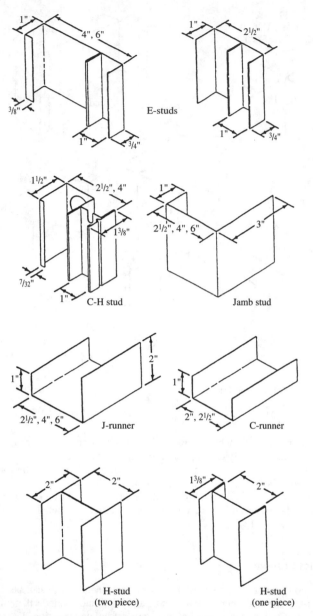

FIGURE 7.2A Metal stud shapes and typical dimensions.

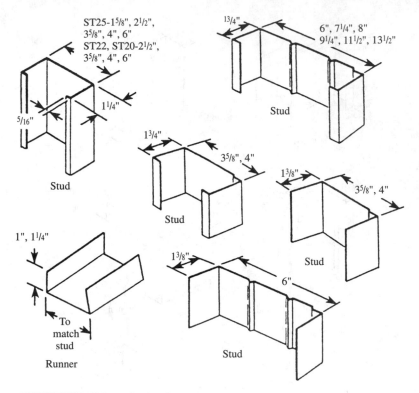

FIGURE 7.2B   Other optional studs.

bottom runners are mounted where partition walls are to be located. Studs are simply twisted into place and typically crimped or screwed into position.

Door openings often are framed in wood to provide a nailable backing for jambs and casings. Wood blocking can also be screwed to the framing between studs to aid mounting of cabinetry or crown molding. Wood base plate or wood blocking inserted in the bottom C-runner can be provided as a nailer if baseboards are not adhesively applied or screw-attached.

Steel product nomenclature

Steel construction products that are used with drywall installations can be load-bearing studs, nonload-bearing studs, curtain wall studs, and joists and channels that might be used in a variety of applications for residential and commercial construction. The stud designs can include special features that permit nesting, simplify electrical and plumbing installation, and facilitate bracing using cold-rolled channel.

Light steel framing should meet ASTM A568 for uncoated steel thickness, and ASTM A 446 grade A (33-ksi yield strength), grade C (40 ksi), or grade D (50 ksi) for stud-joist members, and grade A (33 ksi) for CR members. Metal building components are usually produced from galvanized steel meeting ASTM A525 standards.

Studs

Light steel framing studs are available in two basic types: standard screw studs and curtain wall studs (Table 7.1). The standard screw studs are the most commonly used for interior partitions (Figure 7.3). Some studs of this type are ribbed to provide extra vertical strength for load-bearing applications.

TABLE 7.1 Stud Member Selector

Flange size	1¼"	1¾"	1⅜"	1⅝"	2"	2½"
Suggested application	Nonload bearing interior framing	Curtain wall	Curtain wall, light load bearing	Curtain wall, load bearing joist	Joist-wide flange	Joist-extra wide flange
Gauge range	25–20	20–14	20–14	20–12	20–12	20–12
Available depths*	1⅝", 2", 2½", 3", 3½", 3⅝", 4", 6"	2½", 3½" 3⅝", 5½" 4", 6", 8"	2½", 3½" 3⅝", 4" 5½", 6", 8"	2½", 3⅝" 4", 5½", 6" 7¼", 9¼" 9½", 10", 11½", 12", 13½", 14"	2½", 3⅝" 4", 6", 8", 9¼", 10", 12", 13½"	3⅝", 4", 6" 8", 10", 12", 13½"
Typical punch or knockout design**						

* Availability may vary by geographic region.

** Punch or knockout size will vary on smaller web members.

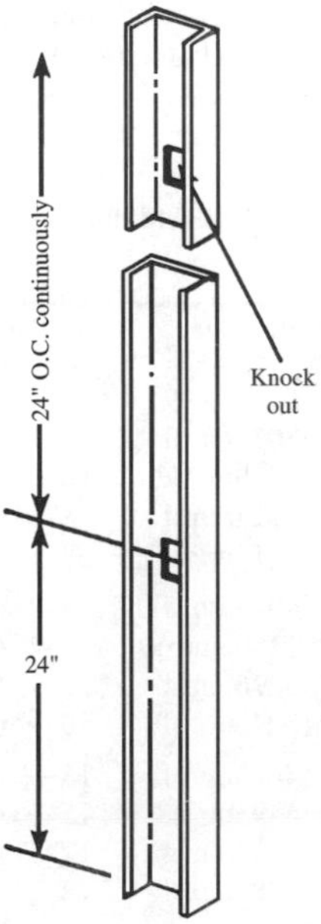

FIGURE 7.3 Typical location of a stud knockout.

Light-steel curtain wall studs are designed for exterior nonload-bearing curtain wall systems, but they are also used for interior partitions to provide more rigidity or greater heights than can be obtained with standard screw studs. These studs are also available in a ribbed style for added strength and with larger flanges for a broader fastening area. The gauge thickness of both types of stud framing members varies from 25 to 12 gauge.

Channel runners (or track) are designed to accompany all stud/joist designs. For instance, they serve as channel runners at the top and base of all curtain wall and load-bearing wall construction, and they work as end caps for joist construction. They also help unitize headers and other structural components that combine members for added strength. To fit design requirements exactly, select galvanized steel from 25, 22, or 20 gauge for nonload-bearing applications or 20 to 12 gauge for load-bearing applications.

Tables 7.2 and 7.3 show the typical maximum partition heights for both screw and curtain wall studs based on specific design criteria. The height limits shown are based on the gypsum wallboard and the screw studs acting as a composite section to provide a maximum deflection of L/120, L/240, L/360 (L= partition height in inches) with a horizontal load of 5 pounds per square foot of partition surface. Even though a stud assembly is structurally capable of withstanding a given load, its use might be restricted if the amount of deflection that would occur when the load is applied exceeds that which the surfacing materials can sustain without damage. Obviously, this deflection factor influences the selection of surfacing materials. For drywall assemblies, it is desirable to limit deflection to L/240 and to never exceed L/120 (L/180 in some codes). The preferred limit for veneer plaster assemblies is L/360 and should not exceed L/240. Using L/240 as an example, and where the length of a span (distance between framing members) is 10 feet, deflection is figured as follows:

$$D = \text{Deflection Limit} = L/20$$
$$D = 120/240$$
$$D = 0.5 \text{ inch}$$

Steel framing members must also withstand any unit force exerted that will break or distort the stud, based on the capacity of the studs acting alone. This action is called *bending stress*.

TABLE 7.2 Limiting Heights/Screw Studs. Design Steel Thickness 0188" (48mm). (Minimum Base Steel Thickness .0179" (.45mm)).

Stud width	Gauge	Stud spacing	Allow deflection	Partition one layer W.B.	Partition two layer W.B.
1⅝" (41.3mm)	25	16"	L/20	10'-1" (3073mm)f	10'-1" (3073mm)f
		(406mm)	L/240	9'-8" (2946mm)d	10'-1" (3073mm)f
		24"	L/120	8'-3" (2514mm)f	8'-3" (2514mm)f
		(610mm)	L/240	8'-3" (2514mm)f	8'-3" (2514mm)f
2½" (63.5mm)	25	16"	L/120	13'-2" (4013mm)f	13'-2" (4013mm)f
		(406mm)	L/240	11'-10" (3606mm)d	13'-2" (4013mm)f
		24"	L/120	10'-9" (3276mm)f	10'-9" (3276mm)f
		(610mm)	L/240	10'-9" (3276mm)f	10'-9" (3276mm)f
3⅝" (92.1mm)	25	16"	L/120	15'-3" (4648mm)f	15'-3" (4648mm)f
		(406mm)	L/240	14'-9" (4495mm)d	15'-3" (4648mm)f
		24"	L/120	12'-5" (3784mm)f	12'-5" (3784mm)f
		(610mm)	L/240	12'-5" (3784mm)f	12'-5" (3784mm)f

Stud width	Gauge	Stud spacing	Allow deflection	Partition one layer W.B.	Partition two layer W.B.
4" (102mm)	25	16"	L/120	15'-8" (4775mm)f	15'-8" (4775mm)f
		(406mm)	L/240	15'-2" (4622mm)d	15'-8" (4775mm)f
		24"	L/120	12'-9" (3886mm)f	12'-9" (3886mm)f
		(610mm)	L/240	12'-9" (3886mm)f	12'-9" (3886mm)f
6" (152mm)	25	16"	L/120	16'-5" (5003mm)f	16'-5" (5003mm)f
		(406mm)	L/240	16'-5" (5003mm)d	16'-5" (5003mm)f
		24"	L/120	13'-5" (4089mm)f	13'-5" (4089mm)f
		(610mm)	L/240	13'-5" (4089mm)f	13'-5" (4089mm)f

Limiting Criteria: Bending Stress = f
                   Deflection   = d

TABLE 7.3 Limiting Heights/Curtain-Wall Studs. Design Steel Thickness .0346" (.89mm). (Minimum Base Steel Thickness .0329" (.84mm))

Stud width	Gauge	Stud spacing	Allow Deflection	Partition one layer W.B.
2½" (63.5mm)	20	16"	L/120	16'-2" (4927mm)d
		(406mm)	L/240	12'-10" (3911mm)d
			L/360	11'-3" (3429mm)d
		24"	L/120	14'-8" (4470mm)d
		(610mm)	L/240	11'-8" (3556mm)d
			L/360	10'-2" (3098mm)d
3⅝" (92.1mm)	20	16"	L/120	20'-10" (3650mm)d
		(406mm)	L/240	16'-6" (5029mm)d
			L/360	14'-5" (4394mm)d
		24"	L/120	18'-11" (5765mm)d
		(610mm)	L/240	15'-0" (4572mm)d
			L/360	13'-1" (3987mm)d
4" (102mm)	20	16"	L/120	21'-5" (6527mm)d
		(406mm)	L/240	17'-0" (5181mm)d
			L/360	14'-10" (4521mm)d
		24"	L/120	19'-6" (5943mm)d
		(610mm)	L/240	15'-5" (4699mm)d
			L/360	13'-6" (4114mm)d
6" (152mm)	20	16"	L/120	27'-4" (8331mm)d
		(406mm)	L/240	21'-8" (6604mm)d
			L/360	18'-11" (5765mm)d
		24"	L/120	24'-10" (7569mm)d
		(610mm)	L/240	19'-8" (5994mm)d
			L/360	17'-2" (5232mm)d

Limiting Criteria: Deflection = d

NONLOAD-BEARING WALLS

There are four phases of framing where steel components can be used:

- Floor joists.
- Exterior and load-bearing walls.
- Interior nonload-bearing partition walls.
- Roof rafters and supports.

While residential building is framed in this order, the major concern of the drywall contractor is with load-bearing and nonload-bearing walls and how gypsum drywall is installed on them.

STEEL STUD FRAMING

Steel stud framing for nonload-bearing interior partitions is secured to the floors and ceilings with runners fastened to the supporting structure, securely attached to:

- Concrete and masonry by using stub nails or power-driven anchors (Figure 7.4).
- Metal concrete inserts using ⅜-inch type-S-12 pan-head screws.
- Suspended ceiling using expandable wall anchors or toggle bolts.
- Wood framing using 1¼-inch type-S oval-head screws or 12d nails.

With all substrate attachments, secure the runners with fasteners located 2 inches from each end and spaced a maximum of 24 inches O.C. Attach the runner ends at the door frames with two anchors when three-piece frames are used. (One-piece frames should be supplied with welded-in-place floor anchors prepunched for two anchors.)

At the partition corners, extend one runner to the end of the corner and butt or overlap the other runner to it, allowing necessary clearance for the gypsum panel thickness. Runners should not be mitered.

Stud frame installation

While interior steel framing can be first assembled and then erected in place, the preferred and easier method is to first position the top and bottom runners as just described, then insert the studs in the proper position. This procedure simplifies the erection of the partition and speeds the process. Here are the steps:

1. Using a chalk line, crayon or other marker, such as a laser alignment tool, mark the position of the partition walls on the ceiling of the structure.
2. Place ladder blocks between joists 16 inches O.C. wherever the top runner cannot be attached directly to the joists (Figure 7.5).
3. Cut the channel runners (CR) to length and screw attach the top plate to the ceiling joists using self tapping pan head or drywall screws (Figure 7.6).
4. Drop a plumb line from the ceiling runners and position the bottom runners directly below the top runners.
5. Insert the metal studs between the top and bottom runners (Figure 7.7) and simply twist into place 16 or 24 inches O.C. as specified. To simplify gypsum-panel installation, insert studs with all legs facing in the same direction.

FIGURE 7.4   Fastening the channel runner.

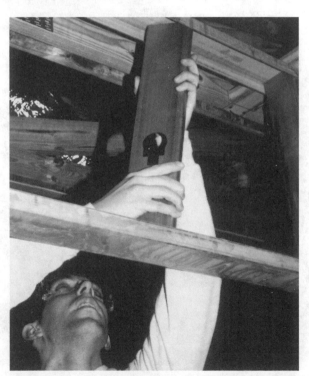

FIGURE 7.5   Place blocks between joists 16 inches O.C. wherever the top runner cannot be attached directly to the joists.

FIGURE 7.6 Cutting metal framing with a chop saw.

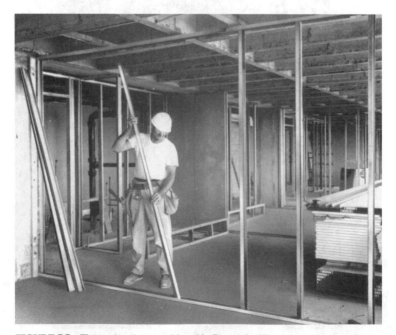

FIGURE 7.7 The steel studs are positioned in floor and ceiling runners.

Note: Steel CR runners accommodate the full height of studs from floor to ceiling less ¾ inch for deflection. For example, 8-foot-high walls use full 8-foot-long (96-inch) studs, rather than precut 92⅝-inch studs typically required with wood construction.

- If the studs fit snugly, no fastener is required. If studs are loose enough to lose their position, they should be fastened in place at the top with a single framing screw.
- Steel studs can be conveniently spliced together when required. To splice two studs, nest one into the other and form a box section to a depth of at least 8 inches. Fasten together with two ⅜-inch type-S pan-head screws in each flange (Figure 7.8). Locate each screw no more than 1 inch from the ends of the splice.
- The stud framing is now ready for the drywall-gypsum panels.

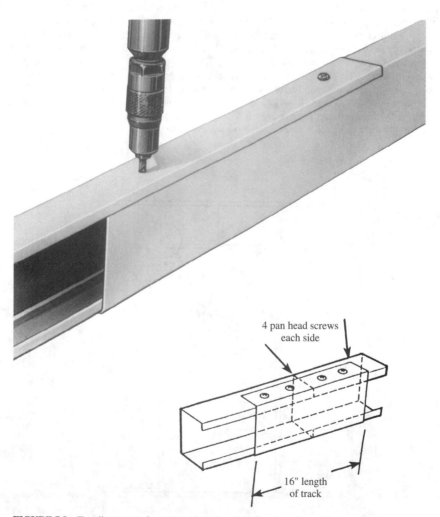

4 pan head screws
each side

16" length
of track

FIGURE 7.8   To splice two studs, nest one into the other, forming a box section.

Door and window openings

Door and window openings require special construction for heads, sills, supports, jamb mountings, control joints, and cripple studs (Figure 7.9). Doors and borrowed light openings should be rough-framed with steel studs and runners. Cut the members for the headers and sills at least 8 inches longer (4 inches per side) than the width of the opening (Figure 7.10). This provides extra metal at each stud to be used as tabs for connecting the cross members to the vertical studs (Figure 7.11). Use snips to cut legs free from the web at the ends, and fold to form tabs.

Position floor-to-ceiling-height structural studs vertically, adjacent to the frames, and anchor securely to the top and bottom runners with the metal lock fastener (Figure 7.12) or screws. Where heavy or oversized doors are used, install additional strut-stud at jambs. Fabricate the sill and header sections from steel runners and install them over less-than-ceiling-height door frames and above and below the borrowed light frames. From a section of runner, cut a piece approximately 8 inches (as previously mentioned) longer than the rough opening, slit the flanges, and bend the web to allow the flanges to overlap the adjacent vertical strut-studs. Securely attach to the strut-studs with metal lock fasteners or screws. For frames with jamb anchors (Figure 7.13), fasten anchors to the strut-studs with two ⅜-inch type-S-12 pan-head screws. Install the cripple studs in the center above the door opening and above and below the borrowed light openings spaced 24 inches O.C. maximum. Wood nailers can be attached directly to the studs if desired. Where control joints in the header boards are required, install cripple studs ½ inch away from the strut-studs, but do not attach the cripple to the runners or strut-studs.

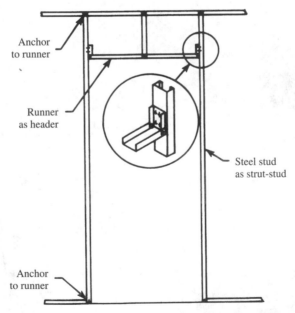

FIGURE 7.9   Door frame with a steel runner as a header, and steel-stud door opening.

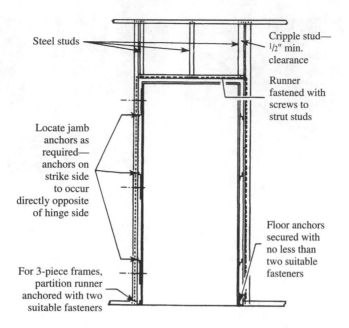

FIGURE 7.10   Frame for a standard door.

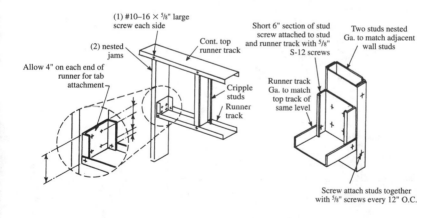

FIGURE 7.11   Added support over door openings.

Corner construction

Position the studs the same as previously described, using the flanges and web of the stud to provide a solid fastening surface (Figure 7.14). Fasten studs together with self-tapping pan-head framing screws.

FIGURE 7.12 Steps required for metal-lock fasteners.

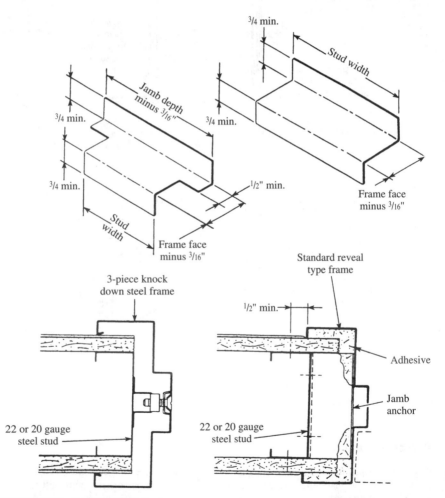

3/4 min.

Stud width

Jamb depth minus 3/16"

3/4 min.

3/4 min.

3/4 min.

1/2" min.

Frame face minus 3/16"

Stud width

Frame face minus 3/16"

3-piece knock down steel frame

Standard reveal type frame

1/2" min.

Adhesive

Jamb anchor

22 or 20 gauge steel stud

22 or 20 gauge steel stud

FIGURE 7.13 Jamb assemblies for doors.

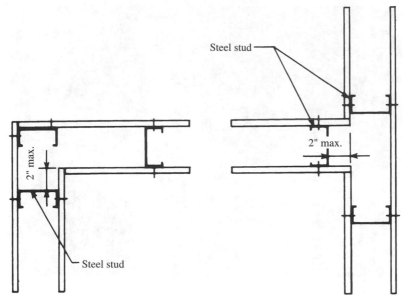

FIGURE 7.14   Proper corner construction reinforcement.

Baseboards

Several methods are used to attach baseboards. Contractors who choose to use nails either lay down a wood plate beneath the steel runner or simply insert sections of 2-x-4-inch wood between the studs in the floor-mounted runner. Others use trim-head screws or simply adhesively attach the baseboard.

Pipe support and wiring protection

Pipes can be fastened to steel studs and bracing with screw-attached straps. Wood can be inserted as a cushion to restrict movement and eliminate rattling. Wherever copper pipes or electrical wire passes through keyhole punch-outs in the stud web, grommets or insulating sleeves are required to protect materials from sharp metal edges and galvanic action (Figure 7.15).

Chase or hollow walls

To simplify the installation of piping and ductwork and to reduce room-to-room noise, a chase or hollow wall system can be used. The many benefits and possible savings available with the use of the hollow wall system are inherent in the nature of the partition system itself. The clear, unobstructed space between partitions provides for pipes, ducts, and conduits (Figure 7.16). No cutting, fitting, or costly adjustments are needed to accommodate the vertical or horizontal runs of piping or ductwork. Because the partition halves are separate units, they can be spaced whatever distance apart is necessary to conceal the fittings to be installed. The system can also be used to build partitions; the three integrated metal parts of the partition are quickly and easily installed, permitting minimum labor

FIGURE 7.15   Typical pipe and wire support.

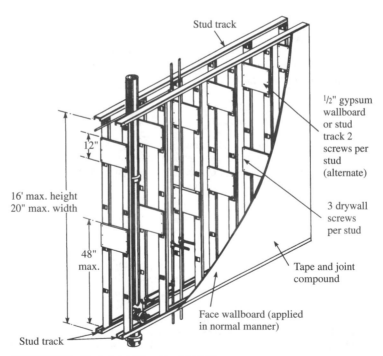

FIGURE 7.16   Typical metal-framing chase wall.

costs for this type of construction. The completed partition generally costs considerably less than masonry walls of the same thickness. No matter what the spacing between partitions, the cost remains the same. Because it is ideal for use in concealing piping and for resisting sound transmission, the chase or hollow wall system is useful in all types of structures where ductwork or plumbing should be hidden. It accommodates all types of electrical fixtures, casings, electrical switches, and outlet boxes.

To assemble a chase or hollow wall-framing system, align two parallel rows of floor and ceiling runners according to the partition layout. Spacing between the outside flanges of each pair of runners must not exceed 24 inches. Follow the previous instructions for attaching runners. Then position the steel studs vertically in the runners with the flanges in the same direction and with the studs on opposite sides of the chase directly across from each other (Figure 7.17). Except in fire-rated walls, anchor all the studs to the floor and ceiling runner flanges with ⅜-or ½-inch type-S pan-head screws.

Cut the cross-bracing to be placed between rows of studs from gypsum board 12 inches high and as wide as the chase wall's width. Space the braces 48 inches O.C. vertically and attach to the stud web with screws spaced 8 inches O.C. maximum per brace.

Bracing of 2½ inches (minimum) steel studs can be used in place of gypsum board. Anchor the web at each end of the metal brace to the stud web with two ⅜-inch pan-head screws. When the chase wall studs are not opposite, install steel-stud cross-braces 24 inches O.C. horizontally, and secure the anchor at the end to form a continuous horizontal 2½-inch runner screw attached to the chase wall studs within the cavity.

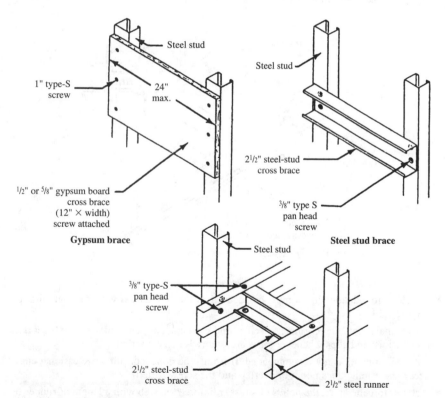

FIGURE 7.17   Three types of chase-wall supports.

STEEL FRAME JOIST ASSEMBLY

While drywall contractors or installers seldom construct steel joist framing themselves, they should know the basics of this type of construction. Steel joists offer distinct advantages for residential construction because they come in sizes and gauges to meet anticipated load and deflection requirements exactly. They also can span longer distances, allowing architects and builders to design open floor plans.

While steel joists provide a great deal of strength overall, that strength can be diminished greatly if the web is not reinforced at points of stress such as ends where the joist rests on the foundation or I-beam. Certain structural features, such as balconies or overhangs, require similar reinforcement. The web of the joist typically can be reinforced at those points either with web stiffeners or with sections of steel runner that is screw-attached in place. Joists must meet the load requirements spelled out in local building codes and must take into account the added load from tile and other floor covering.

To understand the basics of steel frame joist assemblies, consider the following basic construction procedures:

- Cut to length. Joist members can be ordered cut to length for most applications. Shorter members should be field cut, being careful not to cut through a punch hole.

- Allow overlap. Members that will be joined, especially at the I-beam and wall intersections, must be cut to allow for an overlap (Figure 7.18).

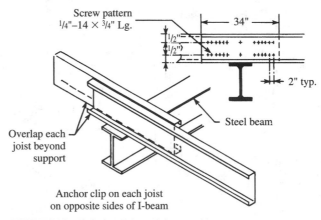

FIGURE 7.18   Typical steel-frame joist assembly.

- Attach to foundation. Joists must be secured to the foundation with foundation clips (Figure 7.19).

- Attach ends. Matching C-runners used as end caps must be screw-attached to the joists. Use the joist end clips whenever joists are otherwise unsupported.

- Splicing. Splicing is not recommended. If it must be done, consult a professional engineer to determine the amount of overlap and the screw pattern.

- Web reinforcement. At the points of stress, reinforce the web with a length of runner or adjustable web stiffener (Figure 7.20). Wood framing material wedged into joist ends as nailers might not provide the necessary long-term reinforcement.

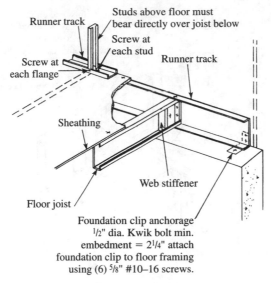

FIGURE 7.19 Typical method of fastening joist to foundation.

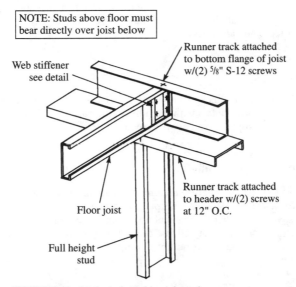

FIGURE 7.20 Method of attaching joist ends.

- Nesting joists. Most steel joist members are designed for nestability. Nested joists increase load-bearing capacity of the members and are essential at header locations (Figure 7.21).
- Stairwell openings. Nested joists are recommended to form headers at stairwell openings.

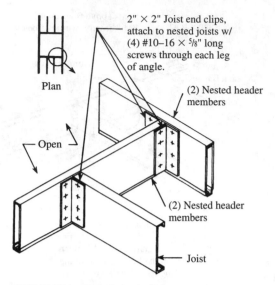

2" × 2" Joist end clips, attach to nested joists w/ (4) #10–16 × ⅝" long screws through each leg of angle.

Plan

(2) Nested header members

Open

(2) Nested header members

Joist

FIGURE 7.21   Method of web reinforcement.

- Bridging. Use 1½-inch 20-gauge flat strapping to bridge across joists or rafters. Solid blocking, using field-cut CR runner sections, screw-attached between the joists, is required at 10-foot intervals or less.

Subflooring

To attach subflooring, use adhesive and screws. Adhesive must be applied along the full length of the joist for firm contact with the subflooring materials. Screws must be installed ½ inch from the edge of panels and at prescribed intervals.

Electrical/mechanical installation

As already mentioned, most steel-product manufacturers provide holes in the web of joist components for installing electrical and plumbing lines. Should larger holes be required for drain lines, vents, or other mechanical installations, reinforcement is required around installed piping to protect against collapse of the web (Figure 7.22). As a rule of thumb, if more than 25 percent of the web is removed, reinforcement is required to add back the required strength.

LOAD-BEARING CONSTRUCTION

The uniformity of steel framing makes it superior to wood for load-bearing construction (Figure 7.23). Steel framing has no knots, cracks, warps, or twists, ensuring reliable performance. With steel's wide range of size and gauge options, studs can be matched to meet even the most difficult requirements for both wind and axial loads. But, like steel-frame

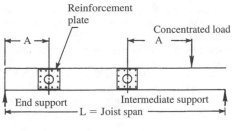

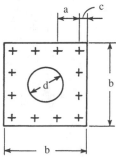

FIGURE 7.22 Reinforcement of larger holes in steel joist.

FIGURE 7.23 Installing load-bearing steel framing.

joist assemblies, load-bearing construction is installed by tradespeople other than drywall contractors or installers. Once again, a knowledge of how this type of construction is assembled will benefit the drywall mechanic covering this framework with gypsum board.

The steel load-bearing framework is assembled in the following manner:

- Runner/stud attachment. Load-bearing walls can be assembled on the ground and then erected, or the bottom runner can be installed and stick-erected. Position the studs in the CR runners top and bottom, and screw-attach using pan-head framing screws. The load-bearing studs must be placed directly beneath joists or trusses to assure load-bearing capacity, and all studs must have their full bearing surface squarely on the bottom track.
- Header-to-jamb attachment. Assemble the load-bearing headers for door and window openings as shown in Figure 7.24 and attach wood nailer to framing members.

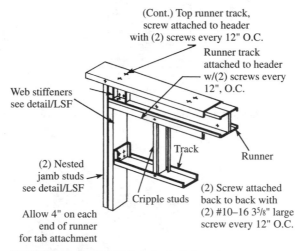

FIGURE 7.24   Typical header-to-jamb attachment.

- Metal window framing. In climates where extremes in summer or winter temperatures might result in condensation on metal frames, gypsum base should be isolated from direct contact with the frame. By placing metal trim between the gypsum-board base and the window frame, protection against moisture damage is provided. Waterproof insulating tape, ¼ inch thick and ½ inch wide, or a waterproof acrylic caulk is required to separate the metal sash and metal trim and provide some measure of insulation between the two different metals (Figure 7.25). Direct contact of an aluminum frame and steel trim in the presence of condensation moisture might cause electrolytic deterioration of the aluminum frame.
- Cripple-to-sill attachment. This is similar to header construction. Attach wood nailers.
- Corner studs. Construct corner studs to secure both wall panels and provide a firm bearing surface for sheathing and gypsum panels. Screw-attach the components with pan-head framing screws.
- Splicing and coping. Splicing members together is not recommended because the splice might alter the integrity of the material. Coping, using shears to remove portions of the

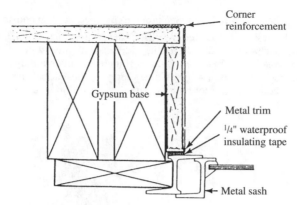

FIGURE 7.25 Installation of metal window framing.

flanges, also is not recommended because it might lessen the bearing strength of the stud. Areas where splicing or coping is required must be reinforced.

- Bracing. Once the assembled wall is erected, leveled, and squared, screw-attach a stud or runner diagonally across the studs and the bottom runner until plywood sheathing at the corners or more permanent bracing can be attached (Figure 7.26). Flat strapping can be used for permanent bracing.

- Sheathing attachment. Sheathing closes in the building and also provides permanent bracing. Position the sheathing lengthwise across the studs and screw-attach them using weather-resistant, self-tapping construction screws.

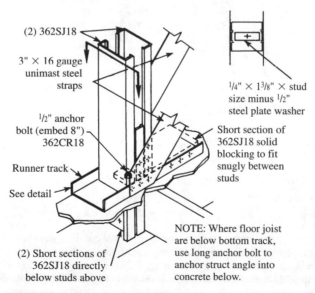

FIGURE 7.26 Bracing of load-bearing wall.

- Electrical/mechanical installation. See previous nonload-bearing construction.
- Insulation. The design of steel studs results in stud cavities that are 1½ inches longer (between studs) than with wood. As a result, wider insulation must be ordered. Insulation manufacturers make batts to fit steel framing (Figure 7.27). A building-products supplier who handles the studs will also be able to supply the insulation. In addition, a ½-inch layer of foam board on exterior flanges can effectively eliminate thermal transmission through the studs.

FIGURE 7.27   Installing insulation in between metal studs.

STEEL CEILING FRAMING

There are three types of steel furring assemblies used for screw-attachment of gypsum-drywall board to ceilings:

- Suspended furred ceiling channel.
- Resilient suspended furring channel.
- Direct screw furring studs.

All three types are suitable for fastening to the lower chord of steel joists or to carrying channels in suspended ceiling constructions. Screw furring channels and resilient furring channels can be secured with tie wires (Figure 7.28) or furring clips (Figure 7.29). Metal screw studs should be attached with wires as shown in Figure 7.30. Installation of resilient furring channel is covered in chapter 9. Table 7.4 indicates maximum spans recommended for each type of furring with ½- or ⅝-inch gypsum panels.

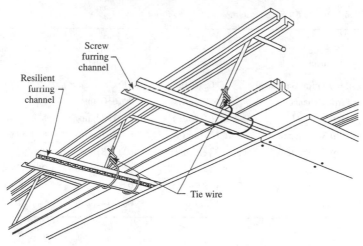

Screw
furring
channel

Resilient
furring
channel

Tie wire

FIGURE 7.28   Installation of hanger wires when using furring channels in a suspended ceiling system.

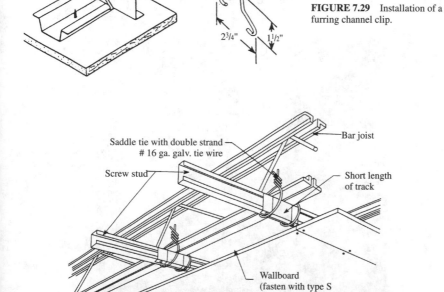

FIGURE 7.29   Installation of a furring channel clip.

$2^{3}/_{4}$" $1^{1}/_{2}$"

Saddle tie with double strand
16 ga. galv. tie wire

Screw stud

Bar joist

Short length
of track

Wallboard
(fasten with type S
drywall screws 12" O.C. max.)

FIGURE 7.30   Installation of hanger wires when using metal studs in a suspended ceiling system.

TABLE 7.4 Furring Member Spacing

Furring member	Furring member spacing	Furring member spacing	Furring member spacing
.0179" (.45mm) min. Base steel	24" O.C. (610mm)	16" O.C. (406mm)	12" O.C. (305mm)
Resilient furring channel	2'-0" (610mm)	2'-0" (610mm)	2'-0" (610mm)
Furring channel	4'-0" (1219mm)	4'-6" (1372mm)	5'-0" (1524mm)
1⅝" (41.3mm) Screw studs	5'-0" (1524mm)	5'-6" (1676mm)	6'-0" (1829mm)
2½" (63.5mm) Screw studs	6'-'0" (1829mm)	6'-6" (1981mm)	7'-0" (2134mm)
3⅝" (92.1mm) Screw studs	8'-0" (2438mm)	8'-6" (2591mm)	9'-0" (2743mm)
4" (102mm) Screw studs	8'-6" (2591mm)	9'-0" (2743mm)	9'-6" (2896mm)
6" (152mm) Screw studs	8'-6" (2591mm)	9'-0" (2743mm)	9-6" (2896mm)

Suspended, furred ceiling channels

The furring channel ceiling, framed to receive drywall, is one of the most popular types of ceiling used in today's commercial structures (Figure 7.31). To start the erection of the suspended ceiling grille, space 8-gauge hanger wires 48 inches O.C. along the carrying channels and within 6 inches of the ends. In concrete, the anchor hangers should be attached to reinforcing steel by loops embedded at least 2 inches or by approved inserts. For steel framing construction, wrap the hanger around or through the beams or joists.

FIGURE 7.31 Commercial application of a suspended ceiling system.

Install 1½-inch carrying channels 48 inches O.C. and within 6 inches of the walls. Position the channels for the proper ceiling height, then level and secure with the hanger wire saddle-tied along the channels as shown in Figure 7.32. Provide 1-inch clearance between the runners and the abutting walls and partitions. At the channel furring splices and the interlock flanges, overlap the ends 6 inches and secure each end with double-strand 18-gauge tie wire (Figure 7.33).

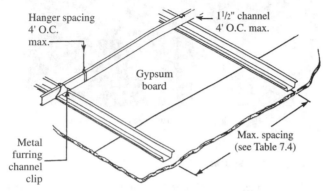

FIGURE 7.32   Installing the gypsum panels to metal furring channels.

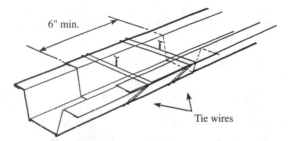

FIGURE 7.33   A furring-channel splice joint.

Erect the metal furring channels at right angles to the 1½-inch carrying channels. Space the furring to within 6 inches of the side walls. Provide a 1-inch clearance between the furring ends and the abutting walls and partitions. Attach the furring channels to the 1½-inch channels with furring channel clips installed on the alternate sides of the carrying channel. Saddle-tie the furring to the channels with double-strand 18-gauge tie wire when the clips cannot be alternated. At the splices, nest the furring channels with an 8-inch overlap and securely wire-tie each end with a double strand of 18-gauge tie wire.

Where required in direct suspended fire-rated assemblies (see chapter 9) install the double furring channels to support the gypsum-board base ends and back-block with a gypsum-board strip. When staggered end joints are not required, control joints can be used.

Apply the gypsum panel with its long dimension at right angles to the furring channels (Figure 7.34). Locate the panel's butt joint over the center of the furring channels. Attach the drywall boards with 1-inch self-drilling drywall screws 12 inches O.C. in the field of the panel and 8 to 12 inches O.C. at butt joints, located not less than ⅜ inch or no more than ½ inch from the edges.

FIGURE 7.34   Installing gypsum panel to a resilient channel.

Exposed grid suspended system

As described in chapter 2, there are predecorated gypsum ceiling panels available that can be laid in a conventional exposed-grid system (Figures 7.35A and 7.35B). Various grid pattern types are shown in Figure 7.36. Because these lay-in panels have a rigid gypsum core, they resist sagging and warping and do not require clips to offset bowing. But compliance with the following cautions and restrictions will ensure maximum performance from gypsum ceiling panels.

- Each panel must be supported on all four edges.
- Do not install panels in areas exposed to extreme or continuous moisture.
- For exterior application, protect the grid panels from direct exposure to weather, water, and continuous high humidity. Under no circumstances should water from condensation or any other source be in contact with the back of the panels.
- Overlaid insulation might cause excessive panel deflection and is not recommended where high humidity is likely to occur.
- Cross ventilation must be provided in unheated or enclosed space above ceiling panels.
- Grid suspension systems must be standard $^{15}\!/_{16}$-inch exposed tee grid or environmental-type grid for severe conditions.
- Extreme lighting conditions might distort texture appearance.
- Common dirt and stains on the vinyl surface can be removed with mild soap or detergent in lukewarm water. Use a light scrubbing action with a cloth, sponge, or soft brush.

Direct screw furring

When installing a direct suspension system, attach the gypsum to the wall angles at the perimeter of the area. Once the ceiling height has been determined, mark this height with a chalk line or the beam of a laster alignment tool. Then install the wall angles along these lines. Locate cross-furring channels within $^1\!/_6$ inch of the walls without wall angles and within 8 inches of the panel end joints.

A

B

FIGURE 7.35   (A) Typical example of an exposed grid system, (B) Another example of an exposed grid system.

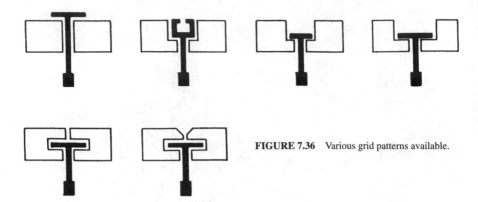

FIGURE 7.36   Various grid patterns available.

Erect the metal furring at right angles to bar joists or other structural members. As an alternative, the studs can be used as furring. Saddle-tie the furring channels to the bar joists with double-strand 18-gauge tie wire at each intersection. Provide a 1-inch clearance between the furring ends and the abutting walls and the partitions. At splices, nest furring channels with at least an 8-inch overlap and securely wire-tie each end with double-strand 18-gauge tie wire (Figure 7.37). Maximum allowable spacing for the metal furring channel is 16 to 24 inches, as required (for ½- or ⅝-inch-thick gypsum board).

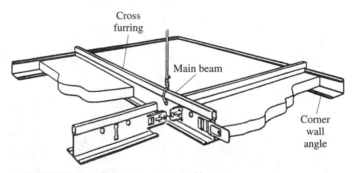

FIGURE 7.37   Installation of an exposed grid system.

For bar joist spacing up to 60 inches, steel studs can be used as furring channels. Wire-tie the studs to the supporting framing. Position the 1⅝-inch studs with the open side up; position the larger studs with the opening to the side. See Table 7.5 for the stud spacing and limiting span.

The installation of gypsum board directly to furring is basically the same as that used with suspended ceilings. Apply the drywall panel with its long dimensions at right angles to the channels. Locate the board's butt joints over the center of the furring channels. Attach the panels with 1-inch self-drilling or tapping screws 12 inches O.C. The screws should not be less than ⅜ inch nor more than ½ inch from the edges. Figure 7.38 shows the installation of a control joint.

TABLE 7.5 Limiting Span—Metal Furring Members

Type furring member	Member spacing (in O.C.)	Single-layer panels (2.5–psf max.)		Double-layer panels	
		1-span	3-span	1-span	3-span
DWC-25	16	5'-9"	7'-1"	4'-7"	5'-8"
(hemmed)	24	5'-0"	6'-2"	4'-0"	4'-11"
DWC-20	16	6'-11"	8'-6"	5'-5"	6'-9"
(unhemmed)	20	6'-0"	7'-5"	4'-9"	5'-11"
158ST25	16	7'-2"	8'-10"	5'-8"	7'-0"
stud	24	6'-3"	7'-9"	5'-0"	6'-2"

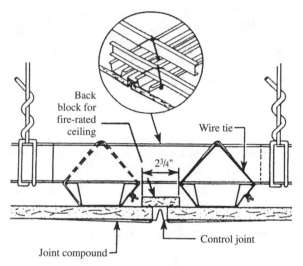

FIGURE 7.38 Installation of control joint in an exposed grid system.

APPLICATION OF WALL PANELS

Once the steel frame studs for a wall or partition are in place, the drywall panels can be installed. The gypsum board, as in applications over wood studs, can be applied horizontally or vertically in single or double layers. With double-layer construction, the face or finish layer can be prefinished gypsum wallboard adhesively applied to the base layer or ply.

Single-layer application

Apply the gypsum-drywall panel with the length parallel or at right angles to the studs (Figure 7.39). Center the abutting ends or edges over the stud flanges. Locate all the attaching screws 12 inches O.C. when the framing is 24 inches O.C. and 16 inches when the metal framing is 16 inches O.C. or less. Attach the gypsum drywall to the studs with type-

FIGURE 7.39   Making a single-ply application on a metal stud.

S drywall screws using an electric drywall screwdriver with a #2 Phillips bit. For vertical panel application with the studs 24 inches O.C., erect the drywall on one side of the partition, screwing it to the studs at the vertical wallboard joints. The first row of screws to be driven at a panel joint should be in the face (flange) of the stud adjacent to the stud web. Complete the drywall panel application to the entire side of the partition in this manner. For the opposite side, cut the first wallboard panel 2 inches so that joints will be staggered. Fasten this and all succeeding drywall panels to all studs on this side. When the partition face is complete, return to the first side and complete screw-attachment of drywall to all intermediate studs.

Make door and window framing openings of such a size that when the drywall is secured to the studs, it will fit snugly into the steel frame. Although one-piece metal door frames can be used with this system, the three-piece metal door frame is preferred by most contractors. This type of frame permits installation after the walls are erected, which normally results in faster completion of the job.

Double-layer application

Two-ply or double-layer drywall construction using steel studs offers some of the best performances in both fire and sound resistance—up to a 2-hour fire rating and a 55-STC sound rating (see chapter 9). These economical, lightweight partitions are adaptable as party walls or corridor walls in virtually every type of new construction.

In these assemblies, a face layer of gypsum-board is job-laminated to the base layer or screw-attached through the base-layer gypsum board to steel studs (Figure 7.40). The installation of steel studs and runners is the same as for single-layer applications described earlier in this chapter.

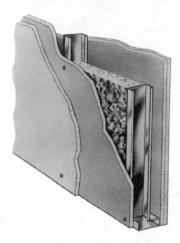

FIGURE 7.40　A double-layer installation on metal framing with insulation placed in the studs.

For double-layer screw-attachment (both layers screw-attached), fasten the face ply to the metal studs with type-S screws spaced 12 inches O.C. Use 1⅝-inch screws for ½- and ⅝-inch-thick gypsum board. As a rule of thumb, screws should be a minimum of ⅜ of an inch longer than the total thickness of the material to be attached to the steel studs. For double-ply laminated drywall construction, attach the face layer using the adhesive lamination described in chapter 6.

CHAPTER 8
SPECIAL DRYWALL CONSTRUCTION

Robert Scharff
Walls & Ceilings Magazine

Gypsum-drywall products are frequently installed to meet special construction applications. For example, they are designed to improve decorative effects, add moisture resistance, improve thermal insulation, reduce sound transmission, provide special construction features, and meet fire-code regulations. To obtain these special drywall construction features, proper framing techniques, fasteners, taping, and finish procedures must be followed as described in this chapter and in chapter 10. In some cases, special drywall materials (see chapter 2) are needed and must be installed following the manufacturer's recommendations.

CURVED-SURFACE DESIGNS

Gypsum panels can be formed to almost any cylindrical or curved surface (Figure 8.1). Panels are applied either dry or wet, depending on the radius of curvature desired. To prevent flat areas between framing, shorter-bend radii require closer-than-normal stud and furring spacing. They are usually horizontally applied, gently bent around the framing, and securely fastened to achieve the desired radius. Table 8.1 supplies the minimum radius of curvature for instances when boards are applied dry. These dry-bending radii are suitable for many curved-surface applications.

Shorter radii (such as shown in Figure 8.2 and given in Table 8.2) can be obtained by thoroughly moistening the face and back papers of the board with water, stacking on a flat surface, and allowing the water to soak into the core for at least one hour. When the board is dry, it will regain its original hardness.

Framing

Figure 8.3 shows a curved wall surface formed with two layers of gypsum drywall on a metal frame. To build the frame, cut one leg and web on the top and bottom steel runner at 2-inch intervals for the length of the arc. Allow a 12-inch uncut steel runner at each end of

FIGURE 8.1   Drywall panels can be formed to almost any cylindrical or curved surface.

TABLE 8.1   Minimum Bending Radii of Dry Gypsum Board

Board thickness		Board applied with long dimension perpendicular to framing		Board applied with long dimension parallel to framing	
Inches	Millimeter	Feet	Meters	Feet	Meters
½	12.7	20[1]	6.1	-	-
⅜	9.5	7½	2.3	25	7.6
¼	6.4	5[1]	1.5	15	4.6

[1] Bending two ¼-inch pieces successfully permits radii shown for ¼-inch gypsum board.

the arc. Bend the runners to the uniform curve of the desired radius (90° maximum arc). To support the cut leg of the runner, clinch a 1-inch-×-25-gauge steel strip to the inside of the leg using metal lock fasteners (Figure 8.4). Select the runner size to match the steel studs; for wood studs, use a 3½-inch steel runner. As shown in Figure 8.5, attach the steel runner to the structural elements at the floor and ceiling with suitable fasteners as previously described in chapters 6 and 7.

Position the studs vertically, with the open side facing in the same direction and engaging the floor and ceiling runners. Begin and end each arc with a stud, and space intermediate studs equally as measured on the outside of the arc. Secure the steel studs to runners with ⅜-inch type-S pan-head screws; secure the wood studs with suitable fasteners. On tangents, place the studs 6 inches O.C., leaving the last stud free-standing. The shorter the radius of the bend or curve, the closer the spacing of the framing members must be.

FIGURE 8.2 A curved stairwell faced with drywall panels forms an attractive design element in this shopping mall.

TABLE 8.2 Minimum Bending Radii of Wet Gypsum Board

Board thickness in inches(1)	Minimum radius in feet	Length of arc in feet(2)	Number of studs on arc and tangents(3)	Approximate stud spacing in inches(4)	Maximum stud spacing in inches(4)	Water required per panel side in ounces(5)
¼	2	3.14	8	5⅜	6	30
¼	2.5	3.93	9	5⅞	6	30
⅜	3	4.71	9	7¹⁄₁₆	8	35
⅜	3.5	5.5	10	7⁵⁄₁₆	8	35
½	4	6.28	8	10¾	12	45
½	4.5	7.07	9	10⅝	12	45

(1) For gypsum board applied horizontally to a 4-inch-thick partition.

(2) Arc length = 3.14R/4 (For a 90-degree arc).

(3) No. studs = arc length/max. stud spacing + 1 (rounded up to the next whole number).

(4) Stud spacing = arc length/no. of studs (measured along outside of runner).

(5) Wet only the side of the panel that will be in compression.

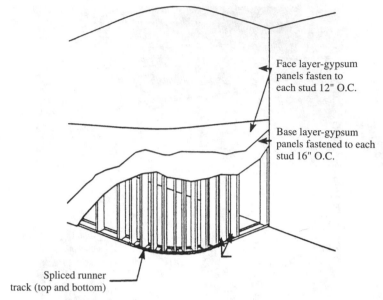

Face layer-gypsum
panels fasten to
each stud 12" O.C.

Base layer-gypsum
panels fastened to each
stud 16" O.C.

Spliced runner
track (top and bottom)

FIGURE 8.3   Board application to a curved surface.

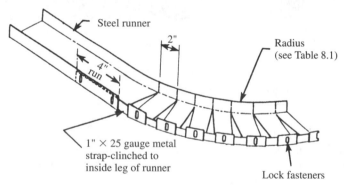

Steel runner

2"

Radius
(see Table 8.1)

4"
run

1" × 25 gauge metal
strap-clinched to
inside leg of runner

Lock fasteners

FIGURE 8.4   Example of the way bottom and top runners are formed for curved-board application.

Panel preparation

Select the panel length and cut the board to allow one unbroken panel to cover the curved surface and 12-inch tangents at each end. The outside panel must be longer than the inside panels to compensate for additional radius contributed by the studs. Cutouts for electrical boxes are not recommended in curved surfaces unless they can be made after the boards are installed and are thoroughly dry.

When a wet-board application is needed, the entire face and back surfaces of the gypsum board to be bent should be moistened with clean water using either a short-nap paint

FIGURE 8.5 Fastening the bottom runner.

roller, a water pump, a spray gun, or a garden sprayer. As a guide, use the quantity of water shown in Table 8.2. Water should not be permitted to stand or puddle on the gypsum board. The moistened panels should be stacked flat on a flat surface and covered with a plastic sheet (polyethylene). Allow the boards to set for at least one hour before application.

Panel application

Apply the panels horizontally with the wrapped edge perpendicular to the studs (Figure 8.6). On the convex side of the partition, one end of the gypsum board should be attached to the framing with nails or screws. The gypsum board should be progressively pushed into contact with and fastened to subsequent framing members, working from the fixed end to the free end. The gypsum board should be held tightly against each supporting framing member while fasteners are being driven.

On the concave side of the partition, a stop should be applied at one end of the curve to restrain one end or edge of the gypsum board during installation. Pressure should be applied to the unrestrained end or edge of the gypsum board forcing the field of the gypsum board into firm contact with the framing. Gypsum board should be fastened by working from the "stopped" end or edge. The gypsum board should be held tightly against the supporting framing while fasteners are being driven.

For single-layer panels, space the screws 12 inches O.C. Use 1-inch type-S screws for steel studs and 1¼-inch type-W screws for wood studs. For double-ply installation, apply the base layer horizontally and fasten to the stud with spacing 16 inches O.C. Center the face-ply panels over the joints in the base layer and secure to the studs with screws spaced 12 inches O.C. Use 1-inch type-S screws for the base layer and 1⅝-inch type-S screws for the face layer. Allow the panels to dry completely (approximately 24 hours under good drying conditions) before applying the joint treatment (Figure 8.7).

FIGURE 8.6   Installing a gypsum board to studs of a curved surface layout.

FIGURE 8.7   How the joints on the radius of a curved gypsum installation are treated.

Archways

Gypsum board can be applied to the inner face of almost any archway. The gypsum board should be precut to the proper length and width. For short radii, the gypsum board should either be moistened or have the back paper scored across the width with parallel score marks spaced at ½-, ¾-, or 1-inch intervals, depending on the size of the radius. After making these "backcuts," the core should be made at each cut so that the board can be bent to the necessary curvature of the arch. The gypsum board should be held tightly against the supporting framing while fasteners are being driven.

A ¼-inch high-flex gypsum board produced by some manufacturers is made specifically for curves (Figures 8.8A and 8.8B). It is used for both inside and outside radii, such as archways, columns, and curved stairways. Except for tight radii work, no wetting of the board is necessary. Check the manufacturer's specifications for the bending-radii limitations of this specialty gypsum board.

Plastic forms or inserts are available that offer a variety of circular or curved shapes for use in drywall surfaces (Figure 8.9). As shown in Figures 8.10A through 8.10D, they are easy to install and result in a perfect surface or arch.

FIGURE 8.8A   A typical drywall doorway arch.

FIGURE 8.8B   A typical drywall window arch.

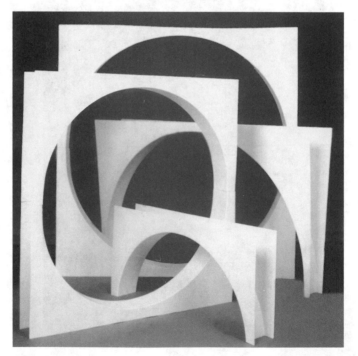

FIGURE 8.9   Various shapes or forms to make instant arches and circular openings in drywall surfaces.

A

B

FIGURE 8.10   (A) Slip the shape into place and nail. (B) Add edge trim.

C

D

FIGURE 8.10 (C) Lightly sand and finish with joint compound.
(D) The complete arch.

SOFFITS

Soffits can be built of gypsum board for either interior or exterior applications. For interior installations, they provide a lightweight, fast, and economical method of filling over cabinets or lockers and housing overhead ducts, lighting systems, pipes, or conduits. They are made with wood framing or with steel stud and runner supports, faced with screw-attached gypsum board. Braced soffits up to 24 inches deep are constructed without supplemental vertical studs. From Table 8.3, select components for the soffit size desired. Unbraced soffits without horizontal studs are suitable for soffits up to 24-×-24 inches. (Figures 8.11, 8.12A, and 8.12B.)

TABLE 8.3 Braced Soffit Design—Maximum Dimensions

Gypsum board thickness(1)		Steel stud size(2)		Maximum vertical(3)		Max. horizontal for max. vertical shown	
Inches	Millimeters	Inches	Millimeters	Inches	Millimeters	Inches	Millimeters
½	12.7	1⅝	41.3	60	1525	48	1220
½	12.7	2½ 3⅝	63.5 92.1	72	1830	36	915
⅝	15.9	1⅝	41.3	60	1525	30	760
⅝	15.9	2½ 3⅝	63.5 92.1	72	1830	18	455

(1) The construction is not designed to support loads other than its own dead weight.

(2) Double-layer applications and ⅜-inch board are not recommended for this construction.

(3) Widths shown are based on construction having supplemental vertical studs.

Braced soffit

Attach the steel runners to the ceiling and sidewalls as illustrated in Figure 8.13, placing the fasteners close to the outside flange of the runner. On stud walls, space the fasteners to engage the stud. Fasten the vertical gypsum face board to the web of the face corner runner and flange of the ceiling runner with type-S screws spaced 12 inches O.C. Place the screws in the face corner runner at least 1 inch from the edge of the board. Insert steel studs between the face corner runner and sidewall runner and attach the alternate studs to the runners with metal lock fasteners or screws. Attach the bottom face boards to the studs and runners with type-S screws spaced 12 inches O.C. Attach the corner bead and finish.

Unbraced soffit

As detailed in Figure 8.14, attach the steel studs to the ceiling and sidewalls, placing the fasteners to engage the wall and ceiling framing. Cut the gypsum board to the soffit depth and attach a soffit-length stud with type-S screws spaced 12 inches O.C. Attach the preassembled unit to the ceiling stud flange with screws spaced 12 inches O.C. Attach the bottom panel with type-S screws spaced 12 inches O.C. Attach the corner bead and finish.

FIGURE 8.11   Special ¼-inch gypsum board can be used for severe bends or turns.

A

B

FIGURE 8.12 (A) Typical interior soffit., (B) How a typical interior soffit is made.

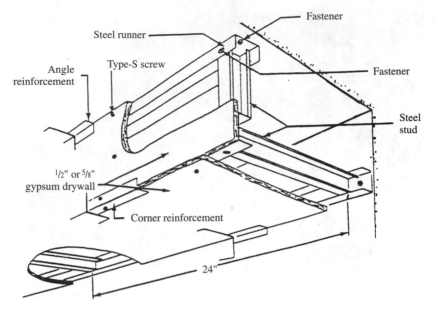

FIGURE 8.13   Typical interior braced soffit.

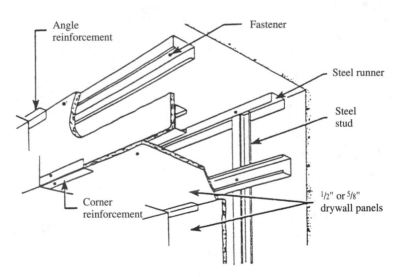

FIGURE 8.14   Typical interior unbraced soffit.

Exterior soffits and ceiling construction

Exterior gypsum soffit board and gypsum wallboard, ½ or ⅝ inch in thickness, are suitable for commercial use as ceilings for covered walkways and malls, large canopies and parking areas, and for residential use in open porches, breezeways, carports, and exterior soffits. These areas must be horizontal or sloping downward away from the building.

When building an exterior soffit, use the longest practical board lengths to minimize the number of butt joints. Framing should be no more than 16 inches O.C. for ½-inch-thick gypsum board, and not more than 24 inches O.C. for ⅝-inch board. Allow a ¹⁄₁₆-to ⅛-inch space between butted ends of the board. Fasten the panels to the supports with screws spaced 12 inches O.C. or nails spaced 8 inches O.C. For steel framed (Figure 8.15), use 1-inch type-S corrosion-resistant screws (type S-12 for 20-gauge or thicker steel). For wood framing, use 1¼-inch type-W screws or 1½-inch galvanized box nails or 1¼-inch aluminum nails. Wood furring that is 1-×-4 inches nominal can be used for screw application of boards where the member spacing does not exceed 24 inches O.C. Furring that is 2-×-2 inches must be used for nail application of boards or when the support member spacing exceeds 24 inches O.C. but is not greater than 48 inches O.C.

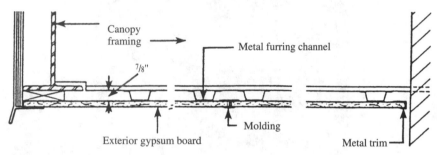

FIGURE 8.15   Typical steel-furred canopy.

Suitable facias and moldings should be provided around the perimeter to protect the board from direct exposure to water (Figure 8.16). Unless protected by metal or other water stops, the edges of the board should be placed not less than ¼ inch away from abutting vertical surfaces. At the perimeter and vertical penetrations, the exposed core of the panels must be covered with metal trim or securely fastened moldings for weather protection (Figure 8.17).

A suspended metal framework for the support of the ceiling board is usually composed of 1½-inch steel channels for the main runners and either steel furring channel or steel stud for cross-furring. Space the main runners as follows: 4 feet O.C. maximum if furring channels are to be used, or 6 feet O.C. maximum for 2½-inch steel studs, or 8 feet O.C. for 3⅝-inch metal studs. Main runners are suspended with 8-gauge (minimum) galvanized wire spaced 4 feet O.C. maximum (Figure 8.18). Secure the metal furring channels to the main runners with 1½-inch channel clips, alternating sides at each intersection or saddle tie with double strands of 16-gauge galvanized tie wire. Secure the metal stud furring to the main runners with double-strand 16-gauge tie wire 16 inches O.C. maximum. For added rigidity, nest an 8-inch length of track at each tie wire location.

The main runners and furring must have a minimum clearance between their ends and any abutting structural element. A main runner must be located within 6 inches of parallel

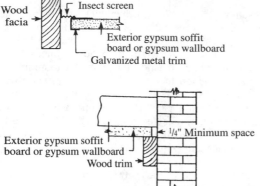

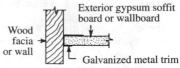

FIGURE 8.16 Gypsum board should be protected from wetting in exterior soffits by facia boards with drip edges. The panel edges should be separated from possible damage by a metal trim or by ¼-inch spacing. Spaces enclosed by gypsum board must be adequately ventilated.

FIGURE 8.17 Installing an exterior ceiling board.

walls. The ends of these runners must be supported by hangers not more than 6 inches from the ends. The closest edge of the furring member must be no more than 2 inches from the parallel wall. At any openings for vents, light fixtures, etc., that interrupt runners or furring, reinforcement must be provided to maintain support equal to that of the interrupted members. Apply the gypsum-board soffit with 1-inch type-S screws, 12 inches O.C. maximum.

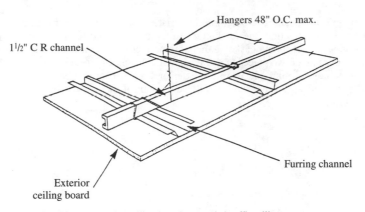

FIGURE 8.18 An exterior ceiling-board suspended-soffit ceiling.

Where the area above ceiling board opens to an attic space above habitable rooms, the space should be vented to the outside in accordance with accepted recommendations of 1 square foot of free vent area per 150 square feet of attic area (Figure 8.19). Where ceiling board is applied directly to the rafters or to the roof ceiling joists (as in flat-roof construction) that extend beyond the habitable rooms, vents are required at each end of each rafter or joist space. The vents should be screened and be a minimum of 2 inches wide by the full length between the rafters (or joists). Vents should be attached through board to 1-x-2-inch (minimum) backing strips installed prior to the board application. Vent openings should be framed and located within 6 inches of the outer edge of the eave. The thickness of the gypsum-board application should be identical to that for the interior ceiling.

As already mentioned, where ceiling board expanse exceeds 4 feet, a space of at least ¼ inch should be provided between the edge of the ceiling board and the adjacent walls, beams, columns, and facia. This space might be screened or covered with molding but must not be caulked.

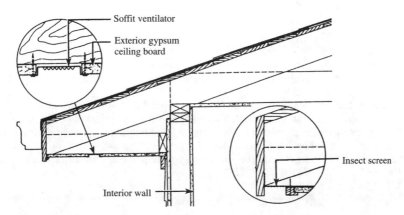

FIGURE 8.19 An exterior-soffit ceiling ventilation system.

Ceiling gypsum board, like other building materials, is subject to structural movement, expansion, and contraction due to changes in temperature and humidity. Install either a casing bead with a neoprene gasket, a manufactured control joint (Figure 8.20), or a control joint consisting of two pieces of metal trim back-to-back in the ceiling board where the expansion or control joints occur in the exterior wall or roof (Figure 8.21). Where aluminum H-moldings are used, they will serve as control joints provided the board is not tightly inserted.

FIGURE 8.20   Control joint installed in an exterior-soffit ceiling.

Long, narrow areas should have control joints spaced no more than 30 feet apart. Wings of L-, U-, and T-shaped areas should be separated with control joints. These joints usually are placed to intersect light fixtures, vents, etc., to relieve stress concentrations. A canopy must be designed to resist uplift.

Treat the fasteners and joints using a joint compound as described in chapter 10. If desired, the panel joints can be concealed with batten strips or by installing the panels with their ends inserted into aluminum H-moldings. After the joint compound has dried, apply one coat of oil-based primer-sealer and one or two coats of exterior oil or latex paint or other balanced finishing system recommended by the paint manufacturer to all exposed surfaces.

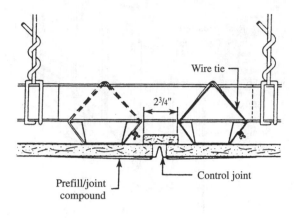

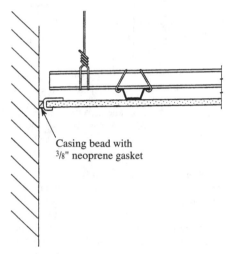

FIGURE 8.21   Details of installing a control joint in a suspended exterior-soffit ceiling.

MR BOARD INSTALLATION

As stated in chapter 2, MR or WR board is a specially processed gypsum wallboard for use as a base for ceramic tile and other nonabsorbent finish materials in wet areas (Figure 8.22). The core, face paper, and back paper of MR or WR board are treated to withstand the effects of moisture and high humidity. A tapered edge is usually provided so that joints can be treated in the normal manner where MR or WR board extends beyond the tiled area. No special tapes or edge sealants are required. Tile adhesive eliminates the need for further corner treatment, nail spotting, edge sealing, or filling the edge taper in the area to be tiled.

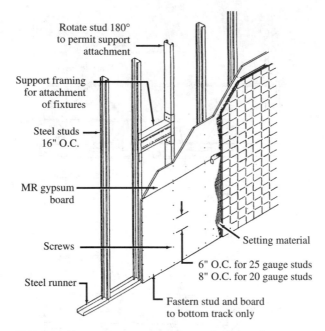

Rotate stud 180°
to permit support
attachment

Support framing
for attachment
of fixtures

Steel studs
16" O.C.

MR gypsum
board

Screws

Steel runner

Setting material

6" O.C. for 25 gauge studs
8" O.C. for 20 gauge studs

Fastern stud and board
to bottom track only

FIGURE 8.22   Details of an MR or WR wallboard installation over steel studs. Installation of MR or WR panel over wood framing is basically the same.

Regular gypsum wallboard can be used as a base for tile and wall panels in dry areas. MR or WR gypsum wallboard should not be used in crucial exposure areas such as saunas, steam rooms, or gang shower rooms. (Cement board should be used in such locations.) Gypsum board used as a base for tile or wall panels in tub or shower enclosures should not be foil backed and should not be applied over any vapor retarder. To satisfy the need for a vapor retarder on exterior walls where water-resistant gypsum backing board is the substrate for ceramic tile, the vapor retarder can be created on the face side of the substrate or tile if installed following one of these procedures (Figure 8.23).

1. Apply a uniform skim coat, not less than ½₂ inch thick, of water-based ceramic tile adhesive over the water-resistant gypsum backing board and allow to dry before installing the tile.
2. Use a silicone caulk as the grout between the tiles to seal the surface.

Framing

Framing members should be plumb and true. Place studs (wood or metal) not to exceed 24 inches O.C. The framing around the tub and shower enclosures should allow sufficient room so that the inside lip of the tub, prefabricated receptor, or hot-mopped subpan will be properly aligned with the face of the gypsum board (Figure 8.24). This might necessitate furring out from the studs the thickness of the gypsum board to be used, ½ or ⅝ inch less the thickness of the lip, on each wall abutting a tub receptor or subpan (Figure 8.25). Interior angles should be framed or blocked to provide a solid backing for interior corners.

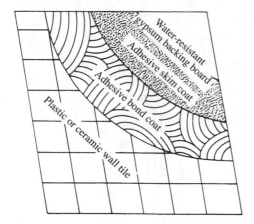

FIGURE 8.23   Details of installing plastic or ceramic tile over MR board.

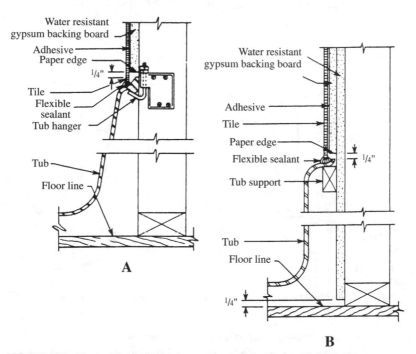

FIGURE 8.24   The installation of wall tile on MR board around tubs. The backing gypsum board must be separated from the tub by at least a ¼-inch gap to prevent moisture wicking.

When the framing is spaced more than 16 inches O.C., suitable blocking or backing should be located approximately 1 inch above the top of the tub or receptor and at the horizontal joints of the gypsum board in the area to receive the tile. The surfacing material should be applied down to the top surface or edge of the finished shower floor, return, or tub and installed to overlap the top lip of the receptor, subpan, or tub and should completely cover the following areas (Figure 8.26).

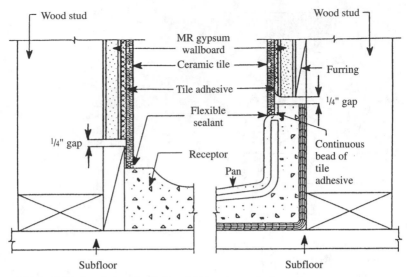

FIGURE 8.25   Installation of wall tile on MR board around a shower receptor or pan.

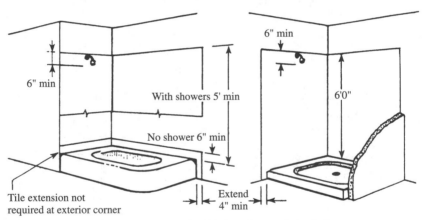

FIGURE 8.26   Tile in baths and showers should be brought up to the levels shown.

- Over tubs without shower heads, 6 inches above the rim of the tub.
- Over tubs with shower heads, a minimum of 5 feet above the rim or 6 inches above the height of the shower head, whichever is higher.
- For shower stalls, a minimum of 6 feet above the shower dam or 6 inches above the shower head, whichever is higher.
- Beyond the external face of the tub or receptor, a distance of at least 4 inches and to the full specified height.
- All gypsum-board walls with window sills or jambs in shower or tub enclosures, to the full specified height.

For plastic-finished wall panels, the recommendation of the manufacturer should be followed.

If necessary, fur out the studs so that the inside face of the receptor is flush with the tile MR or WR backer board. When the surface finish is a ceramic tile, the spacing of the 2½-inch-thick or less blocking should not exceed 16 inches O.C. Studs 3½ inches or more in thickness can be spaced 24 inches O.C., provided blocking described previously is used. Provide appropriate blocking headers or supports to support the tub, other plumbing fixtures, and to receive soap dishes, grab bars, towel racks, and similar items as might be required.

To ensure satisfactory job performance, a fixture attachment should provide sufficient load-carrying capacity within the assembly. Framing and bracing must be capable of supporting the partition elements and fixture additions within L/360 allowable deflection limits. Install bracing and blocking flush with the face of the framing to keep the stud faces smooth and free of protrusions. Heavy-gauge metal straps mounted on the studs are not recommended as supports because they cause bowing in the board and interfere with the flat, smooth application of the MR tile backer board and ceramic tile (Figure 8.27). When heavy plates must be used, fur out the studs with a metal strap or wood shim to provide an

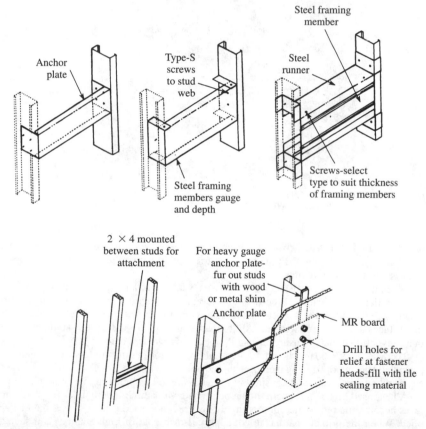

FIGURE 8.27 Supports for heavy bathroom fixtures.

even base for the backer board. If required, the backer board can be ground or drilled to provide relief for projecting bolts and screw heads. Install the shower pans, receptors, tubs, and other plumbing fixtures prior to the erection of the gypsum board.

Applying MR or WR gypsum board

The board is applied horizontally to the framing using nails or screws spaced not to exceed 8 inches O.C., driven flush with the gypsum board. During board application, all cut edges should be coated with approved water-resistant adhesive as recommended for the application. In bath or shower areas, a ¼-inch space should be maintained between the lower paper-bound edge of the board and the lip of the tub or shower receptor. Shimming the tub assures that the tub lip will be in the same plane as the installed MR board (Figure 8.28). The MR board itself is applied to the studs in the same manner as regular gypsum wall-

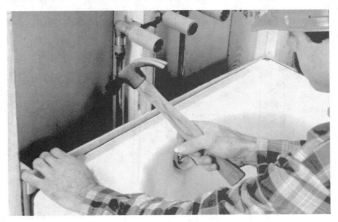

FIGURE 8.28   Shimming assures that the tub lip will be in the same plane as the installed MR or WR board.

board (Figure 8.29). A ¼-inch shim is used to create the necessary space between the MR board and the tub (Figure 8.30). Gypsum board applied with adhesive only should not be used as a base to receive tiles.

When using a water-resistant tile adhesive, lay a bead of adhesive on the tub or shower receptor flange and caulk all corners and around all openings prior to tile application (Figure 8.31). Nail and screw heads should be spotted with water-resistant tile adhesive on the surfaces to be covered with tile. All joints beyond the area to be tiled should be treated in a conventional manner using tape and joint compound (see chapter 10).

The MR or WR board should not be used on interior ceilings unless extra framing is provided; spacing of framing members should not exceed 12 inches O.C., including use as a substrate when ceramic tile or similar materials are to be applied to the ceiling.

All exposed MR or WR board should be primed with a high-quality latex primer. If surfaces become marred or are not thoroughly covered, a second primer coat should be applied. When the primer coat has dried, apply a finish coat of high-quality paint such as latex semigloss enamel.

FIGURE 8.29 MR or WR board is applied to the studs in the same way as regular gypsum wallboard.

FIGURE 8.30 Quarter-inch shims are used to create the necessary space between the MR board and the tub.

When the final finish is to be a wall covering, prime all exposed MR board as described previously, using one or two coats of primer as required to adequately cover the surface, and allow to dry. This treatment serves the dual purpose of ensuring adhesion of the wall covering paste to the board and facilitating subsequent removal of wall coverings when redecorating. Apply wall covering in the conventional manner after primer is thoroughly dry.

FIGURE 8.31 Water-resistant tile adhesive or elastomeric caulking compound is applied around cutouts and the tub lip.

INSTALLATION OF PREDECORATED GYPSUM PANELS

Predecorated gypsum board, as described in chapter 2, consists of gypsum-board panels with a decorative surface covering or coating applied in-plant rather than on site. The decorative sheet or film is usually a plastic (vinyl) film or paper sheet, backed or unbacked, or a combination of these components that has been printed with or otherwise bears a decorative pattern. The decorative coating usually is a paint or other liquid material, with or without aggregate, that has been applied to the paper surface of the gypsum board by spraying, rolling, or other mechanical methods. The face is the side of the predecorated gypsum board that is called the finish side (Figure 8.32).

Several methods of installation can be used with predecorated gypsum wallboard in order to meet specific job requirements. As in regular drywall construction, ceilings are installed first, before predecorated paneling is erected. Panels are attached vertically. Predecorated materials should not be applied to ceilings.

Nailing

Predecorated gypsum panels are easily attached to wood studs or furring with colored nails (color pins), which are available to match most predecorated patterns and colors. For attaching ½- and ⅝-inch panels, use 1⅜-inch color pins. When applying the panels over existing walls, use 1⅞-inch color pins. Space them 12 inches O.C. and drive pins to penetrate the framing a minimum of ½ inch. A plastic-headed or padded hammer should be used.

Adhesive nail-on

To avoid visible fasteners on the exposed surfaces, predecorated panel can be applied to metal or wood studs or furring with adhesive. As described in chapter 6, the panels should be prebowed. That is, the panels must be warped or bowed to give pressure at the center of

FIGURE 8.32   Typical installation of predecorated gypsum board.

the board during adhesive and cementing applications. If the boards were not bowed, temporary bracing would be required. Cut to the proper ceiling height, and stack as shown, with all prefinished surfaces facing up or down, depending on which method of bowing is used. Use padded blocks, cut from 2-×-4s to protect the prefinished surfaces. Stack in such a manner that, when applying, each panel would have a tendency to spring away at the top when nailed at the bottom. Proper bowing can take from one to several days, depending on weather conditions.

Apply adhesive to the metal or wood studs or furring in a continuous ¼-inch bead. Where panel edges abut, apply two parallel beads, one along each edge of the framing member. Press the panel firmly in place against the freshly applied adhesive. Nail or screw at the corners only.

Edge grip clips, also described in chapter 6, can also be used to provide mechanical attachment and positive alignment of wallboard edges over wood or steel framing, concrete block, or any other sound wall surface. The clip is positioned on the back of the board and the prongs are driven into the board edges. Each clip along one edge of the board is in turn attached directly to the studs or wall surface. As each panel is installed, the clips become hidden by the panel edges.

Before application, proper arrangement of panels should be studied. For the most pleasing results, all joints of the panels should be centered on the architectural features of the wall, such as fireplaces, windows, doors, etc. If the wall contains no such openings, arrange for the two end panels to be of equal width. Narrow strips are difficult to install and should be avoided whenever possible.

Where two walls intersect to form an inside corner, the last panel installed at this intersection should have two finished edges to create a professionally installed look. To form such a narrow plank or strip with two finished edges, proceed as follows:

1. Cut the decorative surface with a sharp knife to a dimension that is 1 inch wider than the desired panel width (Figure 8.33A). Then turn the vinyl surface face down.

2. Score the back surface with a knife to the desired panel width. Snap the gypsum core (Figure 8.33B) and peel the 1-inch piece from the decorative surface. Smooth the core if it is uneven.

3. Wrap the excess flap of vinyl or cloth over the exposed gypsum core and staple to the back (Figure 8.33C).

A

B

FIGURE 8.33 (A) Cut the decorative surface. (B) Score the back surface and snap the panel. (C) Wrap excess flap of vinyl or cloth over the exposed core and staple to the back.

C

This treatment can be eliminated by using a snap-on interior trim (Figure 8.34A). Wood, plastic, or metal outside corner moldings, nailed or glued to wood or steel framing, are recommended for edge protection where panels meet to form outside corners. These moldings can be stained or painted in matching or contrasting colors, or use color matching outside snap-on molding (Figure 8.34B). Other decorative trims and moldings that should be considered are described in chapter 10.

Wood and plywood paneling

The use of gypsum board as a substrate when applying wood paneling provides increased fire resistance and sound control (Figure 8.35). In new or existing construction, a ⅜-inch or ½-inch gypsum-board substrate is recommended before applying combustible paneling.

The gypsum-board substrate should be attached parallel to framing using 1⅜-inch drywall nails, 1-inch drywall screws, or a drywall stud adhesive (Figure 8.36). The spacing of fasteners should be the same as given in chapters 6 and 7. The edges of the board should be centered on framing members. The joints need not be taped and finished.

The predecorated panels should be applied using a bead of panel adhesive that is placed midway on each of the studs. Joints in the wood paneling should be staggered from the joints in the base ply of gypsum board. Secure the paneling at the top and bottom with 4d finishing nails, 12 inches O.C. and with one nail at midheight per stud.

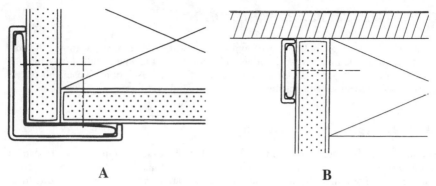

FIGURE 8.34   Snap-on trim application methods. (A) Exterior corner and (B) interior corners.

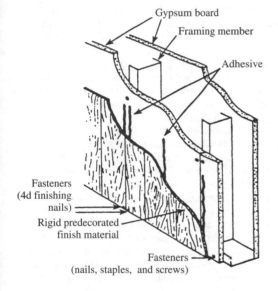

Gypsum board

Framing member

Adhesive

Fasteners
(4d finishing
nails)

Rigid predecorated
finish material

Fasteners
(nails, staples, and screws)

FIGURE 8.35   Predecorated combustible paneling such as plywood panels over a gypsum-board substrate.

FIGURE 8.36   Examples of complete plywood installation over a gypsum-board substrate.

OTHER GYPSUM-BOARD PARTITIONS

There are several other applications of gypsum as a wall surface or as partitions. In addition to being applied over wood framing and steel studs, it can be installed over interior masonry or concrete walls as well as over rigid plastic foam insulation. Gypsum board can also be used to form self-supporting semisolid and solid partitions.

Semisolid gypsum-board partitions

The face panels—either ½ or ⅝ inch— or multiple thicknesses of gypsum board—can be installed on gypsum studs. These studs should not be less than 1 inch thick. They can be of 1-inch material or of multilayer materials laminated to required thickness. They should be a minimum of 6 inches wide and of lengths approximately 6 inches less than the floor-ceiling height unless full lengths are required for fire stops or fire resistance. Runners of wood or steel and of width equal to the partition cavity should be used. Floor and ceiling runners should be securely fastened with fasteners spaced not to exceed 24 inches O.C. Use laminating adhesive, joint compound for tape embedment, or other laminating adhesive as recommended by the gypsum-board manufacturer.

Erect vertical runners or gypsum studs where required to provide proper support at locations such as exterior walls, partition junctions, terminals, external corners, and door frames. The gypsum-board face panels should be positioned vertically. The gypsum studs are laminated to face panels that are not more than 24 inches O.C. and located at the face panel's vertical joints and at the vertical center line of the panel.

The gypsum studs can be laminated to the face panels prior to the erection or as the erection of the partition proceeds. Erect a starter face panel vertically at an exterior wall. The starter panel should be plumb and secured to the floor ceiling and vertical runners. Erect the next face panel adjacent to the starter panel, butting its edge and end firmly to the starter panel and ceiling. Continue erection of the face panels, laminating exposed faces of the gypsum studs as work progresses. Openings in partitions for doors, electrical outlets, etc., should be carefully and accurately marked and cut.

The laminating adhesives should be of a consistency and volume that will cover approximately three-fourths of the gypsum-stud surface after lamination. Type-G screws should be used as required to ensure a continuous bond between the face panels and gypsum studs, and the screws should be placed a maximum of 36 inches O.C. Openings or changes in directions of partitions should be reinforced with additional gypsum studs laminated in place at the following locations:

- External corners. Place between face panels in the corner opposite vertical runners.
- Abutting walls. Place between face panels of a partition to reinforce junctions of an abutting wall.
- Door openings. A vertical gypsum stud should be located within 3 inches of the door frame for reinforcement, and a gypsum stud should be placed horizontally over the door header.

Solid gypsum-board partitions

The face panels of a solid gypsum-board partition can be ½ inch, ⅝ inch, or multiple laminations of regular or type-X gypsum board. The core should be either 1-inch-thick gypsum core board or shaft liner, in single or multiple layers. The laminating adhesive can be joint compound for tape embedment or other laminating adhesive recommended by the gypsum-board manufacturer.

Secure the wood or metal floor runner to the floor with approved fasteners 24 inches O.C. The ceiling runner should be secured in an appropriate manner to the ceiling construction. The L runner should be used as both floor and ceiling runners in fire-rated construction.

The 1-inch gypsum core board shaft liner, cut ¼ inch shorter than the wall height, should be installed vertically and should be fastened to the floor and ceiling runners with two 1⅝-inch type-S screws, each located 2 inches from each edge of the core-board panels (Figure 8.37). A joint compound should be applied evenly with a notched spreader (¼-×-¼-inch notches, 1½ inches O.C.) to the back side of the 4-foot-wide ceiling height of the wallboard face panels and vertically to the sides of the gypsum core board. Stagger the wallboard joints 12 inches from the core-board joints and 24 inches from the joints on each side of the partition wall.

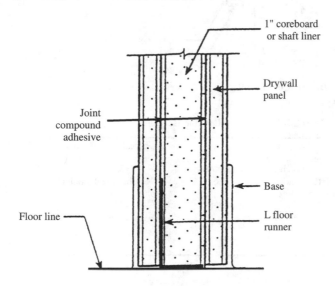

FIGURE 8.37   Installing details of the runners for solid partitions.

Face panels are then screwed 12 inches O.C. to the bottom runners with 1⅝-inch type-S screws and are secured to the core board with 1⅝-inch type-S drywall screws spaced 24 inches O.C. horizontally and vertically to include screws along the vertical edges of each panel. Drywall panel joints should be reinforced with paper tape and finished with joint compound. Door frames should be vertical, plumb, and true, and they should be securely anchored to the floor, wall, and ceiling (Figure 8.38). The completed partition should be straight and plumb.

The solid laminated partition is adapted to any type of building for nonload-bearing partitions. Table 8.4 gives the allowable partition heights based on gypsum board applied to light-gauge steel acting as a composite section. The limiting heights exceeding those shown can be obtained by using deeper studs, spacing the studs closer together, using heavier-gauge studs, increasing gypsum-board thickness, or adding an additional layer of gypsum board.

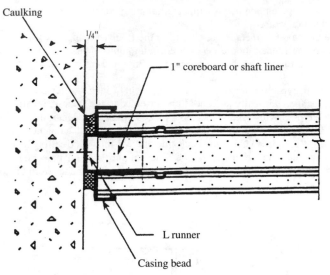

Caulking

1/4"

1" coreboard or shaft liner

L runner

Casing bead

FIGURE 8.38   Installing details of sidewall application for solid-wall partitions.

TABLE 8.4   Allowable Partition Heights

Stud spacing (in inches)	Facing on each side	Stud Depth (in inches)			
		1⅝	2½	3⅝	4
		Height in feet and inches			
16	½" one-ply	11'0"	14'8"	19'5"	20'8"
24	½" one-ply	10'0"	13'5"	17'3"	18'5"
24	½" two-ply	12'4"	15'10"	19'5"	20'8"

Application of gypsum board to interior masonry and concrete walls

Gypsum panels can be adhesively installed over concrete surfaces or applied with metal furring channels or wood furring strips.

Over wood furring strips

Attach the wood or metal furring strips over nailers with cut nails, anchors in holes, power-driven studs, or adhesive-backed anchors. Run the wood furring horizontally at the floor line as shown in Figure 8.39. Then locate and fasten the wood furring on 24-inch centers horizontally or vertically. The long dimension of the gypsum boards should be run at right angles across the furring. Center the end joints over the furring or add blocking. Support the gypsum board with blocking or furring around all openings and cutouts as close to the edge as possible.

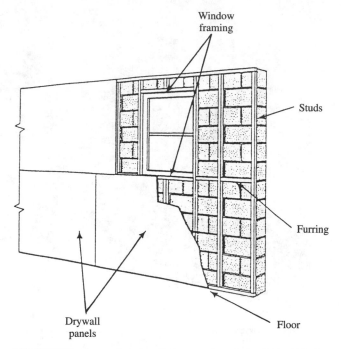

FIGURE 8.39   Gypsum board applied to masonry surfaces with wood furring.

When using metal furring channels, attach them vertically to the masonry or concrete surfaces (Figure 8.40). Space the channels no more than 16 inches O.C. Secure the channels with the fasteners placed on alternate channel flanges and spaced 24 inches O.C. Use a 2-inch cut nail in the mortar joints of brick, clay tile, or concrete block, or in the field of lightweight aggregate block. Use ⅜-inch concrete stub nails or other power-driven fasteners in monolithic concrete. At window and door locations, attach the furring horizontally over the masonry returns to support the gypsum board at the corners.

Adhesively applied

The following are recommended for direct adhesive application: interior masonry or concrete above grade or inside of exterior masonry cavity walls with a 1-inch minimum cavity width between the inside and outside masonry for the full height of the above-grade surface to receive the gypsum board. Interior surfaces to which the gypsum board is to be adhered should be free from any foreign matter, projections, or depressions that will impair bond, and exterior surfaces should be sealed against moisture penetration. Joint compound or a certified subfloor plywood construction adhesive can be used.

Apply the adhesive directly to the back of the gypsum board or on the wall in continuous beads, spaced not to exceed 12 inches O.C. or daubs spaced not to exceed 16 inches. When applying the gypsum board to the monolithic concrete, brick, or concrete block, beads should not be less than ⅜ inch in diameter to provide a continuous bond between the

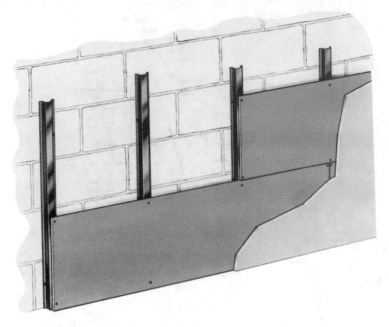

FIGURE 8.40   Gypsum board applied to masonry surfaces with metal furring.

gypsum board and wall surface. The daubs should not be less than 2 inches in diameter by ½ inch thick with a row centered at all vertical joint locations. Position the gypsum board to provide a tight fit at abutting edges or ends. Do not slide the board. Use mechanical fasteners or temporary bracing as required to support the gypsum board until the adhesive sets or adequate bond strength is attained.

As shown in Figure 8.41, gypsum-drywall panels can employ the adhesive nail-on system with wood furring strips. But regardless of whether the panels are directly adhesively held or are applied over furring strips, they must be firmly secured. A variety of clips, runners, and adjustable brackets are available with furring systems to facilitate installation over irregular masonry walls (Figure 8.42). When special clips are used, the manufacturer's instructions should be followed.

Gypsum-board application over foam-insulated masonry

Gypsum board applied over foam insulation as recommended in this section might not necessarily meet all building code requirements. Check with the local authorities.

Gypsum board can be applied over rigid-plastic foam insulation on the interior side of exterior masonry and concrete walls to provide a wall finish and protect insulation from early exposure to fire originating within the building. In applying gypsum board over rigid-plastic foam insulation, the entire insulated wall surface should be protected with gypsum board, including walls above ceilings and in unoccupied spaces (Figure 8.43). The gypsum board can be applied as a single- or double-ply that is fastened by screws to metal furring or fastened by a laminate.

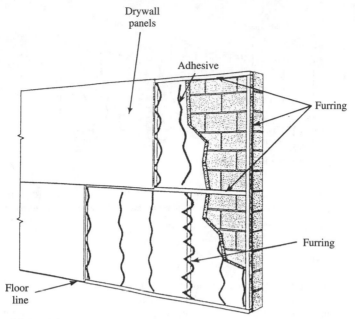

FIGURE 8.41   Gypsum board applied to masonry surfaces with adhesive.

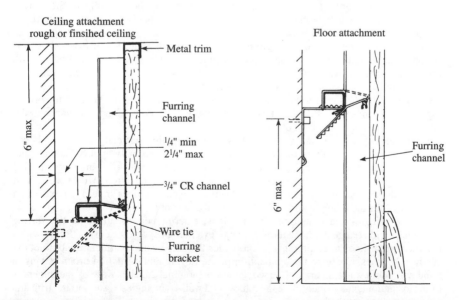

FIGURE 8.42   Adjustable brackets make installation of furring easy over irregular masonry walls.

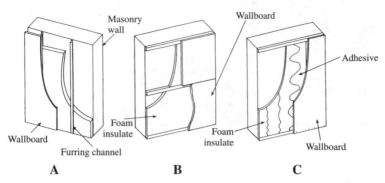

FIGURE 8.43 Installation of foam insulation with (A) Z-type furring channel. (B) Horizontal installation with drywall adhesive. (C) Vertical installation with drywall adhesive.

Metal furring

Metal furring can be used to secure rigid foam insulation and gypsum-drywall panels to masonry walls. Insulation thickness (1, 1½, 2 inches) determines the depth of the furring web. The channel is applied vertically and fastened to the masonry wall through the short (¾-inch) flange with suitable masonry fasteners 24 inches O.C. maximum. Application is progressive. After fastening each furring channel, a 24-inch-wide floor-to-ceiling-high insulation panel is fitted between the wall and the wide (1¼-inch) flange. Many installers prefer to use Z-channels for this type of installation.

Erect the single-ply gypsum drywall either vertically or horizontally to the furring channels. Drywall edges or ends that run parallel to the channels should be centered and abutted over the channels. Fasten the wallboard with 1-inch type-S screws spaced 12 inches O.C. When the wallboard erection is complete, all joints and screw heads should be finished in accordance with the joint-finishing methods described in chapter 10. Prefinished gypsum wallboard panels can be laminated vertically to the channels with screws at the top and bottom. Power-driven fasteners should be used to secure the furring only when the wall is monolithic concrete. Regular concrete nails can be used for fastening to the unit masonry. If the block is old, test nailing should be done in advance to determine optimum size and type of nail.

In double-ply applications, the base ply should be applied vertically. The face ply can be applied either vertically or horizontally. Edge joints of vertically applied face ply and end joints of horizontally applied face ply should be offset one furring-member spacing from base-ply edge joints. The screw spacing for two-ply applications with vertically or horizontally applied face ply that has no adhesive between the plies should not exceed 24 inches O.C. for the base ply and 12 inches O.C. for face ply.

In both single- and double-ply installations, exterior corners attach to the furring through its wide flange, with the narrow flange extending beyond the corner. Begin with a narrow strip of floor-to-ceiling insulation, wider than the insulation thickness but not exceeding 3 inches. Continue the application of the furring and insulation progressively at windows, doors, and trim areas. Use wood nailers (nominal 2 inches wide by the thickness of the insulation, plus ½₂ inch). Use the nailers and wall-floor angles to support the trim and provide backing for the base.

Lamination

Masonry or monolithic concrete should be dry and free of dust, loose particles, oil, grease, or other foreign materials. Joint compound used as an adhesive should be mixed to a consistency thick enough to allow for a 2-inch daub to stick to the underside of a board knife held parallel to the floor.

Apply a 2 to 2½-inch diameter of adhesive ½ inch thick, 16 inches O.C. in both directions to the masonry wall. The adhesive layout must provide for a row of daubs located a maximum of 2 inches from the board ends, and care must be exercised to center daubs on the vertical joints. No more adhesive should be applied to the wall than will be covered with board in 15 minutes.

Cut the gypsum drywall to allow for a ⅛-inch clearance between the board and floor to prevent wicking. Install the wallboard by hand-pressing each panel tight to the wall, making certain that all daubs are in positive contact with the panel. Support the panels at each corner to keep them from slipping to the floor by use of a concrete nail driven through a small block of nominal 1-inch lumber. Butt the panels to each previously positioned panel to ensure flush joints. If necessary to hold the panels straight, plumb, and in proper alignment, drive masonry nails through small wood blocks and into masonry at high points only. After the adhesive is dry (24 to 48 hours), remove temporary nails. To complete the installation, fill all holes and treat joints with tape and joint compound as described in chapter 10.

FIXTURE ATTACHMENT

Gypsum-board partitions provide suitable anchorage for most types of fixtures normally found in residential and commercial construction. To ensure satisfactory job performance, it is important to have an understanding of particular fixture attachments so that sound control characteristics will be retained and attachments will be within the allowable load-carrying capacity of the assembly.

In wood-frame construction, fixtures are usually attached directly to the framing or to the blocking or supports attached to the framing. Blocking or supports should be provided for plumbing fixtures, towel racks, grab bars, and similar items. Single- or double-layer gypsum boards are not designed to support loads imposed by these items without additional support to carry the main part of the load.

Fixture attachment types

Loading capacities of various fixture attachments based with gypsum-board partitions appear in Table 8.5. Fasteners and methods are given here (also see Figure 8.44):

- Number-8 sheet-metal screw. Driven into 25-gauge (minimum) sheet metal plate or strip, laminated between face board and base board in laminated gypsum partitions. Might also be driven through gypsum board into a steel stud. Ideal for preplanned light fixture attachment.

- Hollow wall anchors. ¼-inch anchors installed in gypsum boards only. One advantage of this fastener is that the threaded section remains in the wall when the screw is removed. Also, widespread spider support is formed by the expanded anchor spreading the load against the wall material, increasing load capacity (Table 8.6).

- Toggle bolt. ¼-inch toggle bolt installed in gypsum board only. One disadvantage of a toggle bolt is that when the bolt is removed, the wing fastener on the back will fall down into the hollow wall cavity. Another disadvantage is that a large hole is required to allow the wings to pass through the wall facings.
- Continuous horizontal bracing. Backup for a fixture attachment is provided with a notched runner attached to steel studs with two ⅜-inch pan-head screws.

TABLE 8.5   Fixture Attachment Load Data

Fastener type	Size		Base assembly	Allowable withdrawal resistance		Allowable shear resistance	
	in.	mm.		lbs./ft.	Newton	lbs.ft.	Newton
Toggle bolt or	⅛	3.18		20	89	40	178
hollow wall	3⁄16	4.76	½" gypsum	30	133	50	222
anchor	¼	6.35	panel	40	178	60	267
	⅛	3.18	½" gypsum	70	311	100	445
	3⁄16	4.76	panel and steel	80	356	125	556
	¼	6.35	stud	155	689	175	778
No. 8 sheet metal screw			½" gypsum panel and steel stud or 25-gauge steel insert	50	222	80	356
Type S bugle head screw			½" gypsum panel and steel stud or 25-gauge steel insert	60	267	100	445
Type S-12 bugle head screw			½" gypsum panel and steel stud or 20-gauge steel insert	85	378	135	600
⅜" Type S pan-head screw			25 gauge steel	70	311	120	534
Bolt welded to 1½" channel	¼	6.35	see Figure 8.30	200	890	250	1112
Two bolts welded to steel insert	3⁄16	4.76	½" gypsum board, plate and steel stud	175	778	200	890
	¼	6.35	½" gypsum board, plate and steel stud	200	890	250	1112

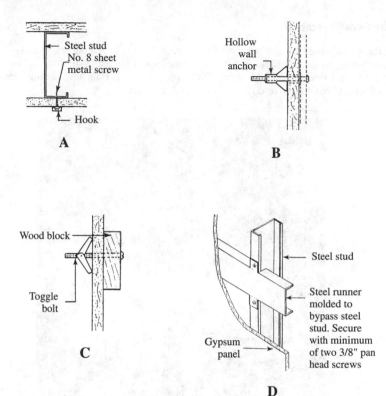

FIGURE 8.44 Fixture attachment types. (A) Number-8 sheet-metal screw. (B) Hollow wall anchor. (C) Toggle bolt. (D) Bolt and channel.

TABLE 8.6 Wall Anchor and Toggle-Bolt Capacities

Type of fastener	Size	1/2" (12.7mm) wallboard	Allowable load ⅝" (15.9mm) wallboard
Hollow wall screw anchors	⅛" (3.18mm) dia. short	50 lbs. (23kg.)	–
	³⁄₁₆" (4.8mm) dia. short	65 lbs. (29kg.)	–
	¼" (6.4mm), ⁵⁄₁₆" (7.9mm)	65 lbs. (29kg.)	–
	⅜" (9.4mm) dia. short	–	90 lbs. (41kg.)
	³⁄₁₆" (4.8mm) dia. long	–	95 lbs. (43kg.)
	¼" (6.4mm), ⁵⁄₁₆" (7.9mm), ⅜" (9.4mm) dia. long		
Common toggle bolts	⅛" (3.18mm) dia.	30 lbs. (14kg.)	90 lbs. (41kg.)
	³⁄₁₆" (4.76mm) dia.	60 lbs. (27kg.)	120 lbs. (54kg.)
	¼" (6.4mm), ⁵⁄₁₆" (7.9mm), ⅜" (9.4mm) dia.	80 lbs. (36 kg.)	120 lbs. (54kg.)

Shelf-wall systems

In the steel-framed assembly shown in Figure 8.45, load-carrying wall shelves are provided for use in stores, offices, schools, and other applications. In steel-framed assemblies, 3⅝-inch steel studs spaced 24 inches O.C. are secured to floor and ceiling runners and faced with either single- or double-layer gypsum board.

FIGURE 8.45   The need for installation of various shelves.

Slotted standards are screw-attached to wood studs or steel reinforcement inserted between the layers (Figure 8.46). In the wood-framed assembly, slotted standards are screw-attached to the studs with 2¼-inch type-S oval-head screws. The partition is load-carrying, but with steel studs, it is not structurally load-bearing. Limiting height is 16 feet.

To install a shelf bracket between wall studs (Figure 8.47), laminate a 1-×-3-×-12-inch wood block, or screw-attach the block to the back of a gypsum wallboard panel. The shelf-bracket-bearing surface is 1 inch (minimum) of the bracket's width. The bracket should be held in place with 1½-inch #10 wood screws.

Cabinet attachment method

The attachment method shown in Figure 8.48 allows kitchen, bathroom, and other cabinets and fixtures (except lavatories and wall-mounted toilets) of moderate weight. The method also allows "Hollywood" style headboards on party walls using resilient channel without

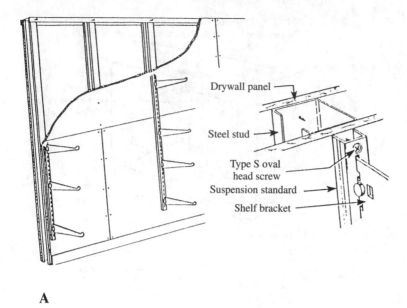

Drywall panel

Steel stud

Type S oval
head screw

Suspension standard

Shelf bracket

A

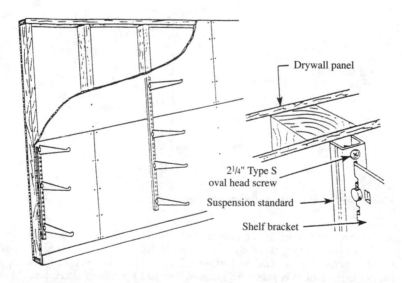

Drywall panel

2¹/₄" Type S
oval head screw

Suspension standard

Shelf bracket

B

FIGURE 8.46   Two popular shelf-wall systems. (A) Steel-framed assembly. (B) Wood-stud-slotted standard assembly.

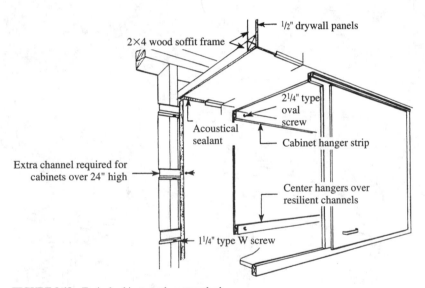

1"×3"×12" wood blocks laminate or screw
attached to back of wallboard between studs

Gypsum wallboard

Screw stud

Shelf bracket
bearing (1" min.
bracket width)

6" min

1¹/₂" #10 wood screws

FIGURE 8.47   Typical between-stud installation.

¹/₂" drywall panels

2×4 wood soffit frame

2¹/₄" type
oval
screw

Acoustical
sealant

Cabinet hanger strip

Extra channel required for
cabinets over 24" high

Center hangers over
resilient channels

1¹/₄" type W screw

FIGURE 8.48   Typical cabinet attachment method.

reducing the sound rating. It is recommended only for residential and light commercial wood-frame construction. It is suitable for loads including cabinet weights of 67½ pounds for studs spaced 16 inches O.C. and 40 pounds for studs 24 inches O.C. Loads are maximum per linear foot of heavier steel channel installed for cabinet attachment. Mounting cabinets back-to-back on a partition should be avoided because this practice creates a flanking path that increases sound transmission. In this system, ⅜-inch gypsum board is installed with the long dimension parallel to the channels and fastened with 1-inch type-S screws spaced 12 inches O.C. along the channels. Cabinets are attached to the channels with 2¼-inch type-S screws spaced 12 inches O.C. and located between the studs. Screws must be driven between the studs. Screws that penetrate the stud cause a significant loss in the partition's sound rating.

Light fixtures

After electrical services have been roughed in and before the gypsum board is installed, make necessary openings in the base and face layers of the board to accept switches, outlets, and fixture boxes, etc. As described in chapter 5, cut the openings with a keyhole saw, an electric router with a drywall bit, or with specially designed cutting tools that produce die-cut openings.

At light troffers or any ceiling openings that interrupt the carrying or furring channels, install additional cross-reinforcing to restore the lateral stability of the grillage (Figure 8.49). When required in fire-rated construction, use light-fixture protection over recessed units installed in direct-suspension ceiling grid. Cut pieces of ½- or ⅜-inch gypsum panels or gypsum-board ceiling with type-X board core to form a five-sided enclosure, trapezoidal in cross section (Figure 8.50). Fabricate a box larger than the fixture to provide at least ½-inch clearance between the box and the fixture, and in accordance with local fire regulations.

Light troughs, such as shown in Figure 8.51, are recessed areas where light fixtures are installed for indirect lighting. They are usually located at the perimeter of a room, and they generally project beyond the wall plane. A wide wood facia hides the lights installed in the trough. The light troughs are framed after the ceiling and wall framing are completed.

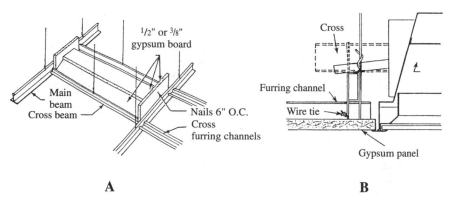

A   **B**

FIGURE 8.49   Typical light-fixture installation.

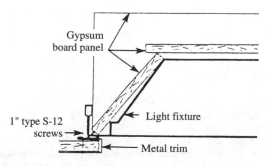

FIGURE 8.50   Typical light-fixture protection.

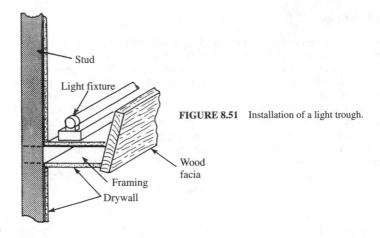

FIGURE 8.51   Installation of a light trough.

REMODELING WITH GYPSUM BOARD

Most of the drywall construction described in this book to this point has dealt with new construction. While most of the techniques given in these chapters are suitable for either new construction or remodeling, let's now take a look at some of the considerations the drywall contractor must keep in mind when tackling a remodeling job.

For example, when gypsum drywall is applied directly over existing walls or ceilings, all loose plaster and wallpaper should be removed. When wall or ceiling surfaces are extremely uneven or unsound, it might be necessary to remove the entire surface. Void areas and areas resulting from removal of loose plaster should be shimmed to the same thickness as the plaster in order to provide uniform backing support to the gypsum board. To maintain fire-resistant characteristics between adjacent living units or public corridors (see chapter 9), void areas should be treated as follows:

- The minimum width of wood shims should be 1½ inches. The minimum width of gypsum-board shims should be 2 inches. Care must be taken to make the shims equal in thickness to the surrounding plaster. Shims should be applied to the exposed framing or wood lath with nails or screws spaced no more than 6 inches O.C. (Figure 8.52).
- Shims can be secured to masonry with masonry nails.
- When voids do not exceed 16 inches across, fill them with plaster or other suitable noncombustible material and cover with a minimum ⅜-inch gypsum board.
- When voids exceed 16 inches across, a minimum of ½-inch type-X gypsum board should be used so that support or framing does not exceed 24 inches O.C.
- When more than 75 percent of the wall or ceiling is not sound, resurface the entire area with ⅝-inch type-X gypsum board.

Gypsum board used over the existing wall and ceiling surfaces should be applied with mechanical fasteners (such as nails or screws) into the framing, or with adhesives in combination with nails or screws (Figure 8.53). It is important to locate the framing member before beginning mechanical attachment of the gypsum board. While there are several ways of doing this, the most simple way is to use either a magnetic, ultrasonic, or electronic stud finder as directed by the manufacturer. Do not nail or screw gypsum board to the plaster only.

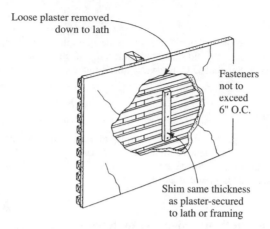

FIGURE 8.52 Treatment of large voids in plaster.

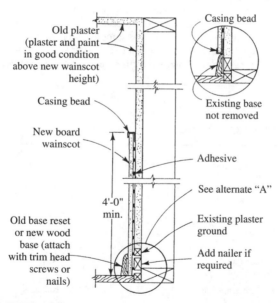

FIGURE 8.53 Wainscot detail shows methods of direct attachment.

Gypsum board can be attached directly over sound-wall and ceiling surfaces with nails or screws. Framing members must be sound, rigid, and aligned, and they should not exceed 16 inches O.C. for ⅜-inch-thick board or 24 inches O.C. for ½-inch or ⅝-inch board. One-quarter-inch and 5/16-inch-thick backer board is intended only for direct application to sound walls and ceilings that are flat, level, and without void spaces.

Nail application

Drywall nails should be of sufficient length to penetrate into the framing ⅞ inch, plus the thickness of the new board, the old surfacing material, and any necessary shims. Nail spacing should not exceed 8 inches O.C. for walls and 7 inches O.C. for ceilings.

Screw application

Drywall screws should penetrate into the framing at least ⅝ inch. Space screws not to exceed 16 inches O.C. for walls and 12 inches O.C. for ceilings where the framing members do not exceed 16 inches O.C. Space screws 12 inches O.C. for walls and ceilings where the framing members do not exceed 24 inches O.C.

Attachment using both adhesive and fasteners

When an adhesive nail-on method is to be used, a test should be made to ensure that the adhesive bond to the surface will be adequate. Loose paint or wallpaper must be removed from the plaster so that the adhesive can be applied directly to a sound surface. Apply a single ⅜-inch-×-3-inch-long bead of drywall adhesive to an 8-inch square sample of gypsum board and press the sample to the surface. Repeat this procedure in several widely separated areas. Allow sufficient setting time (see adhesive manufacturer's directions). The adhesive bond is then tested by pulling the sample away from the surface. The bond can be considered adequate if the gypsum-board back-paper surface is torn from the board sample. After determining that the bond strength is adequate, proceed with the board application as given in Table 8.7.

TABLE 8.7 Attachment Use of Adhesive

Gypsum board	Adhesive with fasteners	Modified contact adhesive method
Gypsum wallboard or veneer base	R,1	R
Water resistant gypsum backing board	R	NR
Predecorated, vinyl faced	R,1	R
Prefinished, paper faced	R,1	R

KEY:
R - Follow manufacturer's recommendations.

NR -   Not recommended.

1 - ⅜-inch-diameter adhesive beads not exceeding 16 inches O.C. applied to back face of boards.

Attachment using furring members

When walls and ceilings are not acceptable for direct application as just described, the use of furring is recommended. Wood furring should have a minimum fastener spacing of not less than 1½ inches. When spanning voids greater than 16 inches in diameter, the wood furring should not be less than 2 inches nominal thickness. When void space is less than 16 inches in diameter, wood furring should be not less than 1-inch nominal thickness. Wood trim can be used as nailer strips along the floor and around door or window openings.

Preparation for attachment using framing members

Trim need not be removed if the new furred-out surface will cover these items and no lead-based paint is left exposed. Bulges in the old surface should be removed so furring is tight against the surface and level across the wall or ceiling.

Attachment of furring

Fasten furring 16 to 24 inches O.C. at right angles to the framing members. Attach the wood furring to each framing member with common nails or type-W screws. Use two fasteners at each intersection.

Attach metal furring channels with screws alternately from top to bottom through flanges at each framing-member intersection. Stop furring 6 inches short of any trim member. Use shims to level. Attach the gypsum board to either the metal or wood furring with appropriate fasteners or adhesives and their recommended spacing.

Corner and exposed-edge treatment

Inside corners should be finished with tape and joint compound or moldings. Outside corners should be treated with 1⅛-inch-×-1⅛-inch (minimum) metal or plastic corner bead attached with fasteners or crimped 12 inches O.C. and filled and finished level with joint compound. Outside corners of predecorated gypsum board should be covered with protective molding as described earlier in this chapter.

Trim the exposed edges around door and window openings with a suitable drywall casing bead or wood molding to hide and protect the cut edge. Where abutting members have a gap not exceeding ³⁄₁₆ inch, a permanent-type flexible sealant can be used to fill the gap (Figure 8.54). When trim is used as a fastener base, suggested methods of treatment are shown in Figure 8.55.

Suspended ceilings

Older dwellings and commercial buildings often have ceilings exceeding 8 feet in height. If ceilings are high, it can be advantageous to use a suspended ceiling system, which will permit covering the old ceiling without removal of ceiling material. The suspension system can be planned so that the new ceiling is 7½ to 8 feet high. Aside from avoiding the mess of tearing down an old ceiling, the decreased height can result in other advantages, such as reduced heating costs, reduced sound transmission between floors, and the provi-

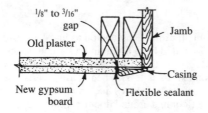

FIGURE 8.54 Door framing details—direct lamination.

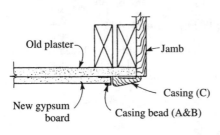

FIGURE 8.55 Door framing details. (A and B) With casing bead. (C) With new casing.

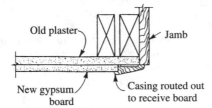

sion of a plenum for electrical or duct work. In the case of existing fixtures, it will be necessary to arrange for adjustment of ceiling electrical fixtures and heating or ventilation ducts. Relocation or adjustment work should be accomplished prior to ceiling installation. The various methods of suspending a ceiling with both wood and metal furring can be found in chapters 6 and 7.

CHAPTER 9
GYPSUM DRYWALL CONSTRUCTION ASSEMBLIES

Robert Scharff
Walls & Ceilings Magazine

There are two important gypsum-board assemblies that the drywall contractor or craftsperson must be familiar with. They are fire-resistant assemblies and sound-control assemblies. Again, while the drywall hangers do not design or erect the actual framework, they will be applying the actual surface to that assembly.

Before considering the actual construction of fire-resistant and sound-control assemblies, let's take a look at some key terminology and definitions:

- *Fire resistance* refers to the ability of an assembly to serve as a barrier to fire and to confine its spread to the area of origin. Spread of fire from one area to another occurs because:
  - ~ The barrier collapses.
  - ~ Openings in the barrier allow passage of flames or hot gases.
  - ~ Sufficient heat is conducted through an assembly to exceed specified temperature limitations. These characteristics form the basis for judging when an assembly no longer serves as a barrier in a test.

- A fire-resistance rating (FRR) denotes the length of time a given assembly can withstand fire and give protection from it under rigidly controlled laboratory conditions. All tests are conducted under standard conditions, and test methods are as described in the *Standard Fire Tests of Building Construction and Materials*, ASTM E119. The standard is also known as ANSI/UL 263 and NFPA 251. The ratings are expressed in hours and apply to floors, ceilings, beams, columns, and walls.

- *Sound control* refers to the ability to attenuate sound passing through a partition.

- The *sound transmission class* (STC) is widely used as a rating of sound attenuation performance. It is accurate for the sounds of speech, but not for music, mechanical equipment noise, or any sound with substantial low-frequency energy. Tested per ASTM E90; rated per ASTM E413.

- The *impact insulation class* (IIC) is a numerical evaluation of a floor-ceiling assembly's effectiveness in retarding the transmission of impact sound, also determined from laboratory testing. Tested per ASTM E492; rated per ASTM E989.

- The *noise reduction coefficient* (NRC) is a measure of sound absorption. This is an important consideration for controlling acoustics within a confined area. It does not generally apply to the performance of a structural system.

FIRE-RESISTANT GYPSUM ASSEMBLIES

As described in chapter 2, fire-resistant gypsum drywall is made with a core formulated to offer greater fire resistance than regular wallboard. Generically, these fire-resistant drywall boards are used to prevent the rapid transfer of heat to structural members, protecting them for specified periods of time, and are designated as "type-X" products.

ASTM C36 is the standard for gypsum wallboard. According to this standard, type-X gypsum wallboard must provide at least a 1-hour fire-resistance rating for a ⅝-inch board or a ¾-hour fire-resistance rating for a ½-inch board applied in a single layer nailed on each face of load-bearing wood framing members. This is the standard when tested in accordance with the requirements of the *Methods of Fire Test of Building Constructions and Materials* (ASTM designation E119). As the number of layers of type-X gypsum covering the framework increases, the fire-resistance rating (FRR) also increases.

A fire-resistant rating denotes the length of time a given assembly can withstand fire and provide protection against it under precision controlled laboratory conditions. Regardless of the thickness of the type-X drywall installed, the wall is still considered combustible as long as wood studs are used in the wall. The wall is termed noncombustible only if none of the materials in the partition will burn.

Floor/ceiling assemblies

Figure 9.1 shows several wall designs that are suitable for all types of wood- and steel-framed residential and commercial buildings, including those with single- and double-layer gypsum-board facings, and other assemblies with sound attenuation, fire blankets, and resilient attachment.

As described for the installation of regular gypsum board in chapters 6 and 7, the type-X panels should be applied first to the ceiling at right angles to the framing members, then to the walls. Boards of maximum practical length should be used so that an absolute minimum number of end joints occur. Board edges should be brought into contact with each other but should not be forced into place. As can be noted, there is little difference between regular and type-X gypsum board as far as installation is concerned.

As in the installation of regular gypsum drywall board, described in chapter 6, when the ceiling size exceeds the following specifications, control joints are needed:

- Interior ceilings with perimeter relief. Maximum 50 feet in either direction.

- Interior ceilings without perimeter relief. Maximum is 30 feet in either direction.

- Exterior ceilings. Maximum is 30 feet in either direction for a run of exterior ceiling panels.

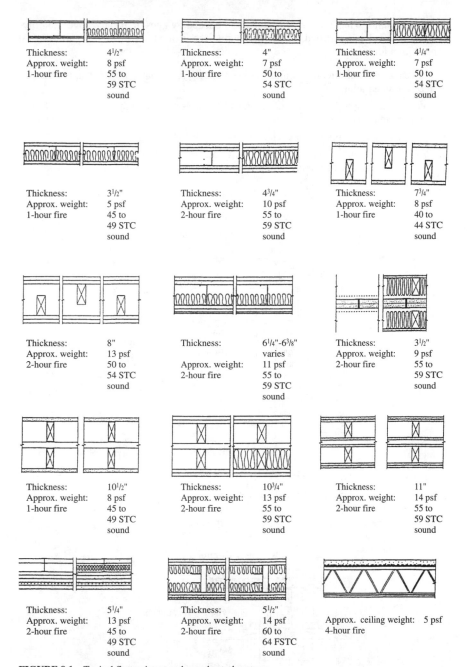

Thickness:	4^1/$_2$"
Approx. weight:	8 psf
1-hour fire	55 to
	59 STC
	sound

Thickness:	4"
Approx. weight:	7 psf
1-hour fire	50 to
	54 STC
	sound

Thickness:	4^1/$_4$"
Approx. weight:	7 psf
1-hour fire	50 to
	54 STC
	sound

Thickness:	3^1/$_2$"
Approx. weight:	5 psf
1-hour fire	45 to
	49 STC
	sound

Thickness:	4^3/$_4$"
Approx. weight:	10 psf
2-hour fire	55 to
	59 STC
	sound

Thickness:	7^3/$_4$"
Approx. weight:	8 psf
1-hour fire	40 to
	44 STC
	sound

Thickness:	8"
Approx. weight:	13 psf
2-hour fire	50 to
	54 STC
	sound

Thickness:	6^1/$_4$"-6^3/$_8$"
	varies
Approx. weight:	11 psf
2-hour fire	55 to
	59 STC
	sound

Thickness:	3^1/$_2$"
Approx. weight:	9 psf
2-hour fire	55 to
	59 STC
	sound

Thickness:	10^1/$_2$"
Approx. weight:	8 psf
1-hour fire	45 to
	49 STC
	sound

Thickness:	10^3/$_4$"
Approx. weight:	13 psf
2-hour fire	55 to
	59 STC
	sound

Thickness:	11"
Approx. weight:	14 psf
2-hour fire	55 to
	59 STC
	sound

Thickness:	5^1/$_4$"
Approx. weight:	13 psf
2-hour fire	45 to
	49 STC
	sound

Thickness:	5^1/$_2$"
Approx. weight:	14 psf
2-hour fire	60 to
	64 FSTC
	sound

Approx. ceiling weight:	5 psf
4-hour fire	

FIGURE 9.1   Typical fire-resistant and sound-rated systems.

Control joints, when properly insulated and backed by gypsum panels, have been fire-endurance tested and certified for use in 1- and 2-hour rated assemblies (Figure 9.2). At control joint locations:

1. Leave a ½-inch continuous opening between the gypsum boards for insertion of the surface-mounted joint.
2. Interrupt the wood floor and ceiling plates with a ½-inch gap, wherever there is a control joint in the structure.
3. Provide separate supports for each control joint flange.
4. Provide an adequate seal or safing insulation (Figure 9.3) behind the control joint where sound and/or fire ratings are prime considerations.

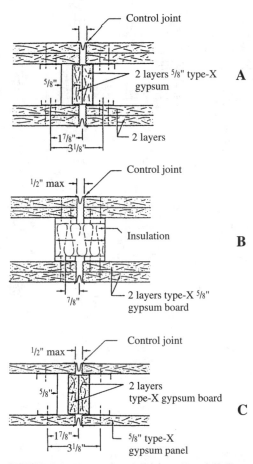

FIGURE 9.2 Fire-rated control joints. (A and B) Two-hour-rated steel-stud partitions. (C) One-hour-rated steel-stud partition.

FIGURE 9.3   Safing insulation is cut wider than the opening to ensure a compression fit. It installs easily with wire support brackets or safing clips.

Wall assemblies

In residential construction, most building codes specifically require fire-resistance-rating walls between attached garages, around heating systems, and in a few other areas. There are more rigid requirements that apply to buildings that house more than one family, such as duplexes, townhouses, apartments, and condominiums. In most cases, restrictions on commercial buildings are even more stringent.

Wood-stud partitions

Suitable for residential and light commercial construction where combustible framing is permitted, these designs include single- and double-layer gypsum-board facings, single- and double-row studs, those with insulating blankets, and those with resilient channel attachments (Figure 9.4). Performance values of up to 4 hours of fire resistance and 59 STC can be obtained.

Steel-stud partitions

Suitable for all types of construction, these designs include single-layer and multilayer gypsum-board facings, with and without sound-attenuation blankets (Figure 9.5). Performance values of up to 4 hours of fire resistance and 62 STC can be obtained. Control joints are required for an FRR partition whose surface exceeds 50 feet in either direction.

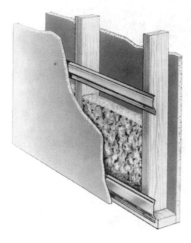

FIGURE 9.4   Single-layer application on resilient channels on wood studs. Installation in between with a fire rating of 1 hour and a sound rating of 50 to 54 STC.

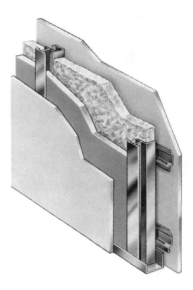

FIGURE 9.5   Cavity shaft walls can provide up to 4-hour fire resistance and sound ratings up to 51 STC.

Single-layer application

This basic construction, described in chapter 6, is used to surface interior partitions where economy, fast erection, and a minimum fire resistance of 1-hour FRR are required features. This use of type-X board is equally suitable for single-layer application in remodeling, altering, and resurfacing cracked and defaced areas.

Double-layer application

Consists of a face layer of type-X board over a base layer of gypsum base that is attached to the framing members. The standard double layer using steel studs and ½-inch type-X board installed as described in chapter 7 has an FRR of up to 2 hours. This rating can be increased by using one of the proprietary or improved type-X boards on the market, which are ⅝ inch thick and have fire-resistant insulation and resilient furring (Figure 9.6). These FRR assemblies are low cost, much lighter in weight, and thinner than concrete block partitions, and the FRR assemblies offer equivalent performance.

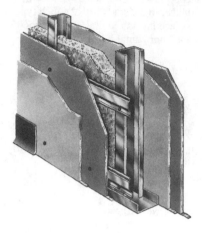

FIGURE 9.6   A so-called double-wall high-performance sound-control system with a 57-STC to 60-STC rating and 3-hour fire rating.

Three-layer application

Apply the gypsum panels vertically with the long dimension parallel to the studs (except the face layer, which can be applied horizontally across the studs). Position the base so that abutting edges are located in the center of the stud flanges (Figure 9.7). Stagger the joints from those in adjacent layers and on the opposite sides of the partition.

Fasten the first layer to the studs with 1-inch type-S screws spaced 48 inches O.C. Fasten the second layer to the studs with 1⅝-inch type-S screws spaced 48 inches O.C. Fasten the face layer to the studs with 2¼-inch type-S screws spaced 12 inches O.C. Horizontally applied face layers require 1-inch type-G screws in the base between the studs and 1½ inches from the horizontal joints.

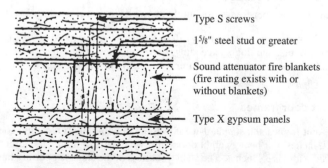

Type S screws

1⅝" steel stud or greater

Sound attenuator fire blankets (fire rating exists with or without blankets)

Type X gypsum panels

FIGURE 9.7   A three-layer application.

Four-layer application

Apply the gypsum boards vertically with the long dimension parallel to the studs (except the face layer, which can be applied horizontally across the studs). Position the base so abutting edges are located in the center of the stud flanges. Stagger the joints from those in adjacent layers and on opposite sides of the partition. Fasten the first layer with 1-inch type-S screws spaced 48 inches O.C. Fasten the second layer to the studs with 1¼-inch type-S screws spaced 48 inches O.C. Fasten the third layer to the studs with 2¼-inch type-S screws spaced 12 inches O.C. Horizontally applied face layers require 1½-inch type-G screws in the base between the studs and 1 inch from the horizontal joints (Figure 9.8).

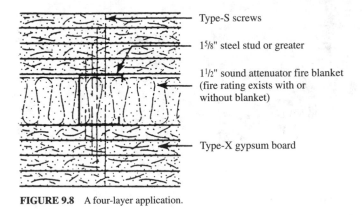

Type-S screws

1⅝" steel stud or greater

1½" sound attenuator fire blanket (fire rating exists with or without blanket)

Type-X gypsum board

FIGURE 9.8   A four-layer application.

Installation of steel fire door frames

The satisfactory performance of steel fire-door frames installed in fire-rated, nonload-bearing interior partitions constructed of steel studs and gypsum-board facings is dependent on proper design and installation of both the door frame and the partition frame at the opening. There are different types of door frames that the drywall contractor might come across when working on fire-rated partitions. They are:

- Single-unit steel door frames for single-swing doors not exceeding 4 feet in width and pairs of doors not exceeding 6 feet in width.
- Three-unit slip-on door frames for single-swing doors not exceeding 3 feet in width.

Frames for wider doors, extra heavy doors (such as X-ray room doors), double-egress doors, sliding doors, and doors exceeding 7 feet 2 inches in height require special detailing. Consult the door-frame manufacturer for specific recommendations.

Single-unit door frames

For single-unit frames and standard-weight doors, the minimum recommended steel stud width is 2½ inches. For heavyweight doors and wide pairs of doors, the minimum recommended stud width is 3½ inches. The steel thickness of the studs supporting the door frame should not be less than 20 gauge.

Frames should be installed with steel-stud anchors as detailed in Figures 9.9A and 9.9B. Frames for pairs of doors 5 feet or more in width should have anchors installed in the door header similar to those in the door side jambs. Anchors should be located 6 to 8 inches from jambs and not exceed 24 inches O.C. (The 8-inch frame header is to receive a door closer.) The details for heavy doors are applicable to pairs of doors 5 feet or more in width and to all heavy doors, such as hospital solid-core doors.

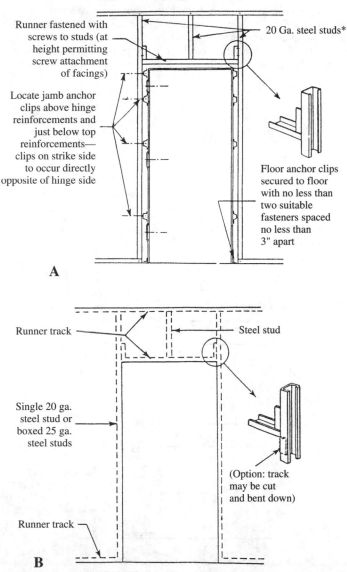

FIGURE 9.9 (A) Single-unit fire-door-frame installation, (B) Another single-unit fire-door-frame installation.

Three-unit slip-on door frames

Three-unit slip-on door frames are designed for installation in a door opening after completion of the steel-stud gypsum-board partition installation.

Details shown in Figures 9.10A and 9.10B are recommended for standard-weight doors not exceeding 3 feet in width and not more than 7 feet 2 inches in height. For larger or heavier doors, consult the door-frame manufacturer for specific recommendations.

Three-unit frames in fire-rated partitions should be a minimum of 16-gauge-steel thickness. The frames should have double back-bend frame-face returns. The frame jamb pieces should be designed for screw anchorage of the jambs to the partition frame (not shown), and the jamb and head pieces should be designed to provide a positive means of aligning and locking the jamb-head intersections in place. For more complete instructions on steel door installation, see chapter 7.

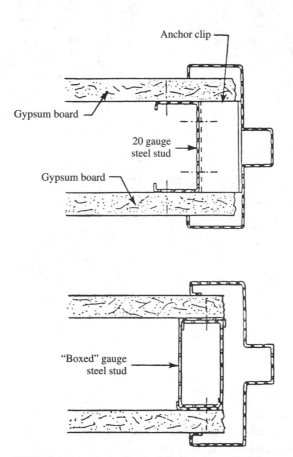

FIGURE 9.10A   Three-unit slip-on fire door frame details.

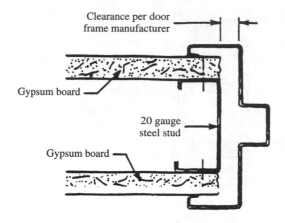

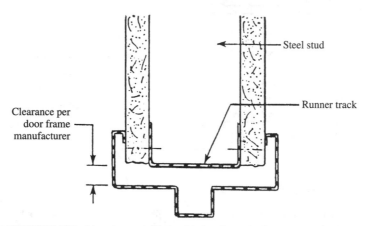

FIGURE 9.10B More three-unit slip-on fire door frame details.

Column/beam fire protection

Type-X gypsum wallboard can also be used as column and beam protection, preventing the rapid transfer of heat so that structural members will not lose strength and fail to carry their intended load.

Column fire protection

Fire-resistant assemblies are obtainable with a 2- or 3-hour fire rating. For instance, a 3-hour fire rating (Figure 9.11) for lightweight columns (10 × 49) can be obtained by using three layers of ⅝-inch type-X gypsum board, while a 2-hour rating can be had with just two layers of ⅝-inch type-X (Figure 9.12). A 4-layer application of ⅝-inch type-X gypsum board will provide a 4-hour rating. The board is held in place by a combination of wire, screws, and steel studs. All attachments are mechanical.

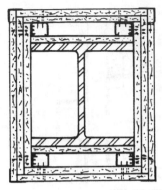

FIGURE 9.11   Three-layer column fire protection.

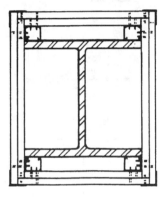

FIGURE 9.12   Two-layer column fire protection.

Beam fire protection

Beam fire protection consists of a double or triple layer of ⅝-inch type-X gypsum board screw-attached to a framework of steel runners and metal angles. These are lightweight, easily and economically installed assemblies that provide 2-hour and 4-hour beam protection (Figure 9.13).

To start the beam protection, install the ceiling runners parallel to and at least ½ inch away from the beam (Figure 9.14). Position the metal angles with the 1⅜-inch leg vertical. Fasten the ceiling runners to the steel floor units with ½-inch type-S-12 pan-head screws spaced 12 inches O.C. Then fabricate the channel brackets from steel runners to allow clearance at the bottom of the beam. For a 3-hour assembly, allow a 1-inch clearance. When the steel runners are used for corner runners, cope or cut away the legs of the runner used for brackets to allow insertion of the corner runner. When metal angles are used for corner runners, slit the channel bracket runner legs and bend the runner to a right angle. Install the channel brackets 24 inches along the length of the beam and fasten to the ceiling runner with ½-inch type-S-12 pan-head screws. The lower corner brackets are installed parallel to the beam. Set the steel corner runner in the coped channel brackets. Apply the metal angles to the outside of the channel brackets with the ⅞-inch leg vertical, and fasten with ½-inch type-S-12 pan-head screws.

For 2-hour assemblies, apply the vertical base-layer type-X gypsum boards and attach to the ceiling and corner runners with 1-inch type-S screws spaced 16 inches O.C. Apply

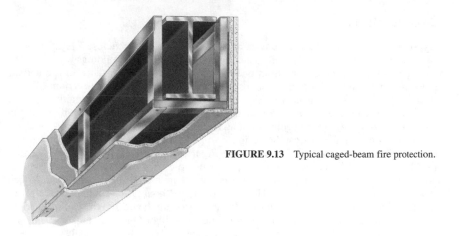

FIGURE 9.13 Typical caged-beam fire protection.

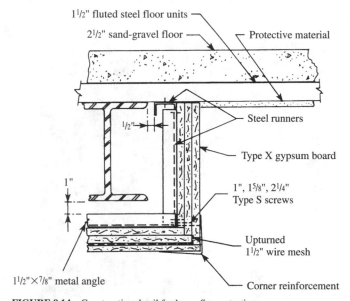

1½" fluted steel floor units

2½" sand-gravel floor

Protective material

Steel runners

½"

Type X gypsum board

1"

1", 1⅝", 2¼"
Type S screws

Upturned
1½" wire mesh

1½"×⅞" metal angle

Corner reinforcement

FIGURE 9.14 Construction detail for beam fire protection.

the middle layer over the base layer and attach to the brackets and runners with 1⅝-inch type-S screws spaced 16 inches O.C. Install a piece of hexagonal mesh over the middle layer at the beam soffit. Extend the mesh 1½ inches up the sides of the beam and hold in place with 1⅝-inch screws used to attach the middle layer. Apply the face layer over the middle layer and wire mesh and fasten to the brackets and runners with 2¼-inch type-S screws spaced 8 inches O.C. Apply all layers so soffit panels support the vertical side boards. Apply corner bead to the bottom outside corners of the face layers and finish with the joint treatment as directed in chapter 10.

Cavity/shaft walls

Gypsum-board cavity shaft-wall systems were developed to enclose elevator shafts (Figures 9.15A and 9.15B), stairwells, and other vertical chases in buildings where it is advantageous to erect these walls from one side only and where resistance to fire and air pressure are required. Shaft-wall systems installed horizontally provide economical construction for fire-resistant duct protection, corridors, and other ceiling and stairway soffits. Shaft-wall systems are also ideal for ceiling office areas in pitched-roof buildings and in modular buildings where the ceiling framing is independent of the floor above.

While cavity shaft walls can be designed to provide up to 4 hours of fire resistance, most installations are for 1- to 2-hour ratings (Figure 9.16). The cavity shaft wall is a non-load-bearing drywall partition system and is made up of two basic components: gypsum board and metal framing. Gypsum board includes 1-inch shaft-liner panels and ⅝-inch type-X gypsum-board face panels. (The most common 2-hour rating contains a face-ply of ½ inch and a second ply of ½-inch or ⅝-inch type-X gypsum board.) In the two most popular shaft wall installations, the metal framing includes either C-H or I-studs with integral tabs that hold the track for runners at the top and bottom, as well as vertically at the partition ends and to the frame openings.

FIGURE 9.15A   Installing gypsum board in an elevator shaft.

FIGURE 9.15B Installing gypsum board in a stairwell. Walls that enclose stairwells, elevators shafts, and other vertical shafts are the most important walls in a building from a life-safety standpoint. Should fire occur, the use of elevators is controlled, and the stairwells provide the only means of egress within the building.

FIGURE 9.16 Typical I-stud cavity shaft wall system.

Framing shaft walls

Locate and lay out the partition floor ceiling lines to assure plumb position. (A laser alignment tool is ideal for layout of these lines.) Then position a top and bottom J-track or runner with the long leg toward the shaft along the ceiling, floor, and vertically at the column and/or the wall where the erection of the shaft wall will begin. Attach with power-driven fasteners, 24 inches O.C. maximum (Figures 9.17A and 9.17B).

Install the first shaft-liner panel by placing the outside vertical edge against the long leg of the vertical track, plumb and attached with type-S 1⅜-inch screws, 24 inches O.C. The metal studs are set within the flanges of the floor and ceiling track; rotate them to hold them in place. Slide the stud tabs snugly over the edge of the shaft liner previously installed. Install the next shaft-liner panel between the tabs of the C-H or I-metal studs. Continue in this manner until the end of the partition run. Occasionally, check the spacing of the wall studs to maintain 24-inch modules.

At the end of the run (Figure 9.18), cut the vertical J-track or runner at least 2 inches short of the partition height. Cut the shaft liner ¼ inch less than the remaining width of the partition and 2 inches short of the full height. Lay a piece of shaft liner 2 inches wide by the length of the opening in the floor track as support for the last shaft-liner panel. Fit the cut edge of the shaft liner into the vertical track and, holding the shaft liner and the track together, slide the paper-bound edge of the shaft liner into the C-H or I-stud. Align the last panel and fasten the vertical track with appropriate fasteners 24 inches O.C. maximum. Fasten the shaft liner to the vertical track with 1⅜-inch type-S or S-12 screws, 24 inches O.C.

Note: Where the shaft wall exceeds 14 feet in height, locate the shaft liner end joints within the upper- and lower-third points of the wall. Stagger the joints from the top to the bottom in adjacent panels by a minimum of 24 inches to avoid a continuous horizontal joint. Shaft-liner panels should be of sufficient length to engage a minimum of 2 C-H or I-stud tabs along each edge.

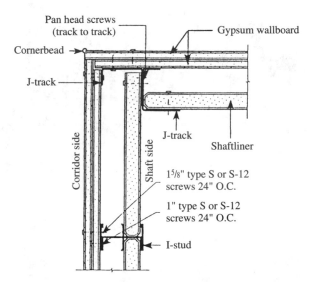

Note: Type S screws for .020" studs
S-12 screws for .0329" and .040" studs

FIGURE 9.17A   Shaft-wall construction, outside corner.

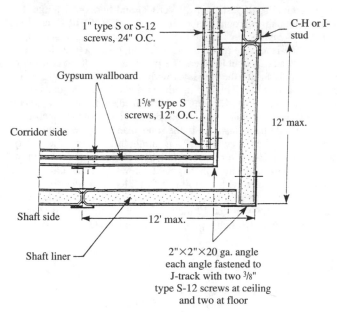

FIGURE 9.17B   Shaft-wall construction, inside corner.

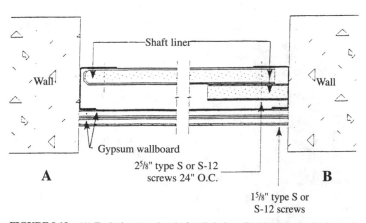

FIGURE 9.18   (A) Typical start and end of wall design. (B) Alternate detail of end of wall.

Gypsum wallboard

In a 2-layer 2-hour-rated shaft wall, apply the first layer of ½-inch type-X board horizontally to the face of the metal C-H or I-stud with screws spaced 24 inches O.C. Apply the second layer vertically with screws spaced 12 inches O.C. (Use 1-inch type-S screws on the first layer and 1⅝-inch type-S screws on the second layer for 25-gauge nominal studs. Use 1-inch type-S-12 screws on the first layer and 1⅝-inch type-S-12 screws on the second layer for 20-gauge nominal studs.) Stagger all vertical and horizontal joints. For proper joint treatment, maintain uniform room temperature between 50°F (10°C) and 70°F (21°C) during cold weather. Treat the joints of the face layer with tape and joint compound.

For a 3-hour fire-resistance rating for a shaft wall, install a triple layer of ½-inch type-X gypsum board instead of a double layer. The panels are installed vertically on the corridor side of the metal studs. Fasten the base layer with 1-inch type-S screws 24 inches O.C. along the vertical edges and in the field. The middle is applied with the joints staggered with 1⅝-inch type-S screws 24 inches O.C. along the vertical edges and in the field. The face layer is applied vertically with the joints staggered and fastened with 2¼-inch type-S screws 16 inches O.C. The shaft liner is installed in the same manner as the double-ply application.

For horizontal installations with a 2-hour rating, three layers of ½-inch type-X gypsum panels are installed on H- and/or I-studs. The base layer is installed with the edges parallel to the studs and attached with 1-inch type-G screws 24 inches O.C. The middle layer is applied in the same manner, with the joints offset 2 feet and attached with 1⅝-inch type-S screws 24 inches O.C. The face layer is installed perpendicular to the studs and attached with 2¼-inch type-S screws spaced 12 inches O.C. Place the face layer end joints between the studs and secure with 1½-inch type-G screws 8 inches O.C.

Caulking

Caulk the cavity shaft wall with acoustical sealant wherever the wall is enclosing shafts where positive or negative air pressure exists (Figure 9.19). Caulk the perimeter of the wall and at any other place where voids create the possibility of moving air causing dust accumulation, noise, or smoke leakage. Caulking should be done in compliance with details specified by the architect/designer.

FIGURE 9.19   Placement of caulking at bottom of cavity shaft wall.

Framing for openings

Frame the elevator doors (Figures 9.20A and 9.20B), borrowed lights, and duct openings (Figure 9.21) with J-track or runner. Use adequate structural support for openings more than 48 inches wide. For openings up to 48 inches wide, use vertical J-track or runner on either side of the openings. For heads and sills of the openings, place the J-track horizontally across the

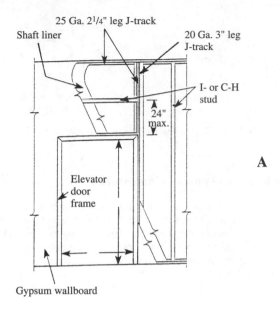

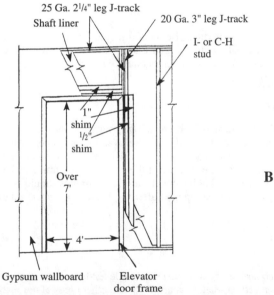

FIGURE 9.20 (A) Door framing for a 7-foot elevator door, (B) Door framing for a door that is more than 7 feet high.

openings. Cut the J-track about 12 inches longer than the openings. Then cut the flanges and fold back to rest over the vertical J-track and fasten the webs or flanges with two ⅜-inch type-S or ½-inch type-S-12 pan-head screws per connection. When nesting J-track to J-track, cut off the short flange of the horizontal J-track so it will fit over the vertical J-track or runner.

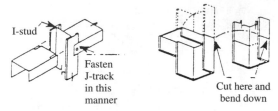

FIGURE 9.21   Typical dual opening recommended for framing.

Call and outlet boxes and position indicators

Protect all call and outlet boxes, position indicators, and fireman's switches (Figure 9.22). Metallic outlet boxes should be permitted to be installed in wood- and steel-stud walls or partitions having gypsum-board facings and classified as 2 hours. The surface area of individual boxes should not exceed 16 square inches. The aggregate surface area of the boxes should not exceed 100 square inches in any 100 square feet. Boxes located on opposite sides of the wall or partitions should be separated by a minimum horizontal distance of 24 inches. Approved nonmetallic outlet boxes should be permitted as allowed by the local codes.

Chases

When possible, locate all vertical rise, conduit, stair hangers, etc. within the wall cavity (Figure 9.23). If the cavity in the 2½-inch stud wall is not of sufficient width, the 4- and 6-inch studs can be used for chases, or erect chase walls.

Elevator doors

Elevator door frames must be braced and supported independently of the shaft wall. However, the shaft wall must be tied into the elevator door frames by being attached to the jamb anchor clips with pan-head screws. The 3-inch leg of the nominal 20-gauge J-track or runner should be used at the juncture of the elevator door frame and the metal wall stud system (Figures 9.24A and 9.24B). All elevator door frames should be spot grouted at the jamb anchor clips with joint compound after the J-track or runner and gypsum shaft liner are in place.

Vent shaft

Type-X gypsum board can be designed to provide a 2-hour fire-rated vent shaft enclosure. It can be used as a vertical shaft in apartments and other types of multistory buildings. The assembly is particularly suited for relatively small and widely separated mechanical, service, and ventilator shafts. Gypsum-board shaft walls are preferred where service and mechanical lines and equipment are consolidated within the building core. The shaft is composed of 1-inch shaft-wall liner, two layers of type-X gypsum, and metal framing to support it.

To support the vent shaft, install 1⅜-×-1⅞-inch 22-gauge galvanized-steel angle runners on the floor and sidewalls by fastening through their short legs (Figure 9.25). Steel angles

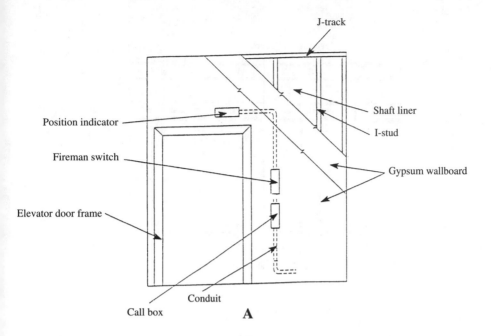

J-track

Position indicator

Shaft liner

I-stud

Fireman switch

Gypsum wallboard

Elevator door frame

Conduit

Call box

A

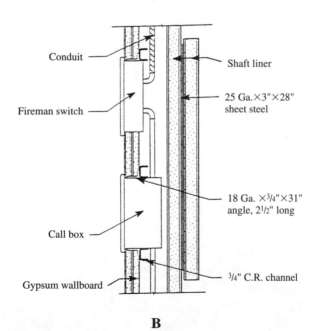

Conduit

Shaft liner

25 Ga.×3"×28" sheet steel

Fireman switch

18 Ga. ×3/4"×31" angle, 2½" long

Call box

3/4" C.R. channel

Gypsum wallboard

B

FIGURE 9.22   Typical shaft-wall elevator electrical-control layout.

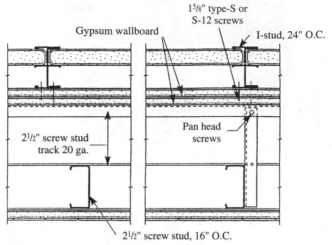

FIGURE 9.23   Details of a typical chase wall.

can also be used as ceiling runners. Install the side angle runners 30 inches long and centered for attachment of the horizontal bracing. Then install 1⅜-×-⅞-inch 22-gauge galvanized steel angles horizontally at the quarter-points between the floor and ceiling, spaced a maximum of 5 feet O.C. Position the long leg vertically for the board attachment and fasten to the sidewall angles with 1-inch type-S screws.

Install the ⅝-inch type-X gypsum board vertically on the shaft side and fasten to the angles and runners with 1-inch type-S screws 16 inches O.C. (Figure 9.26). Apply joint com-

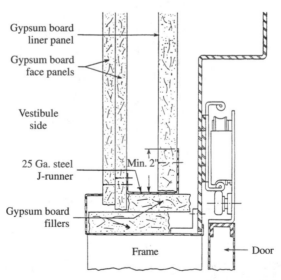

FIGURE 9.24A   Passenger elevator door-frame header and jambs.

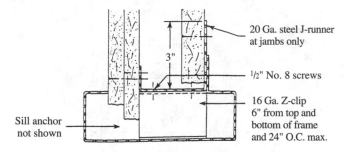

20 Ga. steel J-runner
at jambs only

3"

$^1/2$" No. 8 screws

16 Ga. Z-clip
6" from top and
bottom of frame
and 24" O.C. max.

Sill anchor
not shown

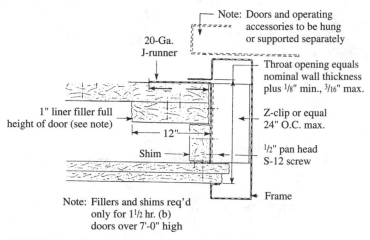

Note: Doors and operating
accessories to be hung
or supported separately

20-Ga.
J-runner

Throat opening equals
nominal wall thickness
plus $^1/8$" min., $^3/16$" max.

1" liner filler full
height of door (see note)

Z-clip or equal
24" O.C. max.

12"

$^1/2$" pan head
S-12 screw

Shim

Frame

Note: Fillers and shims req'd
only for 1$^1/2$ hr. (b)
doors over 7'-0" high

FIGURE 9.24B   More passenger elevator door-frame header and jambs.

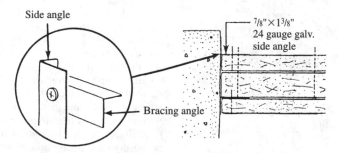

Side angle

$^7/8$" × 1$^3/8$"
24 gauge galv.
side angle

Bracing angle

FIGURE 9.25   Typical vent's bracing angle attachment.

pound and tape on the back side of the liner and strip or sheet-laminate to the shaft-side board. Install the second set of floor and sidewall angle runners (and ceiling angles, if required) with the long legs against the liner. Attach the liner to the runners and angles with 2¼-inch type-S screws 12 inches O.C. and at least 6 inches away from liner edges. Laminate the floor side face board to the liners with joint compound and install vertically.

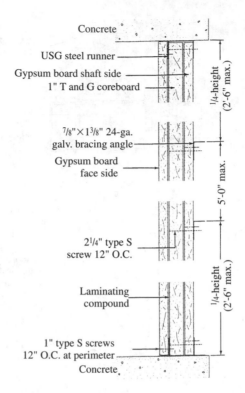

Concrete

USG steel runner

Gypsum board shaft side

1" T and G coreboard

¹/₄-height
(2'-6" max.)

⁷/₈" × 1³/₈" 24-ga.
galv. bracing angle

Gypsum board
face side

5'-0" max.

2¹/₄" type S
screw 12" O.C.

Laminating
compound

¹/₄-height
(2'-6" max.)

1" type S screws
12" O.C. at perimeter

Concrete

FIGURE 9.26   Typical vent-shaft sections.

FIGURE 9.27   Protect duct work with type-X
gypsum board.

The joints should be offset 12 inches from one layer to the next, and moderate pressure should be applied to ensure good adhesive bond. Fasten to the liner with 1½-inch type-G screws. Drive the screws approximately 24 inches from the ends of the board and 36 inches O.C. along lines from the vertical edges. Temporary bracing can be used instead of screws to maintain the bond until the adhesive is hard and dry. Caulk the perimeter with acoustical sealant to prevent air infiltration. Complete the assembly with the appropriate drywall finish application. Ducts can be protected with type-X gypsum board as shown in Figure 9.27.

AREA SEPARATION WALLS

Figure 9.28 illustrates in dramatic fashion the value of breakaway-area gypsum separation walls. The fire destroyed one unit of the townhouse, but the gypsum area-separation

FIGURE 9.28   The fire protection of the gypsum board area separation wall system is demonstrated in dramatic fashion by the results of this actual townhouse fire, in which the 2-hour fire-rated assembly performed as expected in protecting the adjacent properties. The break-away feature allowed collapse of the fire-side structural framing without pulling down the entire wall.

wall protected the two adjacent properties. In addition to providing 2-hour fire protection, area separation walls also are good sound barriers between units in multifamily wood-frame buildings. Some code bodies identify this type of wall by other names, such as fire wall or barrier, lot line wall, or party wall. These systems can be used in buildings up to four stories high, and they offer performance values of up to 3-hour fire resistance and STC 57 (Figure 9.29).

There are two basic area-separation wall systems: solid type and cavity type. Each system can be erected quickly by carpenters and/or drywall tradespeople. Both systems are continuous, vertical, nonload-bearing wall assemblies of gypsum panels attached to steel framing. They extend from the foundation up to or through the roof and act as barriers to fire and sound transmission. These walls are erected one floor at a time, beginning at the foundation and continuing up to or through the roof. At intermediate floors, metal floor/ceiling track should be installed back-to-back to secure the top of the lower section of the partition and the bottom of the next section being installed.

At intermediate floors and other specified locations, the walls are attached to adjacent framing on each side with aluminum clips that soften when exposed to fire (Figure 9.30). These so-called "breakaway" clips are wide, with legs either 1-×-2 inches, 1-×-2½ inches, or 2-×-2 inches. The clips are attached to the wood framing at each vertical steel-framing-stud/wood-framing-intersection using one ⅜-inch type-S pan-head screw to secure it into the steel and one 8d nail or one 1¼-inch type-W drywall screw to secure it into the wood framing. The recommended location of these clips is on the lower side of the structural wood framing. In that location, the clip provides the greatest assurance that the area separation wall will remain in place and structurally sound should one of the adjacent structures fail.

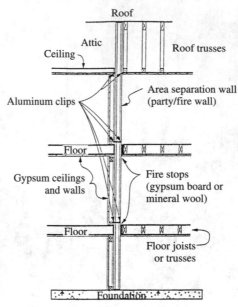

FIGURE 9.29   Typical gypsum-board area separation of wall construction.

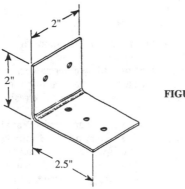

FIGURE 9.30   Typical breakaway aluminum clip.

Solid separation wall

This system is designed for use between load-bearing walls. While the total assembly is thicker than cavity walls, solid walls are no thicker than masonry barriers when used in the same type of construction.

Foundation installation

Position the 2-inch-wide steel C-runner at the floor and securely attach to the foundation with power-driven fasteners at both ends and spaced 24 inches O.C. (Figure 9.31). Space

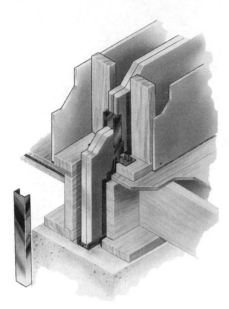

FIGURE 9.31   Foundation of a solid separation wall.

adjacent runner sections ¼ inch apart. When specified, caulk runner at the foundation with a minimum ¼-inch bead of acoustical sealant.

First-floor installation

Install the panels and H-studs cut to length, that is, more than floor-to-floor height. Install two thicknesses of 1-inch liner panels vertically in the C-runner with the long edges in the H-stud. Erect the H-studs and double-thickness liner panels alternately until the wall is completed. Cap the ends of the run with the vertical C-runner and fasten to the horizontal C-runner flange with ⅜-inch type-S screws.

Intermediate-floor installation

Cap the top of the panels and studs with back-to-back C-runners, screw-attached together with double 3.8-inch type-S screws at the ends and spaced 24 inches O.C. Fasten the studs to the runner flange on alternate sides with ⅜-inch screws. Secure the studs to the framing with aluminum angle breakaway clips, screw-attached to both sides of each stud and framing (Figure 9.32). Except at the foundation, install fire blocking between the joists and the fire barrier.

Roof installation

Continue erecting the studs and panels for succeeding stories as previously described. At the roof, cap the panels with a C-runner and fasten to the studs with ⅜-inch screws (Figure 9.33). Fasten the studs to the framing with aluminum breakaway clips.

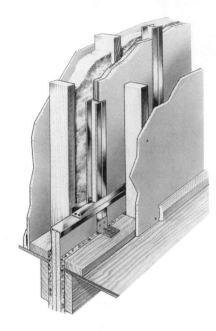

FIGURE 9.32 Intermediate floor of a solid separation wall.

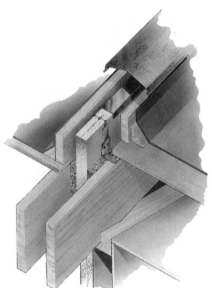

FIGURE 9.33 Roof of a solid separation wall.

To assure a fire-rating assembly without the need for battens, a minimum ¾-inch air space should be maintained between the H-stud assembly and any adjacent framing members. When a ¾-inch air space cannot be maintained, the H-stud and H-stud tracks are covered by screw-attached 6-inch-wide battens fabricated from ½-inch type-X gypsum wallboard, or ½-inch type-X gypsum wallboard panels can be fastened to the H-studs and joints covered with tape and joint compound to provide a finished wall. Mineral wool or glass fiber can be installed in adjacent cavity shaft walls to provide higher STC ratings.

Cavity separation walls

Cavity separation walls are intended for use in buildings where load-bearing walls are not used at the line of separation between units. For that reason they are the thinnest of all fire walls. For instance, a typical 3-hour area separation wall is a mere 4⅞ inches thick, and the 2-hour version is only 3½ inches thick.

Foundation installation

Position the 2½-inch steel C-runner at the floor and attach to the foundation with power-driven fasteners at both ends and spaced 24 inches O.C. (Figure 9.34). Caulk the runner at the floor with a minimum ¼-inch bead of acoustical sealant.

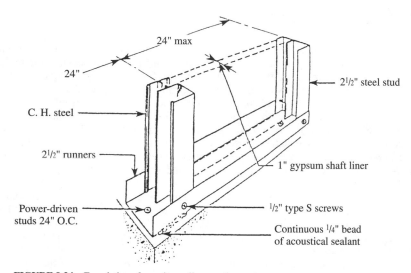

FIGURE 9.34   Foundation of a cavity-wall separation system.

First-floor installation

The 1-inch shaft-liner panels and steel studs are cut to convenient length, but more than floor-to-floor height (Figure 9.35). Erect the liner panels vertically in the C-runner with the long edges in the groove of the C-H stud. Install the C-H studs between the panels and cap the ends of the run with E-stud or C-runner. Fasten the studs to the bottom of the C-runner on alternate sides with ⅜-inch type-S screws.

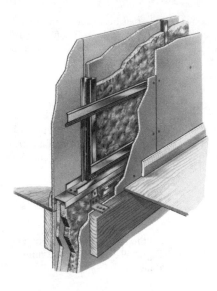

FIGURE 9.35 Intermediate floor of a cavity-wall separation system.

SOUND CONTROL ASSEMBLIES

Structural assemblies, as we have seen, are fire rated for the safety of the building's occupants. Assemblies are also sound rated for the comfort and privacy of occupants in multifamily dwellings, as well as in office buildings. As the drywall contractor, it is important to understand sound control. Noise is unwanted sound. Music generated by one person's stereo might be very pleasing to his/her ear, but it might also be very disturbing to his/her neighbor. The architects or designers of any building take the first step in sound control by following the principles of good room arrangement in the floor plan. They also take the second step by specifying structural systems and finish materials that meet FRR, STC, and IIC requirements. Builders or contractors take the next step by rigidly following plans and specifications. Finally, the drywall contractor completes the task by installing the gypsum board properly.

Sound is produced by a vibrating object. Sound travels in all directions from the source as a pressure wave in the air, the same way ripples travel from a pebble in a lake. The greater the intensity of the vibration—also called the amplitude, pressure, or magnitude—the louder the sound. Sound/noise also has frequency, or pitch, as in a high-pitched squeal or a low-pitched rumble.

Sound control is the art of putting something between a person's ears and the source of the sound to reduce its intensity, or doing something to reduce the sound at its source. Or, if the ears and the sound source are in the same room, treating the room to reduce the amount of sound bouncing off the walls, floor, and ceiling. Sound control is not soundproofing. If something is waterproof, no water can get into it. Similarly, if a room or a structure is soundproof, absolutely no unwanted sound can penetrate into it or escape from it. That degree of sound isolation is neither practical nor affordable for everyday living spaces. In fact, it is not even desirable, for it cuts off all sense of contact with the outside world.

There are three sources of unwanted noise in any given area:

• Noise from outside sources (traffic, children at play, neighbors, barking dogs, aircraft, and the like).

- Noise originating in another part of the building and transmitted through the walls, floor, and ceiling.
- Noise generated inside the same area.

Most sound travels both through the air and through solid objects. For example, the sound of one's voice is airborne sound until it strikes a wall and becomes structure-borne. The wall vibrates and reradiates the sound as airborne sound in an adjacent room or area, but at a lower level because some of the sound intensity has been dissipated inside the wall. At each physical barrier, the cycle repeats until the sound dissipates completely.

There are two types of sound transmission:

- Airborne sound, as the name implies, is sound carried through the air. Conversation, electronic output of television, hi-fi, stereo and radio sets, and the hum of motors are typical examples. As mentioned earlier, each type of construction has a rating, called a sound transmission class (STC), which is a measure of the reduction of the transmission of airborne sound. The higher the rating, the more soundproof that construction is.
- Structure-borne sound, also called *impact sound*, is sound carried by the building's structure. The thud of shoes being dropped, the vibration of some kitchen and laundry appliances, and the noise of plumbing are examples. When measured, the rating is called an *impact insulation class* (IIC).

Airborne sound

Airborne noise can travel over, under, or around walls, through windows and doors adjacent to them, through air ducts, and through floors and crawl spaces below. These flanking paths must be correctly treated to reduce the transmission of sound. Hairline cracks and small holes will increase the transmission of sound.

Sealant application

If a drywall partition is to effectively reduce the transmission of sound, it must be airtight at all points. The perimeter must be sealed with an acoustical sealant (a caulking material that remains resilient and will not shrink or crack).

To properly seal a partition perimeter, cut the gypsum board for a loose fit around the partition perimeter (Figure 9.36). Leave a groove no more than ⅛ inch wide. Apply a ¼-inch round bead of sealant to each side of the runners (Figure 9.37), including those used at the partition intersections with dissimilar wall construction. Immediately install the boards, squeezing the sealant into firm contact with the adjacent surfaces. Fasten the boards in the normal manner. Gypsum panels can have joint treatment applied in a normal manner over sealed joints. Or panels can be finished with base or trim as desired.

To be effective, the sealant must be properly placed; placement is as important as the amount used. The following are some of the important locations where acoustical sealant should be placed:

- Control joints. Apply sealant behind the control joint to reduce the path for sound transmission through the joint (Figure 9.38).
- Partition intersections. Seal the intersections with sound-isolating partitions that are extended to reduce sound flanking paths (Figure 9.39).

FIGURE 9.36   Applying acoustic sealant.

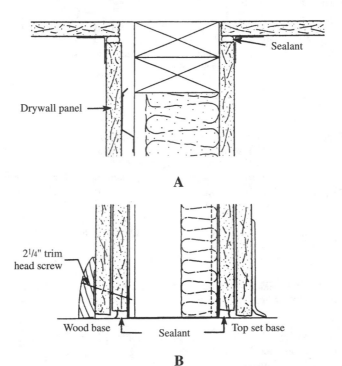

FIGURE 9.37   Use of acoustical sealant.

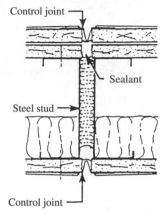

FIGURE 9.38 Use of acoustical sealant on a partition control joint.

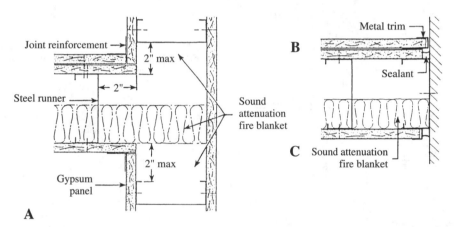

FIGURE 9.39 Use acoustical sealant at (A) the sound-isolating partition intersection, (B) partition-wall intersection, and (C) partition control joint.

- Openings. Apply sealant around all cutouts such as for electrical boxes, plumbing, medicine cabinets, heating ducts, and cold-air returns to seal the opening. Caulk the sides and backs of electrical boxes to seal them (Figure 9.40). Do not install any fixtures back-to-back.
- Door frames. Apply a bead of sealant in the door frame just before inserting the face panel (Figure 9.41).

Perimeter relief, in addition to reducing the likelihood of sound flanking around related construction, should also be provided for gypsum construction surfaces where:

- The partition or furring abuts a structural element (except the floor), dissimilar walls, or ceiling materials.
- The ceiling abuts a structural element, dissimilar partition, or other vertical penetration.
- Ceilings with dimensions exceeding 30 feet in either direction.
- At columns (Figure 9.42).

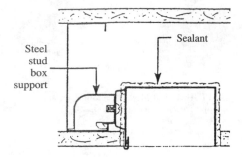

Steel
stud
box
support

Sealant

FIGURE 9.40   Use of outlet sealant around an outlet box.

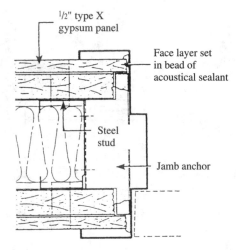

¹/₂" type X
gypsum panel

Face layer set
in bead of
acoustical sealant

Steel
stud

Jamb anchor

FIGURE 9.41   Standard door-frame detail for sealant application.

FIGURE 9.42   Perimeter relief at columns.

Isolation is important to reduce potential joint problems in partitions, ceilings, and beam and column furring (Figure 9.42). Generally, the following procedures for isolating surfaces will remedy any problems:

- Gypsum-board edge treatment. Where boards intersect dissimilar materials or structural elements, appropriate trim should be applied to the face layer perimeter, and acoustical sealant should be applied to close the gap (Figure 9.43). Some acoustical vinyl trim can be used without sealant or joint treatment.
- Partition structural ceiling. Attach the steel runner to the structural ceiling to position the partition. Cut the steel stud ⅜ inch less than floor-to-ceiling height. Attach the gypsum to the stud at least 1½ inches down from the ceiling (Figure 9.44). Allow ⅜-inch minimum clearance atop the gypsum boards; finish as required.
- Partition-exterior wall or column. Attach the steel stud to the exterior wall or column to position the partition. Attach the gypsum board only to the second steel stud erected vertically at a maximum of 6 inches from the wall. Allow at least ¾-inch clearance between the partition panel and the wall (Figure 9.45). Caulk as required with acoustical sealant.

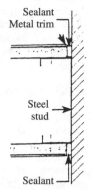

FIGURE 9.43 Details of wall intersection.

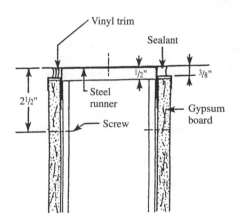

FIGURE 9.44 Details of partition structural ceiling intersection.

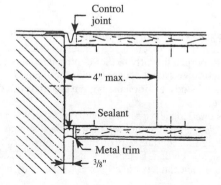

FIGURE 9.45 Details of partition exterior wall or column intersection.

Fixture location

The attachment of fixtures to sound-barrier partitions might impair the sound-control characteristics. Only lightweight fixtures should be attached to resilient wall surfaces constructed with resilient channel unless special framing is provided. Refrain from attaching fixtures to party walls that will provide a direct flow path for sound. Gypsum boards used in the ceiling are not designed to support light fixtures, troffers, air vents, or other equipment. Separate supports must be provided.

Resilient furring channels

One of the ways the drywall contractor can achieve sound-isolation control is by the installation of resilient furring. Whether it is installed by the framing group or the drywall installers, the latter must be very familiar with its installation.

Resilient furring channels are fabricated with galvanized steel with expanded metal legs that provide resiliency to reduce sound transmission through wood-framed wall and ceiling assemblies (Figure 9.46). The steel channels float the gypsum board away from the studs and joists, providing a spring action that isolates the gypsum board from the framing. In other words, these channels act as shock absorbers by reducing the passage of sound through the wall or ceiling, thereby increasing the STC rating. In addition, this spring action also tends to level the panel surface when installed over uneven framing.

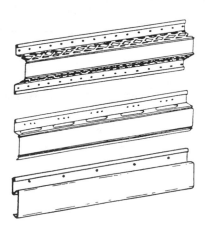

FIGURE 9.46 Typical resilient furring channels.

As mentioned in chapter 2, resilient channels have punched holes, spaced 1 inch O.C. in the leg flanges to facilitate fastening to framing members spaced either 16 or 24 inches O.C. The 12-foot-long channels are applied perpendicularly to the framing members and spaced not more than 24 inches O.C. Attach the resilient channels with the flange down and at right angles (perpendicular) to the metal studs. Position the bottom channel with the attachment flange up for ease of attachment.

Resilient furring channels should be fastened to the wood studs with one type-W screw at each stud in the flange (Figure 9.47). A ½-×-3-inch shim strip of wallboard should be nailed or screwed to the base plate and ceiling line continuously on the resilient side of the partition for attaching the panels at the base and ceiling. Extend the channels into all corners and attach to the corner framing. Splice the channels directly over the studs by nest-

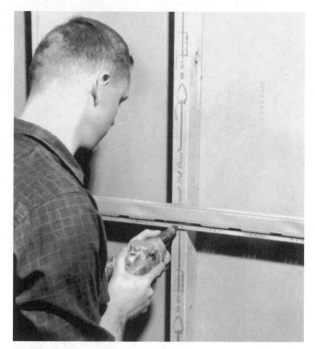

FIGURE 9.47   Installing resilient furring channel on wood studs.

ing (not butting) the channels and driving the fastener through both flanges into the support. Where cabinets are to be installed, attach channels to studs directly behind the cabinet-hanger brackets. When distance between hangers exceeds 24 inches O.C., install additional channel at the midpoint between the hangers.

For wood ceiling-beam installations, the resilient furring channels should be installed perpendicularly to the joists spaced 24 inches O.C. and a maximum of 6 inches from the ceiling-wall line with type-W screws through alternate flanges into the joists. Channel ends can fall on or between the joists but must be fastened to prevent any sliding movement, which could create squeaking noises. When the channel ends fall between the joists, overlap approximately 1½ inches and screw-attach through both legs into a wood block held above the channels, or overlap approximately 6 inches and fasten both channels near the ends with ⅜-inch type-S pan-head screws (Figure 9.48). For a fire-rated double-ply drywall assembly, apply the channels over the base layer and attach with 1⅞-inch type-S screws driven through the channel flange and the base layer into the joists. Fasten the channels to the joists at each intersection. Do not use nails to attach the channels to the joists in either single- or double-layer assemblies.

When applying the drywall panels, attach them to the resilient channels with type-S screws 12 inches O.C. Attach to the framing through the filler strips with drywall screws 12 inches O.C. that penetrate the framing by at least ⅝ inch.

In construction of a cavity area-separation wall, the resilient furring channels can be attached to the flanges of the cavity framing, and the drywall panels are attached to it to provide the higher STC rating.

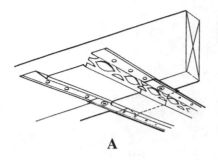

A

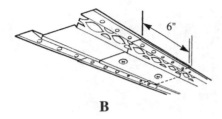

6"

FIGURE 9.48 Splicing resilient furring channels.
(A) Splice on joists. (B) Splice between joists.
(C) Alternate for splicing between joists.

B

1" × 4"
wood block

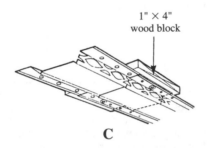

C

Resilient channels on steel frames

When applying resilient channels to steel framing, attach the steel runners on the floor and ceiling to structural elements with suitable fasteners located 2 inches from each end and spaced 24 inches O.C. Position studs vertically with the open side facing in the same direction, engaging floor and ceiling runners, and spaced 24 inches O.C. Anchor the studs to the floor and ceiling runners on the resilient side of the partition. Fasten the studs to the runner flange with metal lock fasteners or ⅜-inch type-S pan-head screws.

Position the resilient channel at right angles to the steel studs, spaced 24 inches O.C., and attach to the stud flanges with ⅜-inch type-S pan-head screws driven through the holes in the channel mounting flange. Install the channels with the mounting flange down, except at the floor, to accommodate the attachment. Locate the channels 2 inches from the floor and within 6 inches of the ceiling. Splice the channel by nesting directly over the stud, and screw-attach through both flanges. Reinforce with screws located at both ends of the splice.

Separate framing

Walls transmit sound vibrations from one face to another through the studs; ceilings and floors transmit sound to one another by vibrations through the joists. Eliminate framing members common to both sides, and the path has been broken. In walls, stagger the studs, or build two walls with a gap in the center, as illustrated in Figure 9.49. A staggered metal-stud arrangement is shown in Figure 9.50.

If a second wall is built, construct it on one side, close to but not touching the existing wall. It helps to add insulation batts between the new studs. (These batts could touch the existing wall.) Also, install a layer of sound-deadening board beneath the new wall's gypsum board.

Heavy materials reduce sound better than light materials. For example, placing sound-deadening board under the gypsum board, applying a second layer of gypsum board, or even adding wood or hardboard paneling to a wall provides increased sound-transmission loss.

Sound-deadening backer board comes in 4-×-8-foot sheets that can be nailed, screwed, or adhesively applied to studs or joists. There are two kinds of sound-deadening board. One is made of organic fibers, and the other is a form of gypsum board. Ordinary gypsum board is applied over the sound-deadening board to provide a finished surface. It must be attached to the sound-deadening underlayer only with adhesive so there is no hard connection to the studs or joists.

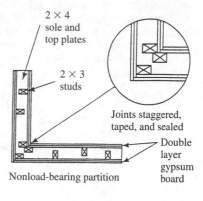

Nonload-bearing partition

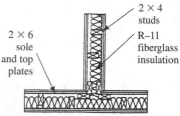

Load-bearing partition

FIGURE 9.49 Split-wall construction. (Insulation has been omitted from the nonload-bearing partition for clarity.)

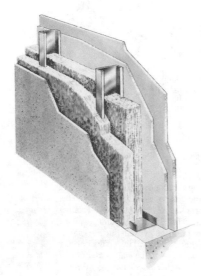

FIGURE 9.50 A staggered metal-stud arrangement.

Insulation blanket applications

Many partition systems have been developed to meet the demand for increased privacy between units in residential and commercial construction (Figure 9.51). Designed for wood-stud, steel-stud, or laminated gypsum-board construction, these assemblies offer highly efficient sound-control properties, yet they are more economical than other partitions offering equal sound isolation. These improved sound-isolation properties and ratings are obtained by using sound-attenuation fire-insulation blankets and decoupling the partition faces. (Decoupling is achieved with resilient application or with double rows of studs on separate plates.)

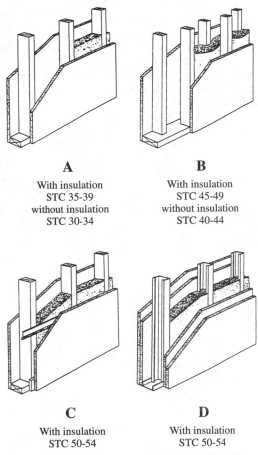

A

With insulation
STC 35-39
without insulation
STC 30-34

B

With insulation
STC 45-49
without insulation
STC 40-44

C

With insulation
STC 50-54

D

With insulation
STC 50-54

FIGURE 9.51   Sound ratings with insulation. (A) Adding a sound absorbing insulation increases the STC four points in the wall. (B) Staggered studs provide partially separated framing for wall surfaces and increase STC about eight points from the wall in A. (C) Resilient mounting of gypsum surfaces raises STC about 12 points above that of the wall in A. (D) Two-ply construction increases the weight of the wall surfaces and helps provide the wall with a higher obtainable sound resistance of STC 50 to 54.

Installation of blankets

In a ceiling, water-based texturing materials should be completely dry before the insulation and vapor retarder are installed. (Under most conditions, drying takes several days.) Then install the blankets to completely fill the height of the stud cavity and with the vapor retarder facing inside or outside of the wall according to job specifications. If necessary to tightly fill the height, cut the stock-length blankets with a serrated knife for insertion into the void. Tightly butt the ends and sides of the blankets within a cavity. Cut small pieces of the blankets for narrow stud spaces next to door openings or at partition intersections. Fit the blankets carefully behind electrical outlets, bracing, fixture attachments, medicine cabinets, etc. In the ceiling, insulation should be carefully fitted around lighting fixtures. Covering the fixtures with insulation causes heat to build up, which could possibly result in a fire.

Insulating blanket to wood studs

Using a power-driven or hand stapling gun, attach the paper flanges to the sides of the studs and at the plates with staples having a ½-inch leg and spaced 6 inches O.C. Do not attach the blanket flanges to stud faces to achieve a continuous vapor retarder. This attachment prevents tight contact between the board and framing and can result in loose boards and fastener defects; it also prevents the adhesive attachment of the board. Where a vapor retarder is required, install type-X foil-backed gypsum board.

Attaching insulating blankets to gypsum board

In steel-stud and laminated gypsum-board partitions, attach only 1-inch-thick blankets to the back side of the boards using staples applied with a pistol-type hand stapler. Apply thicker blankets by friction-fitting between the studs.

Sound-attenuating fire blankets

Install these blankets in the stud cavities of sound-rated partitions. Friction-fit securely between the studs (Figure 9.52). Butt the ends of the blankets closely together and fill all voids. To fit the blankets in the cavity, it is sometimes necessary to make a slit cut down the center and partially through the blanket (Figure 9.53). This allows the blanket to flex or bow in the center, easing the pressure against the studs and transferring it to the face panel, thereby dampening sound vibrations more effectively. The panels are screw-attached.

Aluminum-foil-faced blankets are similar to paper-enclosed regular blankets but with highly reflective aluminum foil laminated to the vapor retarder side to protect against condensation. A minimum adjoining air space of ½ inch in the sidewalls and 1 inch in the ceilings is required to obtain insulating value from the foil reflectivity. It is used in ceilings, walls, and floors with air space; it is most effective with air conditioning and in areas of extreme summer temperatures.

FIGURE 9.52   Installing sound insulation between metal studs.

FIGURE 9.53   If insulation is wider than the space between the studs, a slit-field cut down the center and partially through the blanket will allow it to flex or bow in the center and thus fit.

CHAPTER 10
JOINT TREATMENT AND FINISHING GYPSUM DRYWALL

Robert Scharff
Walls & Ceilings Magazine

After the gypsum drywall board is installed and secured with the proper fasteners, it is necessary to reinforce and conceal the joints, fasteners, and corner beads. Joint compound and reinforcing tape described in chapter 2 and later in this chapter are used for the purpose of achieving the appearance of a monolithic surface.

LEVELS OF GYPSUM-BOARD FINISH

The four major trade associations are the Association of Wall and Ceiling Industries (AWCI), International Ceiling & Interior Systems Construction Association (CISCA), Gypsum Association (GA), and Painting and Decorating Contractors of America (PDCA). They have developed the levels of drywall board finish concerned with the manufacture, erection, finish, and decoration of gypsum-board wall and ceiling systems. They have also developed five levels of specific board finishes. The recommended level of finish of gypsum-board wall and ceiling surfaces varies with the final decoration to be applied and can also be dependent on their location in a structure and the type of illumination striking the surface. Before taking a look at these various levels, the following definitions should be understood:

Accessories. Metal or plastic beads, trim, or molding used to protect or conceal corners, edges, or abutments of the gypsum-board construction.

Critical lighting. Strong sidelighting from windows or surface-mounted light fixtures.

Joint photographing. The shadowing of the finished joint areas through the surface decoration.

Primer/sealer. A paint material formulated to fill the pores and equalize the suction difference between gypsum-board surface paper and the compound used on finished joints, angles, fastener heads, and accessories, and over skim coatings.

Skim coat. A thin coat of joint compound over the entire surface to fill imperfections in the joint work, smooth the paper texture, and provide a uniform surface for decorating.

Spotting. To cover fastener heads with joint compound.

Texture. A decorative treatment of gypsum-board surfaces.

Texturing. Regular or irregular patterns typically produced by applying a mixture of joint compound and water (or proprietary texture materials including latex base texture paint) to a gypsum-board surface previously coated with primer/sealer.

The following levels of finish have been established as a guide for specific final decoration (Figure 10.1).

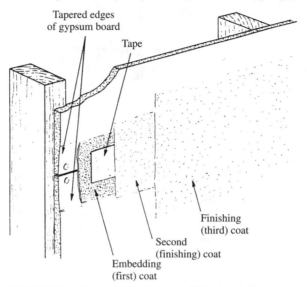

FIGURE 10.1   The levels of gypsum board finish.

Level 0

No taping, finishing, or accessories required. This level of finish is useful in temporary construction or whenever the final decoration has not been determined.

Level 1

All joints and interior angles should have tape embedded in joint compound. The surface should be free of excess joint compound. Tool marks and ridges are acceptable. This level is frequently specified in plenum areas above ceilings, in attics, in areas where the assembly would generally be concealed, or in building service corridors and other areas not normally open to public view. Accessories are optional at the specifier's discretion in corridors and other areas with pedestrian traffic. Some degree of sound and smoke control is provided; in some geographic areas, this level is referred to as "firetaping." Where a fire-resistance rating is required for the gypsum-board assembly, details of construction should be in accordance with reports of fire tests of assemblies that have met the fire-rating requirements.

Level 2

All joints and interior angles should have tape embedded in joint compound, plus a separate coat of joint compound applied over all joints, angles, fastener heads, and accessories.

The surface must be free of excess joint compound. Tool marks and ridges are acceptable. This level is specified where water-resistant gypsum backing board is used as a substrate for tile; it might be specified in garages, warehouse storage, or other similar areas where surface appearance is not of primary concern.

Level 3

All joints and interior angle should have tape embedded in joint compound, plus two separate coats of joint compound applied over all joints, angles, fastener heads, and accessories. All joint compound must be smooth and free of tool marks and ridges. It is recommended that the prepared surface be coated with a primer/sealer prior to the application of final finishes. Typically, level 3 is specified in appearance areas that are to receive heavy or medium texture (spray or hand-applied) finishes before final painting, or where heavy-grade wall coverings are to be applied as the final decoration. This level of finish is not recommended where smooth, painted surfaces, or light- to medium-weight wall coverings are specified.

Level 4

All joints and interior angles should have tape embedded in joint compound as well as three separate coats of joint compound applied over all joints, angles, fastener heads, and accessories. All joint compound must be smooth and free of tool marks and ridges. It is recommended that the prepared surface be coated with a primer/sealer prior to the application of final finishes. This level should be specified where light textures or wall coverings are to be applied, or economy is of concern. In critical lighting areas, flat paints applied over light textures tend to reduce joint photographing. Gloss, semigloss, and enamel paints are not recommended over this level of finish. The weight, texture, and sheen level of wall coverings applied over this level of finish should be carefully evaluated. Joints and fasteners must be adequately concealed if the wall-covering material is lightweight, contains limited pattern, has a gloss finish, or if any combination of these features is present. Unbacked vinyl wall coverings are not recommended over this level of finish.

Level 5

All joints and interior angles should have tape embedded in joint compound as well as three separate coats of joint compound applied over all joints, angles, fastener heads, and accessories. A thin skim coat of joint compound, or a material manufactured especially for this purpose, should be applied to the entire surface. The surface should be smooth and free of tool marks and ridges. It is recommended that the prepared surface be coated with a primer/sealer prior to the application of finish paint. This level of finish is recommended where gloss, semigloss, enamel, or nontextured flat paints are specified or where severe lighting conditions occur. This highest-quality finish is the most effective method to provide a uniform surface and minimize the possibility of joint photographing and of fasteners showing through the final decoration.

JOINT TREATMENT PRODUCTS AND TOOLS

The process of finishing gypsum drywall for paint or wall covering is called *joint treatment*. But taping and finishing operations should not be started until the interior temperature has been maintained at a minimum of 50°F for a period of at least 48 hours. The temperature should be maintained until the compounds have completely dried. Adequate and continuous ventilation must be provided to the area to ensure proper setting and drying of the taping and finishing compounds.

JOINT TREATMENT MATERIALS

As mentioned in chapter 2, two materials are used in joint treatment compound and joint reinforcing tape. These products should conform to ASTM C475 Standard Specifications for Joint Treatment Materials for Gypsum Wallboard Construction.

Joint compound

Choosing the right joint compound for a specific job requires an understanding of a number of factors: job conditions, shop practices, applicators' preferences, types of available joint systems, characteristics of products considered, and recommended product combinations.

Joint compound products are usually named according to function, such as taping, topping, and all-purpose. Taping typically performs as the highest shrinking, strongest bonding, and hardest sanding of the three compounds, and it is used for embedding tape. Topping usually is the lowest shrinking, easiest applying, and easiest sanding of the compounds for use in second and third coats; it might occasionally be designed for texturing. Taping and topping are usually designed as companion products to give the highest-quality workmanship. All-purpose is generally a compromise of taping and topping compounds and might be used as a texturing material. Lightweight all-purpose joint compound is also an all-purpose compound, but is lighter, shrinks less, and sands easier.

Types of joint compounds

Most joint compounds contain water-soluble, dispersible, organic adhesives or synthetic resins often called "vinyls." These latter compounds will keep longer than the organic water-soluble formulations. Both of these mixtures gain their strength and adhesion through drying. The loss of water is accompanied by shrinkage, which can be reduced by applying several thin coats of compound. Each application should be thoroughly dry before applying the next one.

The more common types of joint reinforcing compounds are:

- Two-compound systems. These compounds are formulated for superior performance in each joint-finishing step. The separate taping compounds develop the greatest bond strength and crack resistance. Separate topping compounds have the best sanding characteristics, lower shrinkage, and smoothest finishing.

- All-purpose compounds. They have good performance characteristics at all finishing levels. However, they do not have the outstanding bond strength, workability, and sandability of separate taping and topping compounds. Nevertheless, all-purpose compounds minimize inventories, avoid job-site mixups, and are especially good for scattered jobs.

- Ready-mixed compounds. These compounds offer open-and-use convenience. They save time and prevent mistakes in mixing. They also minimize the necessity of having a water supply at the job site. Ready-mixed compounds have the best working qualities of all compounds; they have excellent performance, plus factory-controlled batch consistency and superior storage life compared to mixed powders. These compounds do require heated storage. Should they freeze, they can be slowly thawed at room temperature, mixed to an even viscosity, and used without damaging effects. However, repeated freeze/thaw cycles will cause remixing to become more difficult.

- Powder compounds. These have the advantage of being storable (dry) at any temperature. If they are stored in a cold warehouse, however, they should be moved to a warm mixing room the day before they are to be mixed. Best results require strict adherence to the manufacturer's proportioning instructions.

- Setting-type compounds. To meet varying job requirements, setting-type joint compounds are offered in a wide choice of setting times. Actually, the set-time choices might be as short as a few minutes and as long as several hours. The quick-set type, having a shorter working time, must be used within the prescribed time limit. (Additional coats are possible before complete drying takes place.) It is common for setting compounds to be used for embedding the tape, and "nonsetting" types are used for the finishing operation. All of the previously mentioned compound types are usually available in setting-type formulations.

Joint tapes

As mentioned in chapter 2, there are two types of joint reinforcement tapes available. One is made of strong fiber paper and the other of fiberglass fibers. The purpose of the joint tape is to reinforce and finish the joints between adjacent gypsum boards (Figure 10.2). They are usually designed for use with ready-mixed or powder-joint compounds.

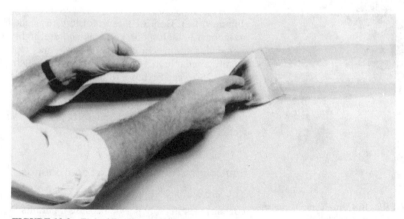

FIGURE 10.2   Embedding the tape in joint compound.

High-strength paper tape is the most commonly used, and its reinforcing-type holes range in size from holes so small they are only visible by holding the tape up to a light to holes about 1/16 inch in diameter. These perforations in the tape allow joint compound to seep through during the embedding process. To serve as a guide when making corner joints, most paper tapes have a crease down the center. Also, some are available with metal strips to reinforce exterior corners.

Fiberglass tape, as the name implies, is fiberglass woven into a coarse mesh. It is available with a pressure-sensitive adhesive backing that can be bonded to the surface by pressing firmly against the joint by running a taping knife or trowel (Figure 10.3) along its entire length. Use a corner tool to press the tape into inside corners. To make concealment easier, do not overlap joints.

FIGURE 10.3   Installing pressure-sensitive fiberglass tape using pressure from a trowel.

FIGURE 10.4 Installing nonadhesive fiberglass tape with staples.

Fiberglass tape is also available with a plain (nonadhesive) back that is usually fastened with staples (Figure 10.4). Both of these moisture-resistant tapes are good for high-moisture areas and are highly recommended for veneer plaster finishes. Paper tapes are usually available in $1^{31}/_{32}$-inch-wide and $2^{1}/_{16}$-inch-wide by 75-, 250-, and 500-foot rolls. Fiberglass tape is generally available in 2- and $2^{1}/_{2}$-inch widths in 300-foot rolls. Coverage for both paper and fiberglass-type tapes is approximately 370 linear feet per 1,000 square feet of gypsum-board base.

Equipment for mixing joint compounds

Mix the powder joint compound in a clean 5-gallon container (preferably plastic because it permits flexing the container walls to break loose hardened compound). While hand mixing of joint compounds is adequate, many applicators prefer electric mixers. Power mixing saves considerable time, particularly on large jobs where mixing in a central location is most convenient. Power is usually supplied by a $^{1}/_{2}$-inch heavy-duty electric drill using a maximum speed of 400 rpm for joint compounds, and 300 to 600 rpm for textures. Drills that operate at high speeds will whip air bubbles into the mix, rendering it unfit for finish-coat purposes. Mixing paddles are usually of open-cage type (Figure 10.5). For small quantities, mix the compound in a mud pan with a potato-masher type mixer (Figure 10.6).

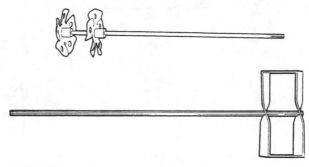

FIGURE 10.5   Typical open-cage mixing paddles.

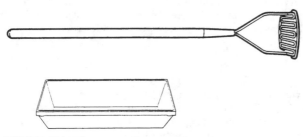

FIGURE 10.6   The potato masher type and a mud pan.

Pour the proper amount of clean, drinkable water into the mixing container. Dirty water (such as that used to clean tools) will contaminate the compound and cause erratic setting of the joint compound. The amounts of water that should be used for the specific application of the product being used are usually shown on the compound package or container.

General mixing directions are to fill the container about half full with water, then sift in the powdered compound, mixing at the same time. Stir until the powder is uniformly damp. This takes less than 3 minutes with most types of powder. Let the mix sit and soak from 3 to 30 minutes, depending on the compound. Then stir again until the mixture is creamy smooth. The mixture can be thinned by adding more water, and thickened by adding more powder, but these additions should not be made until after the mix has soaked. Note: An approved protective respirator (such as the one described later in this chapter) should be worn when mixing powdered joint compound.

Drywall taping knives

Four-, five-, and six-inch knives are designed for taping, fastener spotting, angle taping, and finishing; a 10-inch or wider knife can be used for finish coating. All have square corners needed for corner work (Figure 10.7). The two narrower knives are available with either plain handles (shown on the 4-inch knife) or with hammerhead handles (shown on the 6-inch knife). Other drywall finishing knives are available with blade widths up to 24 inches. Long-handled models are also available. The handles might be made of wood or plastic.

FIGURE 10.7   Typical drywall taping knives.

The drywall taping knife's blade is made of spring steel and is usually available in different degrees of stiffness. Because there is a great difference in "feel" between a very stiff blade and a flexible one, select the one that works best for you.

Sanders

No matter how skilled the drywall applicator is at applying joint compound, sanding will still be required. The hand sander shown in Figure 10.8 has a 3¼-×-9¼-inch base plate to provide for fast, efficient joint sanding. Models also include those with wood or aluminum handles. Long-handled pole sanders (Figure 10.9A) permit sanding of ceiling joints without the necessity of the worker using stilts.

The universal angle sander shown in Figure 10.9B has a spring-loaded center hinge that automatically adjusts this tool to fit corner angles from 82° to 100° to sand both sides at the same time.

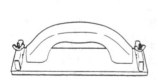
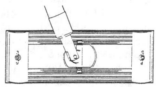

FIGURE 10.8   Typical drywall block hand-sander.

FIGURE 10.9A   A long-handled pole sander.

FIGURE 10.9B   A universal angle sander.

Tape dispensers

The banjo tape dispenser shown in Figure 10.10A applies paper tape and joint compound simultaneously to flat joints. There are two models: One stores the tape and the compound in separate compartments. The other stores the tape and compound together. A tape dispenser and creaser (Figure 10.10B) can hold tape rolls up to 500 feet. It has a built-in creaser to fold tape for corner applications.

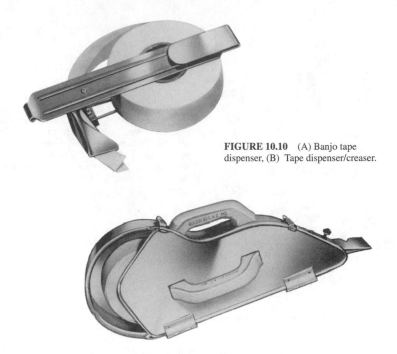

FIGURE 10.10   (A) Banjo tape dispenser, (B) Tape dispenser/creaser.

Other taping/finishing tools

Sometimes called the "mechanical" tools, the specialized tools shown in Figure 10.11 can perform every phase of drywall joint work:

- Automatic taper. Applies the tape and the proper amount of joint compound simultaneously to flat joints or corners. Designed for high-volume machine-tool applications.
- Nail spotter. Efficiently applies joint compound over nail or screw depressions.
- Corner roller. Used to firmly embed tape into 90° interior corner joints on walls and ceiling. It also forces excess compound from under the tape prior to finishing.
- Corner finisher. Feathers joint compound evenly to the wallboard in all 90° internal corners after using the corner roller.
- Flat box. Applies joint compound in correct amounts when operated over flat joints. It automatically "crowns" the joint. Usually available in 8-, 10-, and 12-inch sizes.
- Hand pump. Loads mechanical tools from a 5-gallon pail.

   The use of these mechanical taping tools is covered later in this chapter.
   Care should be taken not to contaminate containers or tools used for different types of joint compounds when mixing or storing. Even a small quantity of one type of joint compound in the seam of a mixing pail or inside a pump or on a tool can adversely affect the adhesive properties of a full mixture of another type of compound. All equipment must be clean. Tools should be disassembled and cleaned after each operation.

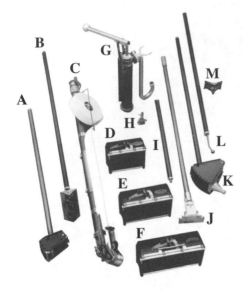

FIGURE 10.11   Mechanical taping tools. (A) Nail spotter with handle. (B) Corner roller with handle. (C) Automatic taper. (D) Eight-inch flat box. (E) Ten-inch flat box. (F) Twelve-inch flat box. (G) Pump. (H) Box-filler fitting. (I) Handle extension. (J) Box handle. (K) Corner box with handle. (L) Corner finisher handle. (M) Corner finisher.

TRIM ACCESSORY APPLICATION

There are several trim accessories available that help to simplify and enhance the drywall finishing process. All are suitable for both wood- and steel-frame construction.

Corner bead application

A metal corner-reinforcement bead provides strong, durable protection for outside wall angle corners, window returns, uncased openings, pilasters, soffits, and beams. The exposed nose of the bead resists impact and forms a screed for finishing (Figure 10.12). Corner bead should be installed in one piece unless the length of a corner exceeds the stock bead length. The easiest way to trim a corner bead to the correct length is to cut through the flanges with tin snips one flange at a time. Then bend and snap.

To apply, force the corner reinforcement bead onto the corner, being careful that the flanges do not spread beyond the 90° angle. Fasten the bead with drywall nails or staples (Figures 10.13A and 10.13B) spaced 9 inches O.C. on both flanges. When using nails, be sure that they are long enough to penetrate the framing members. Drive all the nails below the nose of the corner bead and tightly into the flange so that the joint will be covered smoothly and evenly. Be careful not to dent the metal. The flanges also can be attached with a clinch-on tool (Figure 10.14). Screw attachment is not recommended for corner-bead applications. Finish the corner bead with three coats of joint compound.

Flexible metal corner tape

Flexible metal corner tape is available that ensures straight, sharp corners at any angle (Figure 10.15). It provides durable corner protection on cathedral and drop ceilings, arches, and around bay windows. The tape is 2$\frac{1}{16}$ inches wide and has a $\frac{1}{16}$-inch gap be-

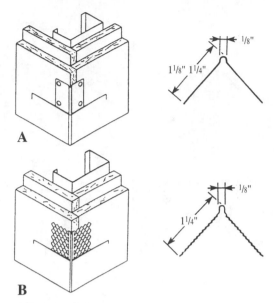

FIGURE 10.12   Corner bead and its typical dimensions.

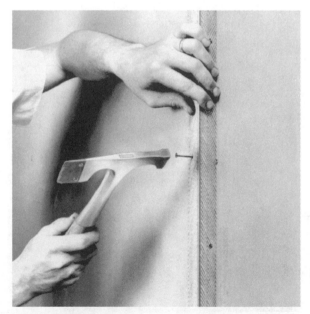

FIGURE 10.13A   Installing corner bead with nails.

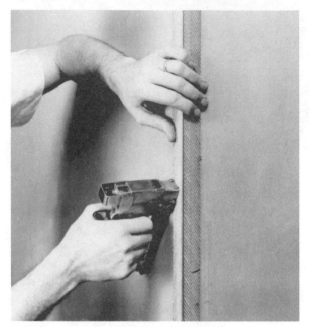

FIGURE 10.13B   Installing corner bead with staples.

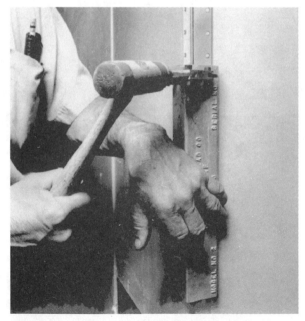

FIGURE 10.14   A clinch-on tool crimps solid-flange beads in place.

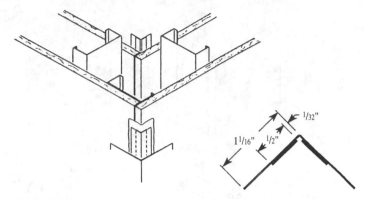

FIGURE 10.15   Flexible metal corner tape and its typical dimensions.

tween two ½-inch-wide galvanized steel strips. When folded, the tape forms a strong corner bead. It is applied with standard joint compound feathered at the edges for a smooth wall surface. It is used to join a drywall partition to a plaster wall in remodeling work and for repairing chipped and cracked corners.

To use, cut the tape to the length desired with tin snips or with a knife, then bend. Notch or angle-cut for arches and window returns. Do not overlap at intersections or corners. Apply the joint compound to both sides of a corner angle, then fold the tape at its center to form a bead and press the metal strip side into the joint compound. Follow immediately with a thin coat of compound over the tape and let dry. Finish the corner in the conventional manner with additional coats of joint compound.

Metal trim application

Metal trim serves to protect and finish gypsum panels at window framing and door jambs. It is also used at ceiling/wall intersections and partition perimeters to form a recess for acoustical sealant. It sometimes is used as a relief joint at the intersection of dissimilar constructions, such as where gypsum board meets concrete (Figure 10.16).

Where metal trim is to be applied, omit the fasteners at the framing member. To space for the installation of the trim, leave a space of ⅜ to ½ inch between the edge of the panel and the face of the jamb. Then place the trim over the edge of the panel with the wide knurled flange on the room side. Attach the trim to the panel using the same type of fasteners that are used to attach the panels. Space the fasteners 9 inches O.C. maximum, and make sure that they penetrate the framing members. Finish the metal trim with three coats of conventional joint compound.

Vinyl trim application

This is a reveal-type trim with flanges of rigid vinyl fins that compress on installation (Figure 10.17). Its fins form a permanent, flexible seal to reduce sound transmission and provides structural stress relief at panel perimeters. In addition, this trim helps to stop condensation where the board terminates at exterior metal surfaces, such as window mullions.

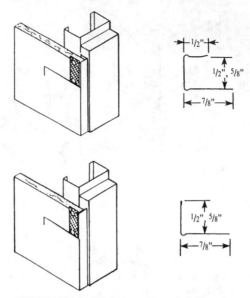

FIGURE 10.16 Metal trim and its typical dimensions.

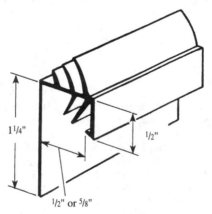

FIGURE 10.17 Vinyl trim and its typical dimensions.

Vinyl trim is available that slips over the edges of either ½- or ⅝-inch gypsum board for friction fitting. Position the panel, press the trim edges against the abutting surface for a snug contact, and attach in the conventional manner. This trim requires no finishing compound; it paints easily.

Trim for prefinished gypsum panels

As described in chapter 8, snap-on two-part outside corner and inside corner trims are available that match the prefinished gypsum panels. One part of the snap-on trim is installed after the panels have been installed. One-piece matching trim is also available (Figure 10.18).

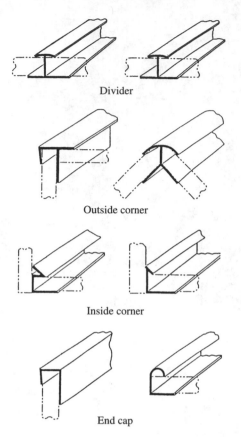

Divider

Outside corner

Inside corner

End cap

FIGURE 10.18 Types of one-part trim used with prefinished panels.

Control joints

Control joints have been mentioned several times, and their installation was described in chapter 6. To finish the joint, Figures 10.19A and 10.19B show how to apply the compound and remove the plastic tape.

HAND-TOOL JOINT TREATMENT PROCEDURE

Before attempting the first level of board-joint finish, check to be sure that all the drywall panels are firmly fastened to the framing members. Press on each panel of drywall along all rows of the fasteners to make sure that it lies against the framing members. To determine if its fasteners are properly seated, run a finishing knife carefully over all surface dimples. If a metallic ring is heard, sink the fastener a little deeper (Figure 10.20). Remove dust and grit from the wallboard surfaces with a damp sponge. Make sure that there are no breaks or cut marks in the surface paper or any fractures of the core. Also make certain that the panel joints are aligned. When one panel is higher than another, it becomes difficult to leave sufficient compound under the tape covering the high panel. Blisters, bond failure, and cracks can easily develop in these areas. Open spaces between panels of ¼ inch or

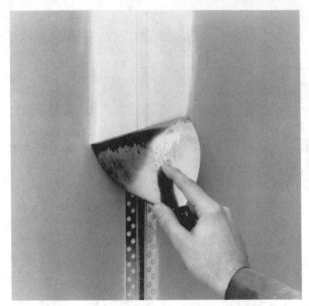

FIGURE 10.19A   Applying joint compound to a control joint.

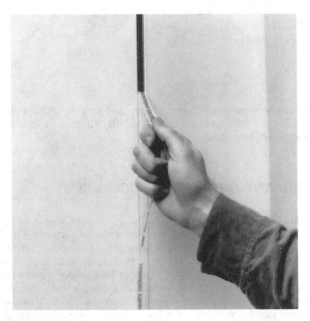

FIGURE 10.19B   Removing the plastic tape.

FIGURE 10.20   Sinking fasteners a little deeper.

more should be prefilled with an all-purpose joint compound at least 24 hours prior to embedding the tape or the first-level finishing. Apply the joint compound directly over the separation with a flexible 5- or 6-inch joint-finishing knife. Wipe off excess compound that is applied beyond the groove. Allow the prefill compound to harden.

To apply joint compound neatly, dip the knife sideways into the mud pan containing compound so that only half the width of the blade is loaded. Keep the blade clean, especially of dried bits of compound, to avoid leaving scratches in the wet joint compound as the knife is drawn over it. Discard any compound containing dried bits of material. Clean the blade by drawing it over the edge of the pan.

Embedding tape

Using a broad, steel finishing knife, apply a continuous coat of taping of all-purpose joint compound to fill the channel formed by the tapered edges of the panels, and lightly press (Figure 10.21). Center reinforcing tape into the fresh joint compound. Working within a convenient arms-reach area, embed the tape by holding the knife at a 45° angle to the panel. Draw the knife along the joint with sufficient pressure to remove excess compound above and below the tape and at the edges (Figure 10.22). Leave sufficient compound under the tape for proper adhesion, but not over ½ inch under the edge. While embedding, apply a thin coat of joint compound over the tape (Figure 10.23). This thin coat reduces edge wrinkling or curling and makes the tape easier to conceal with successive coats. At this point of the treatment, do not worry about a few grooves or streaks in the joint compound. They will be covered over by subsequent coats. Allow the joint compound to dry completely. Do not use a topping compound for embedding tape application.

Spotting fastener heads and filling beads

Use ready-mixed compound at package consistency or powdered joint compounds mixed per bag directions. For each fastener depression, apply joint compound with a 5-inch knife. Holding the blade almost flush with the panel, draw the joint compound across a fas-

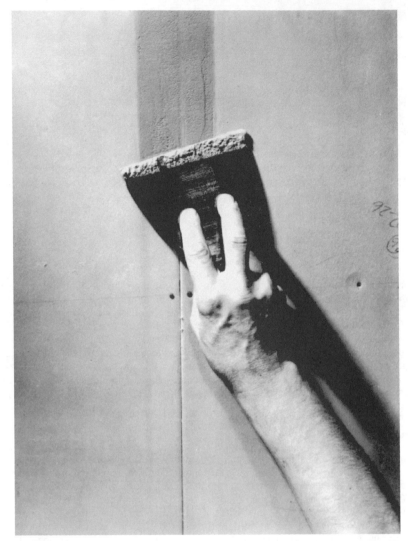

FIGURE 10.21   With a 4-inch to 6-inch finishing knife, butter the joint between panels with joint compound.

tener head and the dimple surrounding it (Figure 10.24). Then raise the knife blade to a more upright position and scrape off excess with a second stroke at a right angle to the first stroke. Fill only the fastener depression. Apply enough pressure on the knife to level the compound with the panel surface. Allow each coat to dry. Repeat application until fastener depressions are flush with the panel surface.

When filling beads and metal trim, apply the joint compound onto one flange of the corner bead (Figure 10.25) using at least a 6-inch knife. Work down the entire length of the bead. Hold the knife at a 45° angle and smooth the compound with one edge of the knife

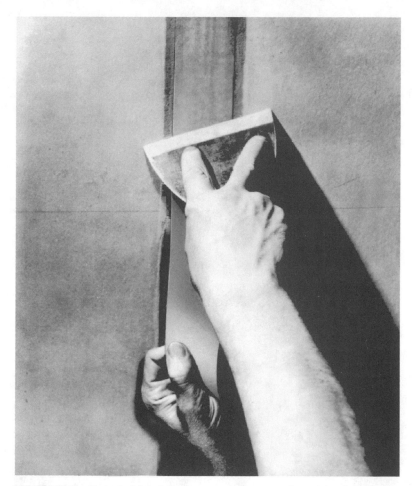

FIGURE 10.22   Center the joint reinforcing tape over the seam, and press it into the fresh compound with a 4-inch or 6-inch knife held at about a 45° angle to the wall.

riding the metal, the other on the surface of the panel. The compound should extend onto the panel a minimum of 4 inches. Repeat the application for the other flange.

If additional coats are needed, allow each coat to dry, and then apply the following coats approximately 2 inches wider than the preceding coats. After filling the first flange, the metal corner edge might have some lumps of joint compound. To remove, run the blade up the bead while also moving it to the side. In this manner, the compound is continuously moved aside as it is scraped off.

Second application

After the embedding coat is completely dry, apply a second coat of topping or all-purpose joint compound. Scrape off bumps, ridges, and other imperfections with the knife. Be

FIGURE 10.23   Apply a thin skim coat over the joint to prevent the edge from wrinkling.

careful not to damage the surface. Using at least an 8-inch knife, apply joint compound to the taped joints, running the knife the length of the joint (Figure 10.26). Apply pressure to the knife edge farthest from the joint and lift the other edge just slightly above the surface. Draw the knife down the joint. Repeat this process for the opposite edge. This technique is called feathering. Joint compound should extend beyond the first coat for a total width of 7 or 8 inches. Be sure to allow enough time between each step to be certain each coat has dried completely or hardened (in the case of setting-type compounds).

Finish coat

After the second coat is dry, if necessary, sand lightly as described later in this chapter, or wipe with a damp sponge and apply a thin finishing (third) coat to joints and fastener

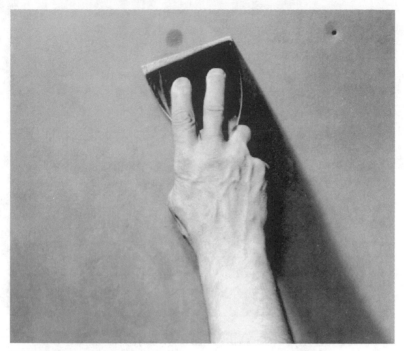

FIGURE 10.24   Spotting fastener heads.

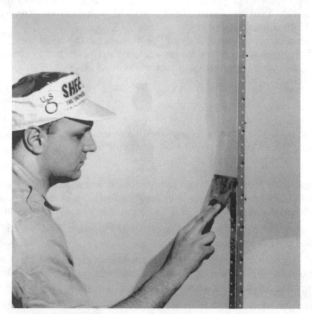

FIGURE 10.25   Filling the beads with joint compound.

FIGURE 10.26   Applying a second coat of joint compound with a 10-inch knife and feathering the edges approximately 2 inches beyond the embedding (first) coat on each side.

heads. Use topping or all-purpose joint compound. Feather the edges of the third coat at least 2 inches wider than the second coat (Figure 10.27). Finish joint compound can be applied at a slightly thinner consistency.

Joints, fasteners, beads, and trim should be finished as smooth as possible to minimize sanding. With joint compound, go over the whole job to smooth and touch-up all scratches, craters, nicks, and other imperfections in the dried finish coat.

End joints

On the end or on field-cut board joints, when there are no tapered edges, the following joint treatment procedure is recommended to minimize crowning and/or ridging of end joints.

1. Before attachment, bevel panel ends approximately ⅛ inch at a 45° angle using a sharp utility knife. This keeps the paper ends apart and reduces expansion problems caused by the raw paper edge. Also peel back and remove any loose paper from the end.

2. The gypsum panel ends should be loosely butted together. Ends should be separated slightly and not touching.

3. Apply the compound and paper reinforcing tape over the joint in the same manner as for tapered joints. Embed the tape tightly to minimize joint thickness, but leave sufficient compound under the tape for a continuous bond and blister prevention.

4. Finish the end joint to a width at least twice the width of a recessed-edge joint. This will make the joint less apparent after decoration, as the crown will be more gradual.

FIGURE 10.27 Applying a thin final (finishing) coat of joint compound with a 10-inch knife, feathering the edges another 2 inches on each side of the second coat.

Finishing inside corners

Fold the tape along the center crease. Apply the joint compound to both sides of the corner, and lightly press the folded tape into the angle. Tightly embed the tape to both sides of the angle with a finishing knife (Figure 10.28). Next, apply a thin coat to one side of the angle. Allow to dry and apply finish coat to the other side of the angle.

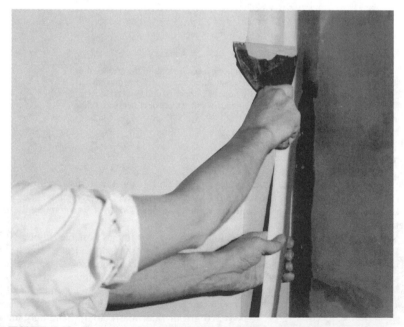

FIGURE 10.28 To tape butt edges, fit the creased tape into the corner and press it into the compound with a 4-inch or 6-inch knife, working first on one side of the corner and then the other.

The use of a corner tool makes finishing inside corners a single operation. As shown in Figure 10.29, the creased tape is fitted into the corner and pressed into the compound with the corner tool. But, it must be kept in mind that as the tape is embedded, a ridge of compound builds up at the edges of the tape. Remove this excess with a knife or either blade of the corner tool. All cutouts should be back-filled with the compound used for taping or finishing so that there is no opening larger than ⅛ inch between the gypsum board and a fixture or receptor.

FIGURE 10.29   When using a corner tool, fit the creased tape into the corner and press it into the compound. Remember that as the tape is embedded, a ridge of compound builds up at the edges of the tape. Remove this excess with a knife or either blade of the corner tool.

Sanding

The final level or step prior to decoration is to lightly sand the joints to eliminate tool marks, high crowned joints, and lap marks where joints intersect. Scratches, craters, and nicks should be filled with joint compound, then sanded. Do not try to remove these depressions by sanding only.

Select sandpaper or abrasive-mesh cloth with a grit as fine as possible (Figure 10.30).

FIGURE 10.30   Typical abrasive mesh cloth used to smooth taped sections.

Excessively coarse sandpapers leave scratches that are visible after decoration. For all-purpose compounds, use a #150 grit or finer sandpaper (#200 grit or finer mesh cloth). For ready-mixed and topping compounds, use a #150 grit or finer sandpaper (#220 grit or finer mesh cloth). Sand only the surfaces coated with joint compound to avoid scuffing gypsum panel paper. Remove sanding dust before decorating. Ventilate or use a dust collector (Figure 10.31) in the work area. Use a NIOSH (National Institute for Occupational Safety and Health) approved respirator specified for mica and talc when air is dusty. Also wear safety glasses or goggles when sanding.

FIGURE 10.31 Typical electric sander with a dust collector.

When only minimal sanding is needed, wet sanding with a sponge, or wet sandpaper and water are often preferred. It eliminates dust and does not scuff the surface paper. One method uses a small-celled polyurethane sponge similar in appearance to carpet padding. Saturate the sponge and wring to prevent dripping. Rub joints to remove high spots, using as few strokes as possible. Clean the sponge frequently during use.

Care should be taken to avoid scuffing or raising the nap of the paper surface of the gypsum board, as these areas might be visible after the decoration. Figure 10.32 simulates the nap raising caused by oversanding at the joint compound edges. An alkyd-based (oil-based) paint will accentuate this condition by freezing the fuzzed paper in its raised position. Joint banding and photographing resulting from this condition are eliminated with a skim coat of ready-mixed joint compound applied before decorating.

Skim coating

The best method to prepare any gypsum drywall surface for painting is to apply a skim coat of joint compound. This leaves a film thick enough to fill imperfections in the joint work, smooth the paper texture, and provide a uniform surface for decorating. Skim coating is currently recommended in the industry when gloss paints are to be used. It is also the best technique to use when decorating with flat paints and for minimizing surface defects under critical lighting conditions. Skim coating fills imperfections in joint work, smooths the paper texture, and provides a uniform surface for decorating.

Finish joints and fasteners in the conventional three-coat method or as in step four of the level of finish. After the joints are dry, mix the joint compound to a consistency approximating that used for hand taping. Using a trowel, board knife, or long-nap texture roller, apply only sufficient amounts of joint compound to cover the drywall surface. Then immediately wipe the compound as tightly as possible over the panel surface using a trowel or broad knife.

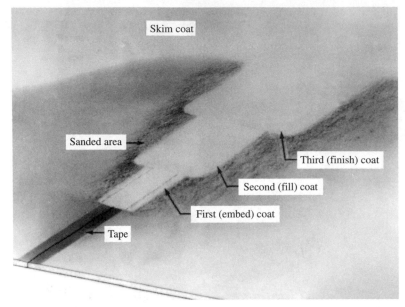

FIGURE 10.32   Guard against raising the nap of the paper surface in the sanded area shown above.

If skim coating is not done, a special primer/sealer coat or a flat latex paint having high solids content (applied undiluted) is recommended as a first (prime) coat. Apply before final paint coat or texture finish application to minimize concealment problems.

Drying time

The drying times are based on an evaporation rate of 10 pounds of water per 250 feet of reinforcing tape, corresponding to $\frac{1}{16}$ to $\frac{5}{64}$ inch of wet compound thickness under the tape. The drying times for thicker (or thinner) coats of wet compound between the tape and the panels will increase (or decrease) in proportion to the wet compound thickness. These drying times apply when the exposed surface of the tape is bare or nearly bare, and when adequate ventilation is provided. A heavy compound coat over tape lengthens drying time.

MECHANICAL TOOL APPLICATION

Several types of mechanical and semimechanical tools are available as shown in Figure 10.11. Such tools are used in the following typical sequence:

1. Using compound of suitable consistency, mechanically tape all the joints; wipe down with a broad knife (Figure 10.33). Allow to dry.
2. Mechanically tape the interior angles. Finish both sides of the angles with a corner roller and corner finisher as shown in Figure 10.34. Touch up with a broad knife as necessary. Apply the first coat to the fastener heads and metal accessories. Allow to dry.

FIGURE 10.33 Using joint compound of suitable consistency, mechanically tape all joints (top). Then wipe down with a broad knife (bottom).

FIGURE 10.34 Mechanically tape interior angles. Finish both sides of the angles with a corner roller and corner finisher as shown. Touch up with broad knife as necessary. Apply the first coat to the fastener heads and the metal accessories. Allow to dry.

3. Apply a fill coat of compound over the tape on the flat joints using a hand finisher tool (Figure 10.35). Using a compound of thicker consistency, spot fastener heads and apply a second coat to the metal accessories. Allow to dry.

4. Apply the finish coat of compound to the flat joints, feathering the edges about 2 inches beyond the preceding coat. Apply the finish coat to the metal accessories and fastener heads. Allow to dry, and smooth lightly as required. Remove all dust before decoration. Do not scuff the face paper by oversanding.

SPECIAL APPLICATION

There are some special finishing applications necessary. For example, while the taping procedure of MR gypsum panel is similar to that for regular gypsum board, there are a few special procedures.

Taping MR or WR gypsum board

In areas to be tiled, for tapered edge joints, embed the reinforcing tape with joint compound and allow to set. Then apply a fill coat of joint compound, making sure not to crown the joint. Wipe excess joint compound from the panel surface before it sets. For butt joints

FIGURE 10.35   Apply a fill coat of compound over tape on flat joints using a hand finishing tool (top). Using a compound of thicker consistency, spot the fastener heads and apply a second coat to the metal accessories (bottom). Allow to dry.

and interior angles, embed the reinforcing tape with joint compound. A fill coat is not necessary. Again, take care not to crown the joint. For fasteners, spot fastener heads at least once with a joint compound.

Fill and seal all openings around pipes, fittings and fixtures with a thinned-down coat of tile adhesive. For best results, follow the manufacturer's installation instructions. With some tile adhesives, it is possible to use them as both a sealer and to set the tile. With such adhesives, add one pint of water per quart of adhesive to make a paintlike viscosity. With a 1-inch brush, apply the thinned compound onto the raw gypsum panel core at cutouts, and allow the areas to dry thoroughly prior to the application of the tile. Before the adhesive dries, wipe excess material from the surface of the gypsum panels.

For areas not to be tiled, embed the tape with joint compound in the conventional manner. Finish with at least two coats of a joint compound to provide joint finishing for painting and wallpapering.

Exterior ceiling-board surfaces

Use the hand application techniques and a joint compound to treat joints and fasteners in exterior ceiling-board applications. During periods of near-freezing temperatures, check weather forecasts before beginning work. Minimum air, water, mix, and surface temperatures of 45°F (7°C) must be assured until the compound is completely dry. Apply the joint compound in the following sequence.

1. Prefill the joints of the exterior gypsum ceiling boards with a joint compound. After the prefill has set, tape all the joints and angles in the ceiling with joint compound and reinforcing tape. When the compound sets (hardens) or completely dries, immediately apply a fill coat of a joint compound; allow to dry before finishing. Note: Remember that the terms "set" and "harden" apply only to setting-type joint compounds. Conventional compounds must dry completely.

2. Apply the joint compound over the flanges of the control joints, metal beads, and trim. Spot all fastener heads.

3. After the fill coat has set (hardened), apply a joint-compound finishing coat. Completely cover all the joints, angles, beads, control joints, and fasteners.

4. After the joint compound has dried, apply one coat of a good-quality latex flat exterior paint. Then follow with at least one coat of a good-quality alkyd or latex exterior paint.

DRYWALL DECORATION

Drywall-gypsum board provides smooth surfaces that can be decorated with paint, wallpaper, textures, fabric, or vinyl wall coverings (Figure 10.36). For satisfactory finishing results, care must be taken to prepare the surface properly to eliminate possible decorating problems commonly referred to as "joint banding" and "photographing." These problems are usually caused by differences between the porosities and surface textures of the gypsum-panel face paper and the finish joint compound, and the problems are magnified by the use of gloss paints. Then, when viewed in direct, natural lighting, the joints and fasteners in painted walls and ceilings might be visible.

To prevent many decorating problems, it is usually recommended that a high-quality latex primer/sealer be applied prior to decoration. Color or surface variations are thereby minimized, and a more uniform texture for any surface covering is provided. The sealer allows the wall coverings to be removed more easily without marring the surface. Glue-size, shellac, and varnish are not suitable as sealers or primers.

While the drywall hanger does not generally apply the final drywall decorative finish, he or she should know something about preparing the surface of drywall panels to receive the different types of final finishes:

For finish paints

A good-quality, white, latex primer/sealer formulated with higher binder solids, applied undiluted, is typically specified for new gypsum-board surfaces prior to the application of texture materials and gloss, semigloss, and flat latex wall paints. An alkali and moisture-resistant primer and a tinted enamel undercoat might be required under enamel paints.

FIGURE 10.36A   Paint finish for gypsum-drywall panels.

FIGURE 10.36B   Wallpaper finish for gypsum-drywall panels.

FIGURE 10.36C   Decorative-panel finish for gypsum-drywall panels.

FIGURE 10.36D   Wainscot finish for gypsum-drywall panels.

For wall coverings

White, self-sizing, water-based, "universal" (all-purpose) wall-covering primers have recently been introduced into the marketplace for use on new gypsum-board surfaces. These products are claimed to make drywall strippable, bind poor latex paint, allow hanging over glossy surfaces and existing vinyls, hide wall colors, and be water washable.

For texture

A ceiling or wall texture finish is an excellent method for masking imperfections and diffusing light across wall and ceiling surfaces (Figures 10.37A and 10.37B). They can be applied by brush, roller, spray, or trowel, or a combination of these tools, depending on the desired result. Textured wall surfaces are normally overpainted with the desired finish; overpainting of textured ceiling surfaces might not be deemed necessary where an adequate amount of material is applied to provide sufficient hiding properties. A primer/sealer might not be required under certain proprietary texture materials; consult the manufacturer of the texture material for specific recommendations (Figure 10.38).

FIGURE 10.37A   Textured finish over a drywall surface.

FIGURE 10.37B Another textured finish over a drywall surface.

FIGURE 10.38   Applying a textured finish to a ceiling.

CHAPTER 11
DRYWALL PROBLEMS AND REMEDIES

Robert Scharff
Walls & Ceilings Magazine

Chapter 4 discussed some of the problems associated with gypsum-board construction, many of which are beyond the control of the drywall contractor or hanger working from construction specifications and documents. Other problems (such as those resulting from improper job conditions and application practices) are the direct responsibility of the contractor and are controllable. In this chapter, these problems and preventive and corrective actions are discussed.

Almost invariably, unsatisfactory results show up first in the areas over joints or fastener heads. Improper application of either the board or joint treatment might be at fault, but other conditions existing on the job can be equally responsible for reducing the quality of the finished gypsum-board surface.

One of the major causes of job problems and poor performance after application is failure to follow the manufacturer's directions and architect's specifications. Application procedures should be checked regularly to conform with current manufacturer's recommendations. Product modifications to upgrade in-place performance might require slight changes in mixing or application methods. New products might require the adoption of entirely new procedures and techniques. Building specifications are designed to provide a given result, but unless specified construction materials and methods are used and the proper details followed, the actual job performance will probably fall short of requirements. Excessive water usage, oversanding, improper surface preparation, substitution of materials, skimping, and shortcuts should not be tolerated because they inevitably lead to problems.

Frequent job inspections by the general or drywall contractor, or both (Figure 11.1) will forestall potential problems and help ensure that project specifications are being met. Wall and ceiling surfaces should be inspected after the gypsum panels are installed, when the joints are being treated, and after the joints are finished before the surface is decorated. These checks will reveal many of the problems that follow.

FIGURE 11.1   The drywall installation should be inspected by all parties concerned.

FASTENER PROBLEMS

Fastener imperfections are very common defects that take on many forms. They might appear as a pop or protrusion of the fastener, a depression over the fastener heads, darkening, or localized cracking of the surface immediately surrounding the faster. It is usually caused by improper framing or fastener application.

Nail pops

Nail pops, the protrusion of nail heads beyond the gypsum surface, are caused by one or more of the following: lumber shrinkage after board application; loose gypsum board; improperly aligned, twisted or bowed framing; and improper nailing. Pops that appear before or during decoration should be repaired immediately. Those that occur after one or more month's heating are usually caused by lumber shrinkage and should not be repaired until the end of the heating season.

Problem: Framing members out of alignment

Probable cause.   Due to misaligned top plate and stud, hammering at points "X" (Figure 11.2) as panels are applied on both sides of the partition will probably result in nail heads puncturing the paper or cracking the board. Framing members that are more than ¼ inch out of alignment with adjacent members make it difficult to bring panels into firm contact with all nailing surfaces.

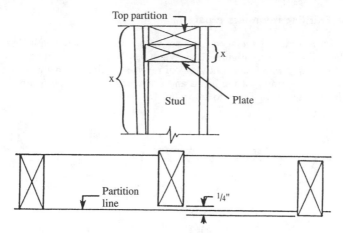

FIGURE 11.2   Framing members out of alignment.

Preventive action.   Provide heat and ventilation to dry framing lumber. Check the alignment of studs, joists, headers, blocking, and plates before applying panels, and correct before proceeding. Straighten badly bowed or crowned members. Shim out flush with adjoining surfaces. Use adhesive attachment. When applying, nail the center of the drywall first. Hold wallboard firmly to the nailing member when nailing. Use the proper nails, as specified for the specific installation. Check all nails before nail spotting. Systems recommended to reduce or eliminate nail pops include: double-layer lamination, double-nailing system, floating-angle system, adhesive nail-on system, and screw application.

Corrective action.   When nail pops occur before decoration, repair immediately. If a problem occurs after decoration, make repairs after the framing lumber is dry (usually one heating cycle). To repair, drive nails 1½ inches from each side of popped nail while holding wallboard firmly to the nailing member. Countersink the popped nail, remove loose joint compound, then apply finishing coats of joint or topping compound.

Problem: Depressed nails

Probable cause.   Depressed nails are probably caused by one of the following: framing out of alignment, lumber expansion due to moisture absorption, improper wallboard application, too few nails, improper furring, structural movement, or nails dimpled too deeply.

Preventive action.   Align framing lumber properly. Allow dry lumber to become acclimated. Correct wallboard application as described for nail pops. Use proper nail spacing. When furring, use no less than 2-x-2-inch furring pieces. Use systems recommended to reduce or eliminate nail pops. Avoid fracturing the paper when driving nails.

Corrective action.   Repair as described for nail pops, unless most nails are depressed and wallboard is loose (usually ceilings). Renail the entire surface using the proper spacing. Dimple depressed nails and apply finishing coats of joint or topping compound.

Problem: Framing members twisted

Probable cause.   Framing members have not been properly squared with plates, presenting angular nailing surface (Figure 11.3). When panels are applied, there is a danger of puncturing the paper with fastener heads or of reverse twisting the member as it dries out, with consequent loosening of the board and probable fastener pops. Warped or wet dimension lumber might contribute to deformity.

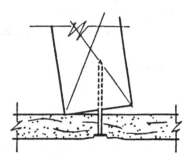

FIGURE 11.3   Framing member twisted.

Preventive action.   Align all twisted framing members before the board application (see chapter 6).

Corrective action.   After moisture content in the framing stabilizes, remove the problem fasteners and refasten with carefully driven type-W screws.

Problem: Framing protrusions

Probable cause.   Bridging, headers, fire stops, or mechanical lines have been installed improperly so as to project beyond the face of the framing, preventing the panels from contacting the nailing surface (Figure 11.4). The result will be loose boards, and fasteners driven in the area of the protrusion will probably puncture the face paper.

Preventive action and corrective action.   Same as for framing members twisted.

Problem: Fasteners puncturing the face paper

Probable cause.   This problem is probably caused by one of the following: poorly formed nail heads, careless nailing, excessively dry face paper or soft core, or lack of pressure during fastening. Nail heads that puncture the paper and shatter the core of the panel (Figure 11.5) have very little grip on the board.

Preventive action.   Correct the framing and properly drive the nails to produce a tight attachment with a slight uniform dimple (Figure 11.6). The nail head will bear on the paper and hold the panel securely against the framing member. Use the proper fastener or adhesive application. Screws with specially contoured heads are the best fasteners known to eliminate cutting and fracturing. If the face paper becomes dry and brittle, its low moisture

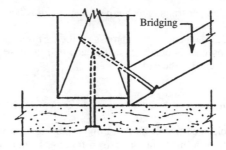

FIGURE 11.4   Framing protrusion.

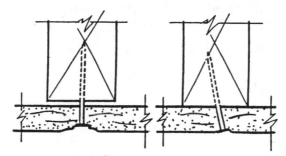

FIGURE 11.5   Fastener puncturing of the face paper.

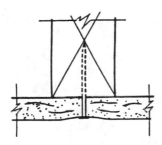

FIGURE 11.6   Properly driven nails will produce tight attachment with a slight uniform dimple.

content might aggravate nail cutting. Raise the moisture content of the board and the humidity in the work area.

Corrective action.   Remove improperly driven fasteners, hold the panel tight, and properly drive the new fasteners.

Problem: Nails loosened by pounding

Probable cause.   Applying panels to the second side of a partition can loosen nails on the opposite side (lack of hand pressure during fastening). This is particularly true when lightweight, soft lumber, undersized studs, or furring are used.

Preventive action.   Use proper framing techniques, screws, or adhesive application.

Corrective action.   Check the panels for tightness on the partition side where the panels were first applied. If looseness is detected, strike each nail head an additional hammer blow. Be careful not to overdrive the nail.

Problem: Unseated nails

Probable cause.   Flexible or extremely hard framing or furring does not permit nails to be properly driven. This might result from undersized framing members, the type of wood used, supports that exceed the maximum allowable frame spacing, or lack of hand pressure during fastening.

Preventive action.   Use proper framing techniques, screw, or adhesive application. Apply pressure to hold the panel tight against the framing while driving the fasteners.

Corrective action.   Replace nails with 1¼-inch screws.

Problem: Loose screws

Probable cause.   Loose screws can be caused by using the wrong type of screws for the application or using an improperly adjusted screw gun, resulting in screw stripping or not seating the screws properly.

Preventive action.   Use screws with combination high/low threads for greater resistance to stripping and pull-out. Set the screw-gun clutch to the proper depth.

Corrective action.   Remove faulty fasteners. Replace them with properly driven screws.

Problem: Bulges around fasteners

Probable cause.   Bulges around fasteners can be caused by overdriving the fasteners, driving them with the wrong tool, or failing to hold the board firmly against the framing while driving the fasteners. This can puncture and bulge the face paper and damage the core of the board. Application of joint compound or texture finish that wets the board paper can result in board bulging or swelling around fasteners.

Preventive action.   Use the correct tools and drive fasteners properly.

Corrective action.   Drive a screw close to the damaged area, clean out the damaged paper and core, repair with a joint compound, and refinish.

Problem: Steel framing panel edges out of alignment

Probable cause.   Steel framing panel edges out of alignment are probably caused by improper placement of the steel studs or advancing in the wrong direction of the panel installation. This can misalign the panel edges and give the appearance of ridging when finished.

Preventive action.   Install the steel studs with all flanges pointed in the same direction. Then install the panels by advancing in the opposite direction to the flange direction (Figure 11.7).

Corrective action.   Fill and feather out the joint with standard joint treatment.

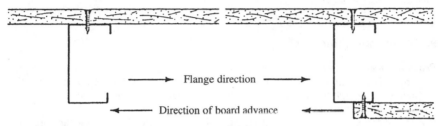

FIGURE 11.7   Steel-framing panel edges out of alignment.

JOINT PROBLEMS

Joint problems generally occur in a straight-line pattern and appear as ridges, depressions or blisters at the joints, or darkening over the joints or in adjacent panel areas. Imperfections might result from incorrect framing or joint treatment, or climatic conditions if remedial action has not been taken.

Problem: Ridging or beading

Probable cause.   *Ridging*, also called beading, is a uniform, fine-line deformation at gypsum-board joints (Figure 11.8). Factors that contribute to this condition include the use of wet lumber, prolonged high humidity, and structural movement of framing members. When this condition develops, it is advisable to wait through a complete heating cycle before repairing. This will permit the wallboard system to stabilize. Repair during warm, dry weather.

Preventive action.   Follow the general recommendations for joint treatment and approved application procedures, which include back-blocking and laminated double-layer application to minimize potential ridging problems (see chapter 6). Pay particular attention to temperature, ventilation, consistency of compound, covering-coat over tape, minimum width of fill, finish coats, and required drying time between coats.

Corrective action.   Lightly sand the ridge down, taking care not to damage the embedded joint-reinforcing tape. Fill the surface over the joint with taping compound as wide as necessary to create an essentially plane surface. After 24 hours of drying, light sanding or wiping with a damp sponge might be necessary to feather edges and remove trowel marks. If examination of the joint with strong side lighting or critical lighting indicates the ridge is not concealed, additional feathered coats of joint compound might be required. Sometimes it is necessary to then float a very thin film of joint compound over the entire area. The repaired joint should receive a coat of high-quality latex primer/sealer before any further decorative finish is applied.

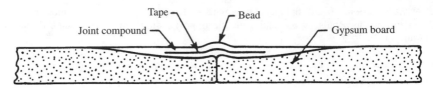

FIGURE 11.8   Joint ridging.

Problem: Tape photographing

Probable cause. This is often caused by slow drying of joint treatment coats. If the joint compound is too thin or too thick or there is overthickness at the edge of the tape, this problem will result. If the tape is too absorbent, photographing could occur also.

Preventive action. Follow correct drying conditions. Be sure to embed the tape properly, and make sure the proper thickness of the joint is maintained.

Corrective action. Sand down the tape outline and seal with joint compound. If necessary, refloat before decoration. Prevent the finish coat moisture from rewetting the tape by applying a thinner coat for fast drying.

Problem: High crown joint

Probable cause. A high crown joint is probably caused by excess piling of the compound over the joint, compound not being feathered out beyond the shoulders, improper bedding of tape, framing out of alignment or panel edges not tight against the framing, improper adjustment of tools, misuse of tools, or worn tools.

Preventive action. Embed the tape properly, using only enough compound to cover the tape and fill the taper depression or tape itself at butt joints. Feather the compound far enough to conceal.

Corrective action. Sand the joint to near flush with the surface without sanding into the reinforcing tape. If necessary, apply a wider joint-compound finishing coat that is properly feathered. Apply a second finishing or skim coat.

Problem: Starved joints

Probable cause. This is generally caused by insufficient drying time between coats of compound. It might also be caused by insufficient compound applied over the tape to fill the taper, overthinning, or oversmoothing of the compound. Shrinkage usually progresses until drying is complete.

Preventive action. Allow each coat of joint compound to dry thoroughly before applying successive coats, or use a low-shrinkage joint compound.

Corrective action. Use a fast-setting joint compound or reapply a full cover coat of heavy-mixed compound over the tape. Since this is the heaviest application, most shrinkage will take place in this coat, making it easier to fill the joint properly. Finish by following the standard procedure.

Problem: Joint shadowing (or see through)

Probable cause.   Temperature differentials in outside walls or top-floor ceilings cause the collection of airborne dust on colder spots of interior surfaces. This results in photographing or shadowing over fasteners, furring, or framing. This condition is most severe in areas with the greatest indoor-outdoor temperature variation.

Preventive action.   Wash the painted surfaces, remove spots with wallpaper cleaner, or decorate the surface.

Problem: Joint darkening or lightening

Probable cause.   This condition occurs as a result of the joints not being dry when painted. Painting under humid conditions or painting with low-grade paint will also cause this problem.

Preventive action.   Be sure that the joints are thoroughly dry before painting, and avoid painting under extremely high humidity. The entire surface should be primed with a sealing latex primer prior to applying the finish decoration. Use good-quality latex paint.

Corrective action.   Select a test area where the condition is most prevalent and repaint with a good-quality sealing latex primer. If the condition persists, prime and seal the affected areas with a good-quality sealing latex primer, then repaint. Further correction will require sealing of the entire surface before painting with a good-quality sealing latex primer.

Problem: Joint yellowing

Probable cause.   Painting over wet joints and slow-drying paint or joint compound will cause this problem. If an auxiliary-type heater is used to warm a room during the finishing operation, its fumes could cause joint yellowing.

Preventive action.   Allow the finished joints to dry thoroughly. Also avoid painting under conditions of extremely high humidity. Use a permanent heat source during cold weather.

Corrective action.   Repaint with a good-quality alkyd flat paint after all the joints are thoroughly dry.

Problem: Joint blisters in the tape

Probable cause.   This problem can be caused by one of the following: Insufficient or overly thin compound was used under the tape. Tape was not initially pressed into good contact with the compound. Too much compound was forced from under the tape by application of excessive tool pressure when embedding.

Preventive action.   Provide sufficient joint compound under the entire expanse of rein-forcing tape.

Corrective action.   Repair the tape by slitting it and filling with joint compound, then smooth out with a finishing knife. Cut out other loose areas and fill with joint compound when necessary. Let dry, then retape and finish.

PANEL CRACKING

Movement of the structure can impose several stresses and cause cracks either at the joint or in the field of the board. Cracks are more likely to occur at an archway or over a door since this is usually the weakest point in the frame construction. In new construction, it is wise to wait until at least one heating season has passed before repairing or refinishing. Another source of cracking in nonbearing walls of high-rise or commercial buildings is the modern trend toward less-rigid structures. Larger deflections in structural members and greater expansion and contraction of exterior columns can impose unexpected loads on nonbearing walls and lead to cracking.

Problem: Edge cracking

Probable cause.   After the joint treatment, straight, narrow cracks along edges of tape re-sult from too-rapid drying because of high temperatures accompanied by low humidity or excessive drafts; improper application, such as overdilution of joint compound; use of wrong compound (topping instead of tapping); excessive joint compound under tape; fail-ure to follow embedding with a thin coat over tape; or cold, wet application conditions, which also might cause poor bonding. This problem, difficult to see when it first occurs, might not be discovered until decoration begins. However, the cause can be attributed to some aspect of the taping operation.

Preventive action.   Correct drying conditions to avoid rapid surface drying. Keep tem-peratures and humidity as consistent as possible by controlling ventilation. Use a roller to wet joints with water prior to each joint treatment operation. Embed tape properly, avoid-ing excessive compound under the tape (a maximum of $\frac{1}{32}$-inch thickness of compound un-der the edges of the tape), and wipe down the tape immediately.

Corrective action.   Especially when poor atmospheric conditions exist, carefully examine all the joints after taping and skimming applications have dried; repairs are more econom-ical at this stage. Cut away any weakly bonded tape edges. Fill any hairline cracks with cut shellac (2 to 3 pound); groove out larger cracks with a sharp tool; coat with shellac and al-low to dry, then refill with joint compound, or cover cracks with complete joint treatment, including reinforcing tape; then feather to surface level with the plane of board.

Problem: Joint cracking

Probable cause.   Joint cracking can be caused by adverse drying conditions, high tem-peratures and low humidity and drafts, or low temperatures and high humidity. Also, joint or topping compound might have been applied in excessive thicknesses.

Preventive action.   Fill all wide wallboard joints with joint compound. Correct drying conditions. Substitute a thick coat of topping or a joint compound with multiple thinner coats. Allow enough time between coats for each coat to dry thoroughly before applying the next.

Corrective action.   Additional coats of joint or topping compound will fill the cracks without reoccurrence.

Problem: Center joint cracking

Probable cause.   Center joint cracking can be caused by abnormal stress buildup resulting from structural deflection or racking. The problem can also be caused by excessive stress resulting from hygrometric and/or thermal expansion and contraction (see chapter 4).

Preventive action.   Provide proper isolation from structure to prevent stress buildup. Install control joints for stress relief in long partition runs and large ceiling areas.

Corrective action.   Correct improper job conditions. Provide sufficient relief; retape and feather the joint compound over a broad area.

Problem: Inside-corner cracking

Probable cause.   This can be caused by the following: joint too wide or not filled, improper drying between coats, excess thickness of joint compound over the tape at the apex of the corners, extremely fast or slow drying conditions, and applying compound to both sides of an inside corner at the same time.

Preventive action.   Fill wide inside corner joints with compound prior to taping. Embed the reinforcing tape properly and allow it to dry thoroughly. Apply compound to one side of the joint and allow it to dry completely; then treat the other side.

Corrective action.   Fill the wide cracks with joint or topping compound. For hairline cracks, run a pointed object (10- or 16-penny nail) along the apex of the corner with adequate pressure to close the crack.

PANEL PROBLEMS

Most so-called panel problems are the result of faulty board, incorrect use of drywall materials, or improper installation procedures.

Problem: Wallboard blisters

Probable cause.   Wallboard blisters are usually caused by a ruptured core in the board or a manufacturing flaw.

Preventive action.   Check the board's field prior to decoration for imperfections. Make any necessary repairs.

Corrective action. Before decoration, cut out the loose area and fill flush with joint compound, if deep. Tape and finish. After decoration, use a polyvinyl acetate (PVA) or white glue to fill the blister(s) adequately to ensure good bonding. Roll smooth with a small, dry paint roller.

Problem: Bond failure

Probable cause. Failure of gypsum board to bond to itself or to another surface can be caused by the following: improper heating and drying conditions, dry powder compounds used too soon after mixing, use of compounds that have been mixed for a prolonged period of time, old stock, excessive thinning of compounds, too little compound under the tape, unbuffed joint tape, oily surfaces, poor-quality compound, mixing with dirt or excessively cold water, and compound that is too dry before embedding the tape.

Preventive action. Provide proper drying conditions. Mix the compound in a cleaner container with clean tap water and allow to stand for 20 to 30 minutes, then remix before using. Avoid using dry powder compounds that have been mixed longer than 48 hours. Avoid overthinning of compounds and removing too much compound from under the tape.

Corrective action. Remove all loose joint tape and compound by sanding or scraping and repairing as necessary.

Problem: End ply separation

Probable cause. This problem could be caused by mishandling of drywall, especially during damp or wet conditions. It could also be caused by a manufacturing flaw.

Preventive action. Allow the drywall panels to dry thoroughly; tear back all face paper prior to taping.

Corrective action. After the joints are finished, determine the distance of looseness from the mill end. Make a cut on each side of the tape across the wallboard and a cut at each end, forming a rectangle around the loose area. Peel off the loose paper, and tape the joint. Once dry, fill flush with joint compound. After the compound dries completely, finish with one or more coats of joint or topping compound, feathering beyond the cutout area.

Problem: Panels improperly fitted

Probable cause. Forcibly wedging an oversized panel into place bows the panel and builds in stresses, preventing it from contacting the framing (Figure 11.9). Result: following fastening, a high percentage of fasteners on the central studs will probably puncture the paper. Another result can be deformation of the joints.

Preventive action. Follow the proper panel installation procedure given in chapter 6.

Corrective action. Remove the drywall panel, cut it to fit properly, and replace. Fasten from the center of the panel, then work toward the ends and edges. Apply pressure to hold the panel tightly against the framing while driving the fasteners.

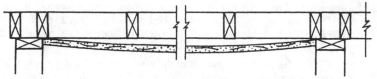

FIGURE 11.9   Gypsum panel improperly fitted.

Problem: Panels loosely fastened

Probable cause.   Framing members might be uneven because of misalignment, warping, or lack of hand pressure on the panel during fastening. The heads of the fasteners alone cannot pull the panel into firm contact with uneven members.

Preventive action.   Correct framing imperfections before applying drywall panels. For more solid attachment, use 1¼-inch type-W screws or an adhesive method. Apply pressure to hold the drywall panel tightly against the framing while driving the fasteners.

Corrective action.   With nail attachments, during the final blows of the hammer, apply additional pressure with the hand to the panel adjacent to the nail (Figure 11.10) to bring the panel into contact with the framing.

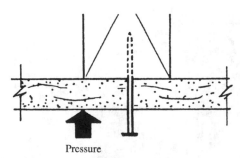

Pressure

FIGURE 11.10   Possible cause of loose panel.

REPAIRING A SURFACE FRACTURE

After gypsum drywall is finished, it will sometimes receive a heavy blow or other abuse that will fracture the surface of the board. If the break is too large for repair with joint compound, the surface fracture can be repaired as follows:

1. Cut a square-shaped or triangular section around the damaged area with a utility knife or keyhole saw (Figure 11.11A). Use a rasp or sanding block to slope the edges inward at a 45° angle. When cutting into stud cavities, use caution to avoid electrical wires or plumbing pipes. Remember that thermal insulation, if present, must be restored.

2. From a section of sound gypsum board, cut a patching piece in the same geometric shape as the opening, but slightly larger than the damaged area. The damaged area is

then further enlarged to match exactly the size of the patching material. If necessary, cement an extra piece of gypsum board to the crack of the face to serve as a brace (Figure 11.11B). If the wall is fire-rated, the patch and brace should be cut from type-X or proprietary type-X board to maintain its integrity.

3. Butter the edges of the patch and insert it in the wall (Figure 11.11C) as a butt joint. To finish the repair, apply joint compound (Figure 11.11D). Note: Some drywall manufacturers have drywall kits available that contain clips to make the job easy.

FIGURE 11.11A Cut a square-shaped section around the damaged area with a utility knife or keyhole saw. Use a rasp or a sanding block to slope the edges inward at a 45° angle.

FIGURE 11.11B Cut a corresponding plug from a sound gypsum panel, then sand the edges to obtain an exact fit. If necessary, cement an extra slat of gypsum panel to the back of the face layer to serve as a brace.

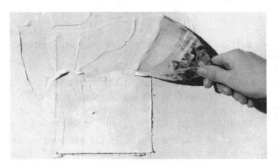

FIGURE 11.11C Butter the edges.

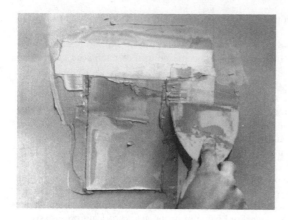

FIGURE 11.11D   Finish as a butt joint with joint compound.

If mechanically or environmentally caused wall or ceiling damage covers more than 100 square inches of a 100-square-foot gypsum system, all material in the damaged area back to the original framing must be removed to make the repair. Framing in the area to be repaired should be inspected and replaced if necessary without increasing the original framing spacing. Replacement material should be cut to fill the opening and mechanically attached to the framing. Ends and edges of the board that are not backed by framing materials should be supported with metal runner track. The repaired area should be finished with tape and joint-treatment compound as necessary.

WATER DAMAGE

During transit or storage, if care is not taken, the drywall panels might receive water damage. Prolonged soaking or exposure to water can soften the core. If stored wet, the gypsum might be subjected to mildew or might sag. Therefore, it is important that wet board be completely dry before using. Check incoming board shipments for water stains or dampness. Protect the panels carefully during shipment and storage (see chapter 4). Because of the probability of paper-bond failure and softening cores, never erect damp panels.

Drywall contractors today are often faced with the situation of assessing and repairing major water damage problems to gypsum board. Roofs and pipes can leak, toilets and sinks can overflow, rivers and creeks can rise, and rain, tornadoes, and hurricanes can strike at any time. All of these, and many others, are potential sources for water entry into buildings in places where water was never intended to go. Although a little water might not be a problem, building contents and building materials, including gypsum board, can be damaged by exposure to water, depending on the duration and severity of the exposure and the source of water.

Always work safely in and around water and flood-damaged buildings, following the safety guidelines issued by the Federal Emergency Management Agency (FEMA), the American Red Cross, or your local civil defense organization. Since extensive visible and hidden hazards might exist, depending on the severity and source of the water, do not enter a flooded or potentially water-damaged structure until you are sure it is safe to do so. Foundations might have become weakened, electrical systems can be shorted out, and certain floodwaters might have left contaminants behind that can cause sickness. Many materials that absorb water can hold mud and contamination for an extended period of time.

When in doubt, throw it out. Do not risk sickness or infection from the residue left behind by contaminated floodwaters.

Prior to beginning any repair work, drain standing water out of wall and ceiling cavities. Wall cavities can be drained by cutting holes at the bottom of each stud cavity just above the bottom plate. To check for water, take off the baseboard. Stick an awl or knife into the wall about 2 inches above the floor (just above the wood sill plate). If water drips out, cut a hole large enough to allow the water to drain freely. Repeat this process at each stud cavity. (With metal framing, the metal channel at the bottom of the wall can act like a gutter. Drill through the channel at the floor line to drain the water.) To prevent shock or electrocution, do not use an electric drill or saw.

Sagging or saturated ceilings can be dangerous and must be drained with care. Ceilings can be drained by poking holes through the gypsum board with a long-handled poker made by attaching a nail or other pointed object to the end of a long stick. Begin by poking a hole at the edge of the area being drained while standing away from any sagging areas. Do not start at the center of a sagging area, or the ceiling might collapse without warning. As the water drains out, poke another hole closer to the center of the area, working progressively toward the center until the area is fully drained.

The Federal Emergency Management Agency recommends that flood-soaked gypsum board be removed and thrown away since floodwaters are frequently contaminated and can cause illness. If dirty floodwaters have soaked the gypsum board 4 feet or more above the floor level, remove the gypsum board from the entire wall surface and replace it. If floodwater contact was limited to less than 4 feet, remove the lower 4 feet of gypsum board and replace it with 4-foot-wide gypsum board installed horizontally.

Visually inspect wet gypsum board that has been exposed to clean water for signs of damage. Some types of damage that might require removal and replacement include gypsum-board paper delamination, fastener pull-through, and sag. Carefully tear down any damaged gypsum board only after it has been fully drained. In order to extract insulation, remove any gypsum board from walls and ceilings that contain wet fibrous insulation.

Certain types of damage might not appear until after the gypsum board has dried. This includes rusting fasteners and mold or mildew that is either visible on the gypsum-board face or concealed on the back surface of the gypsum board or on the framing. The presence of concealed mildew or mold might require the removal of the gypsum board, depending on the success of removal efforts and the types of mold-producing organisms present. Some mold-producing organisms might cause illness.

In the absence of damage or exposure conditions that would make removal necessary, wet gypsum board can generally be salvaged. After drying out the building, if the gypsum board is clean and in good shape, drill or cut ventilating holes near the bottom of each wall cavity, even those that did not need to be drained. Place the holes low enough so they will be covered by the baseboard after the wall dries out. Open up both sides of interior walls and the interior side only of exterior walls. Lower humidity to facilitate drying. Humidity can be lowered by opening up the building when the outside air is drier than the inside air. Open all closets and cabinets to allow for air circulation. Use fans to increase air movement (do not use the central HVAC system for this purpose if the ducts were under water). Run dehumidifiers and use desiccants throughout the building to remove moisture from the air. Adequate ventilation, air circulation, and drying are of crucial importance to minimize the potential for mildew or mold growth. Remove vinyl wall coverings from wet or moist gypsum board to allow water to move out through the surface of the gypsum board.

Caution: When repairing a wall that is required to have a given fire-resistance and/or sound rating, take care to ensure that all repairs are consistent with the specific fire or sound-rated design to which the wall was initially constructed (gypsum board type, fasteners and spacing, and staggering of joints). Do not begin the restoration work until the area has dried out completely.

Inspect the dried gypsum board for signs of damage that might have been missed earlier. Remove any gypsum board that exhibits damage that cannot be easily repaired. Remove and replace fasteners exhibiting corrosion or rust.

Start cleaning where the damage was most severe. Some areas will be stained and will either need to be sealed or replaced to prevent bleed-through after decoration. Particular attention should be paid to mildewed areas. Remove surface mildew using a commercial mildew remover or mildewcide, a solution of trisodium phosphate (5 tablespoons per gallon of water), or a bleach solution (¼ cup of laundry bleach per gallon of water). Exercise care and observe warning labels and manufacturer's instructions when cleaning with any of these materials.

After the gypsum board is cleaned, repair all holes, including those made for drainage and drying, and those left where fasteners were removed. Install new gypsum board to replace the gypsum board that was removed. Using a sealer recommended for this use by the sealant manufacturer, seal the surface where necessary to prevent bleed-through. Tape and finish all joints, repairs, and fasteners in the usual manner as described in earlier chapters. The walls and ceilings are now ready for redecoration.

APPENDIX A
ILLUSTRATION CREDITS

All photographs and drawings, except for those listed below, were furnished by the United States Gypsum Company.

Hyde Manufacturing Co.: Figures 9.6, 9.7, 9.8 and 9.9.

Black & Decker Corp.: Figures 3.20, 3.21, 3.23, 3.24, 3.57, and 10.31.

Delmharst Instrument Co.: Figure 4.12.

Georgia-Pacific Corporation: Figures 2.4, 2.12, 9.11, 9.12, and 10.36.

Gypsum Association: Figures 1.4, 2.2, 2.4, 2.18, 4.6, 4.7, 4.8, 4.9, 4.11, 5.15, 5.17, 5.18, 6.3, 6.4, 6.5, 6.6, 6.23, 6.24, 6.30, 6.31, 6.32, 8.13, 8.16, 8.20, 8.21, 8.23, 8.32, 8.39, 8.49, 8.50, 8.51, 8.52, 9.1, 9.24, 9.29, 9.46, 9.51 and 10.1.

Home Plan for Today, Inc.: Figure 4.1.

Insta-Arch Corporation: Figures 8.9 and 8.10.

Leica Inc.: Figure 3.3.

National Gypsum Company: Figures 1.5, 1.8, 1.9, 2.3, 2.13, 2.25, 5.4, 5.6, 5.7, 5.10, 5.21, 6.1, 6.9, 7.1, 7.3, 7.16, 7.28, 7.30, 7.33, 8.8, 8.22, 8.25, 8.26, 8.28, 8.29, 8.30, 8.31, 8.34, 8.35, 8.40, 8.44, 9.10, 9.11, 9.15, 9.30, 9.48, 10.4, 10.26, 10.27, and 10.36.

Pla-Cor, Inc.: Figures 1.10, 8.8, and 10.36.

Premier Drywall Tool Co.: Figure 9.11.

Ridge Tool Co.: Figure 3.42.

Spectra-Physics Laserplane, Inc.: Figures 3.12 and 3.14.

Stanley Tool Works, Inc.: Figures 3.1, 3.4, 3.5, 3.10, 3.18, 3.25, 3.24, 3.32, 3.33, and 3.39.

Telpro Inc.: Figure 6.16.

The Celotex Corp.: Figures 7.35 and 7.36.

Unimast Incorporated: Figures 7.2, 7.6, 7.5, 7.7, 7.11, 7.15, 7.18, 7.19, 7.20, 7.21, 7.22, and 7.24.

Vaughan & Bushnell Mfg. Co.: Figure 3.31.

APPENDIX B
CONVERSION TABLES

As noted in chapter 3, metric math has moved into the drywall field. That is, a 4-foot-×-6-foot-×-½-inch-thick gypsum-board panel under the metric (SI) system would be 1219mm × 1828mm × 12.7mm. To convert the United States Conventional Units to metric units using Table B.1. divide by the U.S. equivalent.

TABLE B.1 Metric Terms

Basic Units

Quantity	Metric (SI) Unit	Symbol	U.S.A. equivalent (nom.)[1]
Length	millimeter	mm	0.039 in.
	meter	m	3.281 ft.
			1.094 yd.
Area	meter	m^2	10.763 ft.^{2}
			1.195 yd.^{2}
Volume	meter	m^3	35.314 ft^3
			1.307 yd.^{3}
Volume (Fluid)	liter	L	33.815 oz.
			0.264 gal.
Mass (Weight)	gram	g	0.035 oz.
	kilogram	kg	2.205 lb.
	ton	t	2,204.600 lb.
			1.102 tons
Force	newton	N	0.225 lbf.
Temperature (Interval)	kelvin	K	1.8°F
	degree celsius	°C	1.8°F
Temperature	celsius	°C	(°F-32)5/9
Thermal Resistance	K•m^2		5.679 ft^2•hr•°F
		W	Btu
Heat Transfer	watt	W	3.412 Btu/hr.
Pressure	kilopascal	kPa	0.145 lb./in.^{2} (psi)
	pascal	Pa	20.890 lb./ft.^{2} (psf)

GLOSSARY

acoustics Science dealing with the production, control, transmission, reception, and effects of sound, and the process of hearing.

adhesive A compound, glue, or mastic used in the application of gypsum board to framing or for laminating one or more layers of gypsum boards.

airborne sound Sound traveling through the medium of air.

anchor Metal securing device embedded or driven into masonry, concrete, steel, or wood.

annular ring nail A deformed shank nail with improved holding qualities specially designed for use with gypsum board.

ASTM Formerly American Society for Testing and Materials, now ASTM, a nonprofit, national technical society that publishes definitions, standards, test methods, recommended installation practices, and specifications for materials.

atomization The use of compressed air to break up (atomize) a spray texture at spray gun orifice/tip.

attenuation Reduction in sound level.

back blocking A short piece of gypsum board adhesively laminated behind the joints between each framing member to reinforce the joint.

back clip A specially designed clip attached to the back of gypsum board that fits into slots or other formations in the framing to hold the gypsum board in place. Often used in demountable partition designs.

backing board (1) A gypsum board designed for use as the first or base layer in a multilayer system. (2) A base layer in ceilings for the adhesive application of acoustical tile. 3) A type of water-resistant gypsum board.

backup strips Pieces of wood nailed at the ceiling-sidewall corner to provide fastening for ends of plaster base or gypsum panels.

balloon frame Method of framing outside walls in which studs extend the full length or height of the wall.

bar joist Open-web, flat-truss structural member used to support floor or roof structure. Web section is made from bar or rod stock, and cords are usually fabricated from "T" or angle sections.

batten Narrow strip of wood, plastic, metal, or gypsum board used to conceal an open joint.

beading A condition where flat joints become visible under critical lighting, showing a narrow bead or ridge in the center of the joint. No loss of bond. Synonym for ridging, picture framing.

beam Load-bearing member spanning a distance between supports.

bearing Support area upon which something rests, such as the point on bearing walls where the weight of the floor joist or roof rafter bears.

bed coat First compound coat after taping. Same as first finish coat.

bed To set firmly and permanently in place.

bending Bowing of a member that results when a load or loads are applied laterally between supports.

breakdown (1) How well material mixes into a lump-free homogeneous solution. (2) Loss of viscosity a few hours after mixing.

brick veneer Nonload-bearing brick facing applied to a wall to give the appearance of solid brick construction. Bricks are fastened to backup structure with metal ties embedded in mortar joints.

bridging Members attached between floor joists to distribute concentrated loads over more than one joist and to prevent rotation of the joist. Solid bridging consists of joist-depth lumber installed perpendicular to and between the joists. Cross-bridging consists of pairs of braces set in an "X" form between joists.

butt joint Joints formed by the mill-cut ends or by job cuts without a tapered edge. Synonym for end joint.

camber Curvature built into a beam or truss to compensate for loads that will be encountered when in place and load is applied. The crown is placed upward. Insufficient camber results in unwanted deflection when the member is loaded.

cant beam Beam with edges chamfered or beveled.

cant strip Triangular section laid at the intersection of two surfaces to ease or eliminate the effect of a sharp angle or projection.

carrying channel Main supporting member of a suspended ceiling system to which furring members or channels attach.

casement Glazed sash or frame hung to open like a door.

casing The trim around windows, doors, columns, or piers.

chalk line Straight working line made by snapping a chalked cord stretched between two points, which transfers the chalk to the work surface.

cladding Gypsum panels, gypsum bases, gypsum sheathing, cement board, etc. applied to framing.

column Vertical load-bearing member.

compression Force that presses particles of a body closer together.

compressive strength Measures maximum unit resistance of a material to crushing load. Expressed as force-per-unit cross-sectional area, e.g., pounds per square inch (psi).

corner brace Structural framing member used to resist diagonal loads that cause racking of walls and panels due to wind and seismic forces. Might consist of a panel, diaphragm, or diagonal flat strap or rod. Bracing must function in both tension and compression. If the brace only performs in tension, two diagonal tension members must be employed in opposing directions as "X" bracing.

corner cracking Hairline fracture or wider crack occurring in the apex of inside corners. Synonym for shrinkage cracking, angle cracks.

coverage Usually measured in square footage, an area a given material will cover (i.e., 10 gallons per 1,000 square feet of wallboard). Synonym for mileage distance.

deflection Displacement that occurs when a load is applied to a member or assembly. The dead load of the member or assembly itself causes some deflection, as might occur in roofs or floors at midspan. Under applied wind loads, maximum deflection occurs at midheight in partitions and walls.

delayed shrinkage Shrinkage of preceding coats of particularly wet joint or topping compound after joints are completed or painted.

depressed nails Depressions in the joint or topping compound directly over the head of a nail. Synonym for dimpled nail heads, recessed nail heads. Sometimes incorrectly referred to as shrinkage.

design load Combination of weight and other applied forces for which a building or part of a building is designed. Based on the worst possible combination of loads.

dirt collection A condition where dirt collects on the decorative coating directly over a nail head. Synonym for nail spots.

dry hide The ability of a coating or texture to completely hide substrate when dry.

drywall Generic term for interior surfacing material, such as gypsum panels, applied to framing using dry construction methods (e.g., mechanical fasteners or adhesive).

edge cracking Straight hairline cracks at one or both edges of the joint tape. Shows through finishing coats and/or painting. Synonym for hairlines.

end-ply separation Loss of bond between gypsum and wallboard face paper resulting in butt joints showing as high joints or starved joints. Joint will have a hollow sound. Synonym for end-joint separation. Sometimes incorrectly referred to as ridging or high joint.

feathering Blending of finishing coats along the edges to minimize ridges and sanding. Synonym for cutting, wiping.

fire resistance Relative term, used with a numerical rating or modifying adjective to indicate the extent to which a material or structure resists the effect of fire.

fire taping The taping of gypsum board joints without subsequent finishing coats. A treatment method used in attic, plenum, or mechanical areas where aesthetics are not important.

first finishing coat Application of the first coat of joint or topping compound over tape, bead, and nails. Synonym for second coat, filling, bedding, floating, bed-coat, prebedding, first-bed.

flat spots Areas on textured surfaces that have little or no aggregate. Synonym for holidays.

fogging in Spraying a ceiling with a fog coat or light overspray of spray texture.

furring Member or means of supporting a finished surfacing material away from the structural wall or framing. Used to level uneven or damaged surfaces or to provide space between substrates. Also an element for mechanical or adhesive attachment of paneling.

halo effect Overspray from wall texture or wall paint on ceiling texture that leaves a different color around the perimeter of the room.

header Horizontal framing member across the ends of the joists. Also the member over a door or window opening in a wall.

hide The ability of paints and textures to conceal minor imperfections, allowing a surface to appear uniform in color and texture.

high joint Butt or tapered-edge joint protruding above the plane of the board. Synonym for crowned joint, crowning fat joint.

horizontal application Application of gypsum wallboard with the length perpendicular to the nailing members. Synonym for around the room, across the joists or studs.

jamb One of the finished upright sides of a door or window frame.

joint darkening Joint and nail spots that appear darker than the surrounding areas.

joint lightening Joints and nail spots that appear lighter than the surrounding areas.

joint shadowing Joints that appear darker when viewed from an oblique angle, yet show no color differentiation when seen from a right angle. Usually caused by texture variation, low joints, or high joints. Incorrectly referred to as burning, flashing, photographing, and joint darkening.

joint yellowing Joint and nail spots that appear yellowish. Severity of discoloration might vary, depending on paint color. Synonym for flashing bleeding, yellowing.

joint blisters Looseness of paper appearing after the first finishing coat. Synonym for bubbles.

joist Small beam that supports part of the floor, ceiling, or roof of a building.

let down Drop in viscosity of the joint or topping compound after mixing. Synonym for thinning, watering down, drop off, slack off, milking.

limiting height Maximum height for design and construction of a partition or wall without exceeding the structural capacity or allowable deflection under given design loads.

lintel Horizontal member spanning an opening such as a window or door. Also referred to as a header.

load Force provided by weight, external or environmental sources such as wind, water, and temperature, or other sources of energy.

miter Joint formed by two pieces of material cut to meet at an angle.

nail dimpling Depression in the wallboard surface resulting from setting nails with a wallboard hammer. Synonym for dimple, depression.

nail pops Protrusions or bumps directly over a nail head. This condition normally occurs when wallboard is not in close contact with the nailing members. Synonym for pops.

nail pop The protrusion of the nail usually attributed to the shrinkage of or use of improperly cured wood framing.

nominal Term indicating that the full measurement is not used; usually slightly less than the full net measurement, as with 2-×-4-inch studs that have an actual size when dry of 1½-×-3½ inches.

open time Length of time after applying joint or topping compound in which joint can be crossed without roughing the surface of the compound. Synonym for tearing, scuffing, roll up.

photographing joint and nail spots Joints and nail spots that appear as a different color or sheen after painting. Synonym for photographs, poor hide, flashing, picture framing.

pilaster Projecting, square column or stiffener forming part of a wall.

pillar Column supporting a structure.

plate "Top" plate is the horizontal member fastened to the top of the studs or wall on which the rafters, joists, or trusses rest; "sole" plate is positioned at the bottom of the studs or wall.

pock marking Small openings in the surface of the joint or topping compound. Synonym for air bubbles, cratering, pocking, bubbling, balloons.

pumpability Ease with which a spray material pumps through spray equipment.

putrefication Souring of joint or topping compound. Synonym for souring, smelling, spoiling.

racking The forcing out of plumb of structural components, usually by wind, seismic stress, or thermal expansion or contraction.

rough framing Structural elements of a building or the process of assembling elements to form a supporting structure where finish appearance is not crucial.

safing Fire-stop material in the space between the floor slab and curtain wall in multistory construction.

second finishing coat Application of the second coat of joint or topping compound over tape, bead, and nails. Synonym for third coat, finishing, finish bed, polishing, feather coat, skimming.

shaft wall Fire-resistant wall that isolates the elevator, stairwell, and vertical mechanical chase in high-rise construction. This wall must withstand the fluctuating (positive and negative) air-pressure loads created by elevators or air distribution systems.

sheathing Plywood, gypsum, wood fiber, expanded plastic, or composition boards encasing walls, ceilings, floors, and roofs of framed buildings. Might be structural or nonstructural, thermal-insulating or noninsulating, fire-resistant or combustible.

sheen variation Joints or nail spots that appear with more or less sheen than the wallboard. Commonly seen with semigloss paints, but can also show with latex or oil flat paints without prime coating. Synonym for high-sheen, low-sheen, highlighting.

shooting fat Applying spray material at a heavy consistency.

shooting loose Applying spray material at a thin consistency.

shrinkage cracking Cracking that occurs with joint or topping compound when applied too thick in one application. Cracks are irregular and common along metal corner bead and over wide joints. Synonym for map checking, map cracking.

sill Horizontal member at the bottom of door or window frames to provide support and closure.

skimming Applications of a thin coat of joint or topping compound to the entire wall and ceiling after joint treatment. Provides a uniform smoothness of paper and joints. Synonym for milk coat, wash coat, skim coat.

solution time Time required after mixing joint or topping compound to obtain optimum working qualities. Synonym for take up, let down.

span Distance between supports, usually a beam or joist.

spotting nails Application of joint-finishing compound to nail heads and dimples. Synonym for spotting, nail coating.

starved joint Depression in the joint over tapered joints. Also seen as depressions on each side of the tape on a butt joint. Synonym for low point, delayed shrinkage, concave joint.

stop Strip of wood fastened to the jambs and head of a door or window frame against which the door or window closes.

stress Unit resistance of a body to an outside force that tends to deform the body by tension, compression, or shear.

stud Vertical load-bearing or nonload-bearing framing member.

substrate Underlying material to which a finish is applied or by which it is supported.

surging Spray equipment problem that results in material not pumping in a steady stream.

tape photographing Outline of tape is visible in corners and flat joints after joints are finished. Synonym for railroading, tape floating, tape ghosting. Sometimes incorrectly called shrinkage.

taping Application of joint compound and joint tape on gypsum wallboard joints. Synonym for embedding tape, first coat, hanging, laying tape, bedding, roughing, joint finishing.

texturing Application of texture by roller, spray, brush or other method. Synonym for stripling.

tooth Surface porosity and its ability to promote bond with joint or topping compound, textures, and paints. Synonym for porosity, suction, grab.

vapor retarder Material used to retard the flow of water vapor through walls and other spaces where this vapor might condense at a lower temperature.

vertical application Application of gypsum wallboard with the length parallel to the nailing members. Also means with the studs and joists.

wet hide The ability of a coating or texture to completely hide substrate when wet.

wet edge Length of time joint or topping compound can be worked while maintaining a smooth, feathered edge. Synonym for fast drying, poor water retention, bodying, thickening, roll up, ragging.

wet sand To smooth a finished joint with a small-celled wet sponge. A preferred method to reduce dust created in the dry sanding method.

wipe down After spraying ceilings, cleanup of overspray on walls using a long-handled, wide steel blade.

working life Length of time joint or topping compound can be worked and reused. Synonym for water retention, plasticity.

INDEX

Boldface numbers indicate illustrations

About the authors

Robert Scharff has been a regular contributor of articles to leading "how-to" and trade publications for almost 50 years. He wrote his first book, *Plywood Projects for the Home Craftsman*, for McGraw-Hill in 1954. Since that time he has written almost 300 books, most of them in the building and construction field. In addition, he has served as a consultant for various building materials manufacturers.

Walls & Ceilings Magazine is independently owned and published for contractors, suppliers, and distributors engaged in drywall, lath, plaster, stucco, ceiling systems, partitions, steel fireproofing, seamless flooring, poured roof decks, concrete pumping, and specialty finish systems, among others. With a circulation of 40,000, the magazine has been known as the "voice of the industry" since 1938.